BLOOD FROM STONES

BLOOD
FROM
STONES

The Secret Financial Network of Terror

DOUGLAS FARAH

BROADWAY BOOKS

NEW YORK

PRINTED IN THE UNITED STATES OF AMERICA

BROADWAY BOOKS and its logo, a letter B bisected on the diagonal,
are trademarks of Random House, Inc.

Visit our website at www.broadwaybooks.com

First edition published 2004

Book design by Scott Santoro/Worksight
Map designed by Jeffrey L. Ward

Photographs on title spread and page xiv (bottom): © 1999,
Washington Post, by Michel duCille. Reprinted with permission.
Photograph on page xiv (top): © 2001, *Washington Post,* by Douglas
Farah. Reprinted with permission.

Library of Congress Cataloging-in-Publication Data
Farah, Douglas.
    Blood from stones : the secret financial network of terror /
Douglas Farah.—1st ed.
        p. cm.
    Includes bibliographical references.
    1. Terrorism—Economic aspects—Africa, West. 2. Diamond mines
and mining—Africa, West. 3. Diamond industry and trade—Africa,
West. 4. Islam and terrorism—Africa, West. 5. Political corruption—
Africa, West. 6. Africa, West—Politics and government. 7. Africa,
West—Social conditions. 8. Africa, West—Economic conditions.
I. Title.
HV6433.A358F37 2004
303.6'25'0966—dc22

                                                              2003064627

ISBN 0-7679-1562-3

10 9 8 7 6 5 4 3 2 1

*This book is dedicated with love and deepest appreciation
to Leslie Bumstead, Raquel Farah-Robison, Jonas Farah-Bumstead,
and Gillian Farah-Bumstead.*

CONTENTS

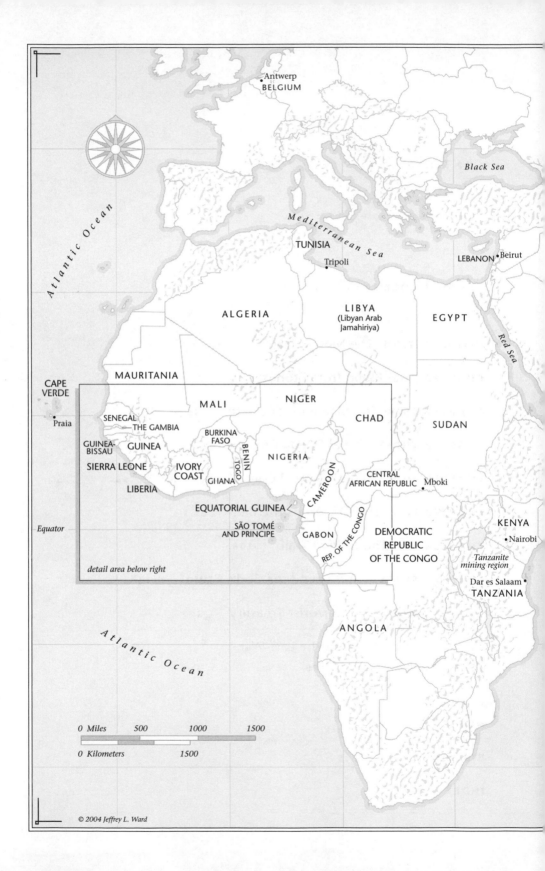

Antwerp
BELGIUM

Black Sea

Mediterranean Sea

TUNISIA
Tripoli

LEBANON •Beirut

Atlantic Ocean

ALGERIA

LIBYA
(Libyan Arab
Jamahiriya)

EGYPT

Red Sea

MAURITANIA

CAPE
VERDE

MALI

NIGER

CHAD

SUDAN

•Praia

SENEGAL
THE GAMBIA

BURKINA
FASO

GUINEA-
BISSAU

GUINEA

BENIN
TOGO

NIGERIA

SIERRA LEONE

IVORY
COAST

GHANA

CAMEROON

CENTRAL
AFRICAN REPUBLIC

•Mboki

LIBERIA

EQUATORIAL GUINEA

Equator

SÃO TOMÉ
AND PRINCIPE

GABON

REP. OF THE CONGO

DEMOCRATIC
REPUBLIC
OF THE CONGO

KENYA
•Nairobi

*Tanzanite
mining region*

detail area below right

Dar es Salaam•
TANZANIA

Atlantic Ocean

ANGOLA

0 Miles   500   1000   1500

0 Kilometers   1500

© 2004 Jeffrey L. Ward

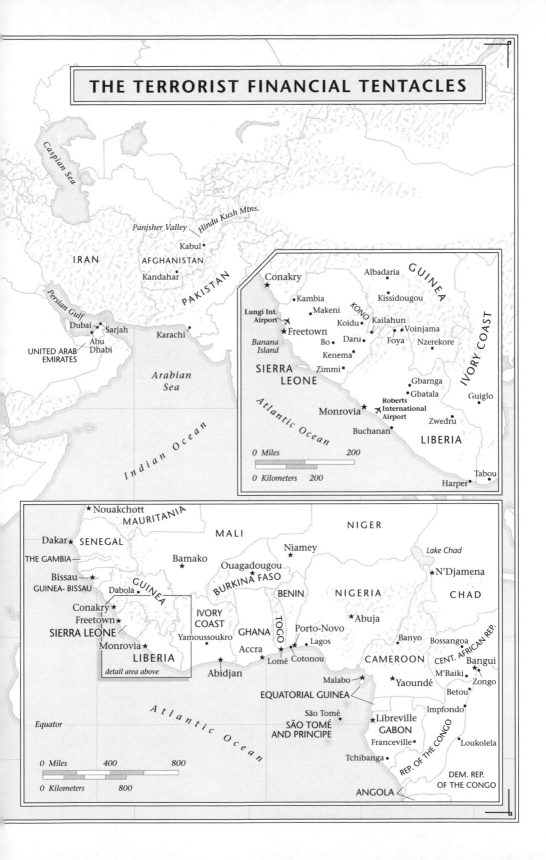

THE TERRORIST FINANCIAL TENTACLES

Detail map (upper right inset):

Caspian Sea

IRAN

Panjsher Valley — Hindu Kush Mtns.

Kabul

AFGHANISTAN

Kandahar

PAKISTAN

Persian Gulf

Dubai
Sarjah
Abu Dhabi
UNITED ARAB EMIRATES

Karachi

Arabian Sea

Indian Ocean

Inset (upper right):

Conakry

Albadaria
Kissidougou
GUINEA

Kambia
Makeni
KONO
Kailahun
Koidu
Voinjama
Nzerekore

Lungi Int. Airport
Freetown
Bo
Daru
Foya

Banana Island

Kenema
Zimmi

SIERRA LEONE

IVORY COAST

Gbarnga
Gbatala
Guiglo

Roberts International Airport
Monrovia
Zwedru

Buchanan

LIBERIA

Atlantic Ocean

0 Miles 200
0 Kilometers 200

Tabou
Harper

Lower map:

Nouakchott
MAURITANIA
MALI
NIGER
Lake Chad

Dakar
SENEGAL
Niamey
N'Djamena

THE GAMBIA
Bamako
Ouagadougou
BURKINA FASO

Bissau
GUINEA-BISSAU
Dabola
GUINEA
BENIN
NIGERIA
CHAD

Conakry
Freetown
SIERRA LEONE
IVORY COAST
TOGO
Abuja

Monrovia
LIBERIA
Yamoussoukro
GHANA
Porto-Novo
Lagos
Banyo
Bossangoa
CENT. AFRICAN REP.

detail area above
Accra
Lomé Cotonou
CAMEROON
Bangui

Abidjan
Malabo
Yaoundé
M'Baiki
Zongo

EQUATORIAL GUINEA
Betou

São Tomé
SÃO TOMÉ AND PRINCIPE
Libreville
GABON
Impfondo

Equator

Atlantic Ocean

Franceville
Loukolela
REP. OF THE CONGO

Tchibanga

0 Miles 400 800
0 Kilometers 800

ANGOLA

DEM. REP. OF THE CONGO

ACKNOWLEDGMENTS

This book would not have been possible without my courageous friend CR. His life has changed dramatically from the days when we met at the Mamba Point Hotel in Monrovia and he was a swashbuckling, gunrunning, diamond-dealing insider in a rogue regime. Because of our friendship, the lives of CR, his wife, Precious, and daughter, Leslie, have been turned upside down. They are safe now, thanks to people who cannot be named, but they live far from home, perhaps forever. Agents of my own government betrayed CR. I hope he and his family can return to a free Liberia someday.

Jeff Leen at the *Washington Post* is one of the best editors in the business. Without his careful eye, constructive criticism, and willingness to help make a complex story understandable and interesting, this book would be far less.

Charles Conrad at Broadway Books has a great editing touch and guided me in making the rough drafts cohesive and readable. Alison Presley was unfailingly gracious, funny, and comforting during my panic attacks.

My deepest gratitude to Joe Melrose, who has defended my reporting, helped corroborate its accuracy, and pushed the story forward.

I owe a particular debt to Global Witness, especially Alex Yearsley and Alice Blondel. Their brave and dogged reporting on the illicit diamond and timber trades in West Africa set the agenda for desperately needed reforms. Alex's unflagging enthusiasm for the diamond story, doing the work of the FBI, CIA, and MI6, was awesome.

Alan White, David Crane, and the Special Court on Sierra Leone supported me and helped warn Washington of al Qaeda's Africa involvement. All this while doing the invaluable service of investigating and bringing to trial some of the world's worst war criminals. That their evidence and warnings have been ignored is a true scandal.

Johan Peleman, one of the few true experts on the twilight zone of illegal arms and diamond trades, has been a good friend through the years whose critical analysis and encyclopedic memory have been invaluable.

Rep. Frank Wolf of Virginia cares deeply about stopping the blood diamond trade. He has done heroic work raising pressure on the diamond industry and holding the FBI and CIA accountable for their unwillingness to confront the problem.

My talented and patient agent, Gail Ross, saw the potential for a book in the scraps I first presented her, then guided me through the process while dealing with my anxieties and insecurities.

Washington Post editors Len Downie, Steve Coll, and Phil Bennett trusted me and let me run where the stories took me. They helped make sure we all got out alive.

Issa Kamara, my intrepid driver in Sierra Leone, kept us both alive in numerous situations through his wisdom, humor, and ability to make the right decisions under pressure.

Many colleagues at the *Washington Post* have been generous. Coll and Michel duCille first met CR and put me in touch with him. Without Dana Priest's push to write this book I would not have attempted it. Marilyn Thompson gave me the time I needed and pushed my stories on diamonds into the paper. Lenny Bernstein ably edited many of the terrorist financing pieces. John Mintz was generous with his time, knowledge, and documents. Margot Williams, who has the ability to conjure up stories, files, and timely facts on a moment's notice, was more helpful than I can say. Andy Mosher is a gifted editor whose knowledge of Africa and concern for getting its stories into the paper are invaluable. His editing eye, both in the stories and early drafts of the book, was helpful. Sue Schmidt was always willing to share information.

Stephen Ellis corrected numerous errors of fact and interpretation on Liberia and Sierra Leone. Gayle Smith always had time to share her knowledge of Africa. Neely Tucker's eye for trimming a rough draft was helpful. Davene Grosfeld got me organized.

A special thanks to Ronald Sandee and Henk Dop for their great help. Dimitri Antonissen at the *De Nieuwe Gazet* in Antwerp was generous in sharing his knowledge. The staffs at the Investigative Project and the SITE Institute were extraordinarily helpful in providing documents and interpretations of the ties among radical Islamic groups in the United States.

My wife, Leslie Bumstead, spent many late nights reading and editing drafts, giving emotional support, and helping me put this book together. Thank you.

Many diamond dealers, UN officials, aid workers, Congressional aides, fellow reporters, mercenaries, intelligence officers, investigators, and private sources in Africa, Pakistan, and the United Arab Emirates contributed to this work. Many important sources who should be acknowledged by name cannot be at this time. My deepest thanks to all of them.

Norbert Zongo, the fearless journalist murdered by government thugs in Burkina Faso, shows how real the threats in West Africa are to those who care too much about the truth.

INTRODUCTION: The Money Trail

Years before the September 11 attacks on New York and Washington, Osama bin Laden's al Qaeda organization and other terrorist groups had systematically built financial networks capable of sustaining their aim of bringing their war to the United States on its own soil. Indeed, bin Laden initially rose to prominence not as a fighter but as the most influential financier of the mujahideen fighting to drive the Soviet army out of Afghanistan.

"It is this financial architecture that continued with him when he turned to terrorism, and it's this financial architecture that is at the heart of how al Qaeda today gets its finances," said William F. Wechsler, who specialized in tracking terrorist funding while at the National Security Council during the last two years of the Clinton administration.

When bin Laden was given sanctuary by the Taliban in Afghanistan in 1996, he was able to use his Rolodex to solicit funds while building a stable base of operations. Within a few years the al Qaeda money trail stretched from the tropical diamond fields of West Africa to the gold markets of the United Arab Emirates, from the money merchants of Pakistan to the suburbs of Washington, D.C. The melding of the financial resources with the control of a country made al Qaeda a terrorist organization without peer.

But the network itself is little understood. Even the source of the money that paid for 9/11 remains a mystery. The FBI and CIA have traced the money flow from Dubai, the wealthy desert sheik-dom that forms part of the United Arab Emirates. But U.S. officials have not discovered where the funds originated beyond that. From Dubai, the money flowed by wire transfer and debit card to bank accounts and ATMs in the United States, as the hijackers attended U.S. flight schools, rented homes, and passed largely unnoticed in this country.

Intelligence officials have been able to describe the wire transfers from the paymasters to the foot soldiers in great detail, because the money moved through traceable financial systems. They know that on June 23, 2001, Mustafa Ahmed al-Hawsawi, al Qaeda's chief money handler, and another man, Fayez Banihammad, opened accounts in the Dubai branch of Hong Kong's Standard Chartered Bank. Al-Hawsawi identified himself as a businessman, used a Saudi passport, and requested two debit cards on his account. Two days later Banihammad flew to Florida and later became one of the hijackers who flew into the World Trade Center. Al-Hawsawi was in the UAE each time one of the hijackers transited there and provided them with funds to buy travelers' checks. A few weeks after al-Hawsawi opened his account, another debit card was issued on it in the name of Abdulrahman A. A. al-Ghamdi, who the FBI later identified as Khalid Shaikh Mohammed. Mohammed was the master-mind behind the 9/11 attacks. Within days of opening the account, a series of deposits totaling $102,000 flowed into it. Within a couple of weeks, al-Hawsawi wired $15,000 to the al Qaeda cell in Hamburg, Germany. There the money was picked up by Ramzi bin al-Shibh, another of the 9/11 plotters. Within days bin al-Shibh wired $14,000 to Zacarias Moussaoui, the alleged "twentieth hijacker," in the United States.

Moussaoui is awaiting trial in the United States for terrorist activities. Khalid Shaikh Mohammed and al-Hawsawi were arrested together in Pakistan in March 2003. Bin al-Shibh is also in U.S. custody.

U.S. officials found other money transfers. From July 1999 to

November 2000, about $100,000 flowed from another bank account in Dubai to the cell of hijackers living in Germany. They know that in July 2000 two of the terrorists opened a joint checking account at the SunTrust Bank in Florida and over the next ten weeks the account received four money transfers totaling $109,500. The money was sent from Dubai. Al-Hawsawi had power of attorney over several of the hijackers' accounts. Hours before the attacks of 9/11, al-Hawsawi consolidated the money left in the accounts he controlled, about $42,000, and withdrew it. Then he immediately flew to Karachi and went into hiding.

U.S. officials know the hijackers were disciplined and conscientious in their use of money. This was shown in the final days leading up to the attacks when several hijackers, aware they would not live to spend the remaining money, returned about $18,000 to their paymasters in Dubai.

"There were no slip-ups," FBI director Robert S. Mueller III told Congress. "Discipline never broke down. They gave no hint to those around them what they were about. They came lawfully. They lived lawfully. They trained lawfully. They boarded the aircraft lawfully. They simply relied upon everything from the vastness of the Internet to the openness of our society to do what they wanted to do without detection."

But the money trail stops cold with al-Hawsawi. Where he got it remains as much a mystery as the terrorist financial network itself. Yet this subterranean web of money provides the lifeblood for the most formidable threat the United States has seen since the end of the Cold War.

I stumbled on the al Qaeda diamond trail a few weeks after the September 11 attacks, while working as the *Washington Post*'s bureau chief for West Africa. Over lunch in Abidjan, Ivory Coast, Cindor Reeves, a veteran of West Africa's murderous underworld of diamond trading and black-market arms deals, described a safe house he had rented in the Liberian capital of Monrovia on behalf of a new group of diamond dealers protected by Liberian president Charles Taylor. He was alarmed because the new Arab residents, buying millions of dollars' worth of diamonds from rebels in neighboring Sierra Leone, had put pictures of bin Laden on their walls and spent much of their free time watching videos of Palestinian suicide bombings.

That conversation ultimately launched me on a journey across four continents that gave me a unique window into the uncharted world of terrorist financing. What began as an investigation into terrorist ties to the diamond trade eventually led around the world and back to the United States. The information I obtained was often far ahead of what U.S. intelligence agencies knew as they scrambled to understand al Qaeda's money in the aftermath of the 9/11 attacks.

I learned how high-quality diamonds, preferred for engagement rings and abundant in parts of West Africa, are an integral part of al Qaeda's finances. Overall, West Africa's diamonds make up less than 10 percent of the world's $7 billion diamond trade. Most of these are "blood diamonds," or stones mined and sold by warring factions in Africa, from Sierra Leone to the Congo to Angola. Altogether, blood diamonds amount to about 4 percent of the global diamond trade. Al Qaeda's investment in the West African trade was most likely less than $50 million, a fraction of the world trade but an enormous windfall to terrorists.

It is clear the terrorists understood how to take advantage of the rapid deregulation that came with globalization, where international financial transfers are instantaneous and hard to trace. There is no manual on how to track goods that move from collapsed states like Sierra Leone and Liberia into the world market.

In exchange for diamonds, the terrorists paid cash to some of the most brutal killers in Africa. Some of the same weapons merchants who armed the Taliban and al Qaeda delivered guns and ammunition to Charles Taylor in Liberia and other international criminals who have perpetrated massive crimes against humanity.

Al Qaeda left plenty of clues to its involvement in the gemstone trade, but they were overlooked by intelligence agencies. Court transcripts of the trials of the few al Qaeda members brought to justice before the attacks of September 11, reviewed in the aftermath, outline in great detail the terrorist interest in precious stones going back to at least 1996. But vital evidence—the numerous Arabic notations in notebooks and on the business cards of diamond and tanzanite merchants—was largely untranslated and ignored by the FBI and CIA until too late.

Even as the terrorist threat grew, the Central Intelligence Agency missed several key chances to understand what was happening in Africa. None of the available information would have prevented the 9/11 attacks, but it would have left the nation less unprepared for the war it now wages.

For al Queda, the pivotal moment came in the aftermath of its August 1998 attacks on the U.S. embassies in Kenya and Tanzania. Until then, the terrorist organization and its partner, the Taliban in Afghanistan, kept much of their money in the formal banking sector. It was a mistake that would cost them dearly. They would not repeat it.

In July 1999 the Clinton administration froze $240 million belonging to the Taliban and al Qaeda in Western banks. Most of the money was in the form of gold reserves on deposit with the U.S. Federal Reserve. Realizing their vulnerability, al Qaeda leaders subsequently moved tens of millions of dollars from banks into commodities: diamonds, gold, tanzanite, emeralds and sapphires. All are essentially parallel currencies: easy to transport, smuggle, and convert. U.S. and European intelligence missed the shift completely. In fact, until a 1999 multiagency assessment of bin Laden's financial empire was commissioned in the aftermath of 1998 attacks, conventional wisdom in the intelligence community was that bin Laden was using his personal funds—essentially writing checks—to pay for al

Qaeda's expenses. "After the bombings we asked the entire bureau-cracy, 'What do we know about terrorist financing,' and the answer was 'almost nothing,' " William Wechsler of the NSC said.

By the time the assessment was complete, it was clear al Qaeda had a structure in place. Only now is that structure beginning to be understood.

With the diamonds and other commodities in hand, al Qaeda operatives turned away from Western-style banks toward home-grown money merchants in Saudi Arabia, Dubai, Karachi, and Lahore. Through a network of sympathetic and enterprising gold merchants and gemstone buyers, and through *hawala*, a traditional Arab and Asian system of moving money through brokers, al Qaeda turns cash into commodities and commodities into cash. The cash also can be turned into weapons, ammunition, television sets, or satellite telephones. Or it can be turned into gold. As a commodity, gold is exempt from most reporting requirements that govern cash. Once the cash is converted, the goods and commodities are then put into the *hawala* system. Often, the money never actually moves. Yet with a simple e-mail or telephone call among business associates in the *hawala* system, hundreds of thousands of dollars changes hands with no record kept.

In the late 1990s, with bin Laden's personal fortune largely ex-hausted and new Muslim uprisings spreading across the globe, al Qaeda and other Islamic terrorist groups turned increasingly to Muslim charities for financing. Many Islamic charities are honorable and work hard to safeguard themselves from abuses. But others are allied with a handful of extremely wealthy Saudi families who be-lieve in spreading the radical Wahhabi vision of Islam. Wahhabism is rooted in Saudi Arabia and preaches a literal interpretation of the Koran. Embraced by bin Laden and the Taliban, it promotes intoler-ance, often to the point of violence, of people who do not follow its absolutist teachings.

Islamic charities are adept at raising funds and moving them around the world. While much of the money goes to worthy causes, some is siphoned off to fund violence and terror. Many of the charities under scrutiny in the United States and Europe were set up over the past twenty years by members of the loosely knit Muslim Brotherhood. Founded in the 1920s, the Brotherhood has aided and abetted violent Muslim groups for generations through a web of businesses, offshore banks, and charities. The Brotherhood opened up a new, sophisticated financial front for bin Laden's group. Ultimately, these charities moved millions of dollars for al Qaeda and other terrorist organizations and provided the groups' operatives with identification cards and safe passage across Afghanistan, Europe, and Africa.

Thanks to al Qaeda's diversification strategy, President George W. Bush's vow to "choke off the flow of terrorist money" and his order to freeze all terrorist assets in the aftermath of 9/11 were blunted. More than $112 million was seized in the three months after the attacks. Of that amount, $34 million was taken in the United States. But much of the money was ultimately unfrozen because governments found their own laws did not allow them to keep the assets. In some countries it was not even illegal to fund terrorists. In other cases the governments cast too wide a net and could not tie businesses and individuals to terrorist activities. Seizures quickly trailed off.

Al Qaeda's resourcefulness allowed its financial structure to survive a near-complete military defeat in Afghanistan. The size of al Qaeda's bankroll after 9/11 remains a mystery. Estimates range from $30 million to $300 million. Nor is it clear how much al Qaeda spent at the height of its influence in Afghanistan. Intelligence analysts believe the organization needed an annual budget of about $100 million to prop up the Taliban, run training camps, pay salaries, and fund related groups in the Philippines and Southeast Asia.

My *Washington Post* stories on the diamond trade and similar stories by veteran *Wall Street Journal* correspondents Robert Block and the late Daniel Pearl on al Qaeda's ties to the tanzanite trade proved to be ahead of the intelligence community's information. The stories sparked congressional inquiries and demands for explanations, largely directed at the CIA. In response, the government agencies went on an offensive unlike anything I had experienced in my seventeen years of dealing with U.S. officials in controversial conflicts in El Salvador, Nicaragua, Colombia, and Haiti. Instead of investigating the veracity of the stories, the CIA and other agencies began to attack our personal credibility and quietly spread the word we had fabricated our stories, either for fame or fortune, or perhaps both. They spent time and money trying to discredit sources rather than following the trail of precious stones.

Today, almost three years after 9/11, the extent of the terrorist foothold in the United States is emerging. Two men in Detroit were convicted of belonging to an al Qaeda cell. Six people in New York pleaded guilty to terrorist associations with al Qaeda. In Ohio, a truck driver pleaded guilty to planning to sabotage the Brooklyn Bridge and derail trains on behalf of al Qaeda. In Chicago, the director of one of the largest Muslim charities in the world reached a plea bargain with federal officials over funding fundamentalist Islamic violence abroad. A Hezbollah cell in North Carolina, funneling money back to the Middle East, was taken down. Charities and businesses associated with Hamas were forced to close.

But the interlocking web of commodities, underground transfer systems, charities, and sympathetic bankers is still in place. The financial resources of al Qaeda are carefully hoarded and scattered around the world, but accessible. They remain ready to support al Qaeda's next plot.

CHAPTER ONE: Blood from Stones

I was doing my monthly expense reports at the *Washington Post*'s West Africa bureau, based in Abidjan, Ivory Coast, on September 11, 2001. From Abidjan I covered some twenty countries in Western and Central Africa, traveling and writing stories on everything from wars to HIV/AIDS to politics and human interest. A friend called in the middle of the afternoon and asked if I was watching television. No, I laughed, I was doing my bookkeeping so I could get to my 5 P.M. tennis date. She urged me to watch, saying something very bad had happened. Stunned, I turned on CNN and watched as events unfolded.

In the following days the foreign desk at the *Post* was interested in anything and everything related to terrorism, but I didn't see how my beat, covering largely poor and obscure West African countries, fit into that. I knew thousands of Lebanese lived in West Africa, controlling much of the commerce and monopolizing the diamond trade. I also knew that most of the Lebanese community was Shi'ite

Muslim but that there was also a sprinkling of Christians. My grand-father, a Christian born in Damascus, Syria, had migrated to the United States in the early 1900s. He was part of the same exodus from what was called Greater Syria that landed many Lebanese on the coast of West Africa.

From the beginning of my time on the beat I had heard rumors that radical groups from the Middle East used diamonds to fund their activities. But I had no idea that my beat was at the center of some of al Qaeda's most vital financial operations and that my story would land me there too.

•

In June 2001, all around the gutted town of Kono in eastern Sierra Leone, thousands of young men, dressed only in tiny strips of underwear and tattered T-shirts and armed with buckets and shovels, swarmed into streams and over hills of mud in search of diamonds. Working in teams, one group would dig up mounds of earth and gravel. Another group would move the mud to the round screen sifters held by others. Carefully, the gravel was washed in rivers and streams and examined for the precious stones. The difference be-tween a piece of gravel and a rough diamond is invisible to the un-trained eye.

In a frenzy of barely harnessed labor, some worked in narrow, deep pits surrounded by twenty feet of mud. Deaths from cave-ins were frequent. In the mad scramble, workers dug under the founda-tions of abandoned, burned-out houses, causing collapses. The inter-vention of recently arrived United Nations peacekeepers prevented a greater tragedy by halting the digging under the pylons supporting the only bridge that connected the region to the outside world. At the end of each day the miners, watched by heavily armed guards of the Revolutionary United Front, had to strip and wash every body cavity where a stone could be hidden.

The RUF had been founded in 1991 as part of the strategy of Libyan leader Mu'ammar Gadhafi to spread revolution across Africa.

While claiming to fight to end to Sierra Leone's notorious corruption, the rebels had quickly degenerated into a brutal occupation force in parts of the tiny nation. It was an army that had neither a coherent ideology nor a revolutionary credo.

The rush on one of the world's richest diamond fields in the steaming West African tropics was spurred by strangers offering exorbitant prices for the better-quality stones. Few knew who the buyers were. The remote mining region had been under the control of the hermetic and brutal RUF since 1997, and few outsiders had been there in the previous four years. Long used to selling diamonds to outside buyers chosen by their secretive leadership, the rebel commanders on the ground didn't ask many questions. They just dubbed the new patrons "bad Lebanese," believing them to be part of the Lebanese diamond-buying network that had controlled diamond sales in that country for decades. The buyers were thought to be "bad" because they seemed to wield inordinate power and provided the rebels with large quantities of weapons in exchange for the stones.

Most of the miners were illiterate peasants, either combatants for the RUF or young men held as RUF slaves, a fate marginally better than that of their countrymen who had the misfortune to run into the rebels. Thousands of people, ranging from two-year-old children to grandmothers, had had their arms and legs hacked off by the rebels in the spasm of brutality that had rocked the impoverished nation for twelve years. Women were systematically raped and towns razed to the ground. Water tanks, electrical plants, hospitals, and schools were destroyed. The miners, handling diamonds worth tens of millions of dollars, were lucky to eke out enough rice for themselves and their families. The RUF claimed to want to build a rural, agrarian utopia and end the power of the small, ruling urban elite. The rebels promised an end to corruption. But they were incapable of winning large-scale military victories or the backing of the people, so the RUF turned to terror to maintain order in the areas it controlled.

•

The RUF supervisors were not happy to see me and my driver, Issa, that June day when our Land Rover appeared in the warm tropical drizzle. It had been a long eight-hour trek from the capital of Freetown, over once-paved highways that were now overgrown by jungle, littered with burned-out vehicles, and cratered from bombing. Once the nation's main artery, the road ran through what had been Sierra Leone's breadbasket, past the abandoned fields and destroyed homes, the acres of derelict palm tree stands, grown for their palm nut oil, and overgrown rubber tree lots.

Just as the road emerged from the lush green hills onto a flat plain, we stopped beside a large group of miners near the town of Koidu. Stunned by the swarming laborers, I got out and began taking pictures.

I was among the first foreign journalists to travel by road into the diamond fields as a fragile UN-brokered peace agreement was taking hold in Sierra Leone. The agreement was monitored by 16,500 UN troops on the ground, the biggest such peacekeeping force in history. While the UN troops were fanning out across the country, a Pakistani unit had helicoptered into Kono just a few days ahead of me and was still setting up its camp.

Vehicles of any sort were rare on the strip of potholes turned to mud that passed for a road to Kono. As we ground our way through the low hills and broad, shrub-covered savannah, the sight of our mud-covered jeep brought all activity to a halt. Children would point and shriek in amazement *"Oputu,"* meaning "white man," at me as we passed. Hardly a house had been left standing, and the few people who remained in the area during the war looked gaunt and haunted.

I barely had time to take off the lens cap after we stopped when a young man in wraparound shades and an AK-47 assault rifle slung over his shoulder yelled at me to stop. Yelling in Krio, the patois spoken across Sierra Leone, the boy kept pointing and grabbing my arm.

My driver Issa translated. Just down the road an RUF officer calling himself Major Nikol, wearing a denim vest and red baseball cap, sat at the foot of one of the few trees still standing. One of his young bodyguards held an umbrella over his head. The major had ordered us brought to him. He demanded to know who I was and why I was taking pictures. He scowled when I told him I was a reporter for the *Washington Post*. "During the war we took journalists like you into the bush and they did not come back," he said in a heavily accented English laced with Krio. As he spoke in a rumbling, deep voice, he drew one of his enormous, callused fingers across his throat with a thin smile. "But now that we are having peace, you are welcome." However, he said, pictures were not.

He proudly said that most of those I saw mining were his war captives, working as slaves. He said the RUF was mining more diamonds than ever before. Then the major harangued us with a sermon equating RUF founder Foday Sankoh—a barely literate cashiered army corporal whose revolutionary strategy consisted primary of abducting children and turning them into killers—with Nelson Mandela. God had chosen Sankoh to bring justice to Sierra Leone, Nikol said. RUF thugs temporarily abandoned their positions to crowd around and glimpse the outsiders, especially the white one. Workers took an unauthorized break to watch the scene.

As the major lectured us, the sullen combatants stared at us, gauging our response. I sensed the precariousness of our situation. Issa, who I trusted and had often worked with in delicate situations, sensed the same thing and knew what to do. Even though he hated the RUF, he began vigorously nodding his head and saying, "Yes, yes, that is true." My more muted response drew stares from the unblinking eyes behind the cheap plastic wraparound sunglasses. So I soon chimed in with Issa, sounding like the Amen choir in a Pentecostal church as the major rambled on.

We agreed the RUF was the world's premier revolutionary force. We accepted that Sankoh was a divine messenger. We cheerfully conceded that all that had been reported about RUF atrocities by the BBC—the only outside news, via shortwave radio, that the RUF had access to—was a pack of despicable lies. After forty minutes, satisfied that we understood each other, Major Nikol shook my hand and pronounced us "bosom friends forever." But he had a favor to ask.

"I want you to get me a visa to the United States," he said. "That is where I want to live." I promised to use my personal influence with President Bush in repayment for his hospitality, but said I still needed to take pictures. He reluctantly agreed I could take five, but only after I threw a pack of cigarettes and the equivalent of one dollar into the deal. I waded out into the mud while the major held an umbrella over my head. I shot until I sensed he was getting uneasy, then retreated to the jeep amid handshakes and hugs from the major and his entourage. Issa already had the engine running. He barely waited until I was seated before hitting the gas.

•

The mysterious buyers in the summer of 2001 were only the latest actors in the saga of West Africa's blood diamonds. Among the wars that have been largely tugs-of-war over rich diamond fields are the especially brutal, interwoven conflicts in Sierra Leone and Liberia.

In most places, diamond fields require a substantial investment before mining can commence, and the extraction process is expensive. In Sierra Leone and Liberia the diamonds wash out of the riverbeds. The only investment necessary is about $15 for a shovel and "shake-shake," a simple screen sifter to sift the gravel. Control of these diamond fields almost automatically means easy access to great riches.

But in recent decades the diamonds have brought little wealth to the people of Sierra Leone. Instead, they have benefited profiteers such as warlord-turned-president Charles Taylor in neighboring Liberia. Taylor was urbane, U.S.-educated, and had a penchant for finely tailored suits, silk ties, and calling visitors "my dear." Liberia, settled by freed U.S. slaves in the nineteenth century, shares an extensive, porous border with Sierra Leone that runs through the diamond fields. Years ago, Taylor set out to exploit his neighbor's riches. A graduate of Bentley College in Massachusetts, Taylor had led an army in Liberia's civil war, where he honed the practice of using children as cannon fodder by forming SBUs, or Small Boy Units, for his savage military campaigns against his rivals.

Taylor got his start in Liberian politics while serving as chief procurement officer for the corrupt, U.S.-backed government of Liberian president Samuel K. Doe. Taylor absconded with $900,000 in Liberian government money and headed to the United States. At the request of the Liberian government he was arrested and imprisoned in Somerville, Massachusetts, in May 1984. But fifteen months later he mysteriously escaped from the Plymouth House of Corrections and made his way back to Liberia to lead the revolt that toppled Doe. His prison escape, which he has hinted was carried out with the collaboration of the CIA, greatly enhanced his aura in Liberia as a "big man," or a person protected by a great foreign power. In a nation constantly at the mercy of world powers, especially the United States, this myth was a valuable asset.

In the ensuing years Taylor's government became a functioning criminal enterprise, exploiting Liberia's natural resources of diamonds, gold, and timber for the enrichment of Taylor and his closest cronies. In the process, he turned Liberia into a pariah state. Taylor, his family, and all senior government officials in Liberia have been banned from international travel by the United Nations. In June 2003 a special UN-backed court indicted Taylor for crimes against humanity, making him only the second sitting head of state, after Slobodan Milosevic, to suffer that fate.

On August 11, 2003, with armed rebels closing in on the capital and the country near starvation, Taylor departed for a gilded exile in Nigeria after turning the government over to his vice president and longtime confidant, Moses Blah. As a jet loaded with luxury cars and household goods sat on the tarmac to carry him, Taylor issued knighthoods for his cabinet and closest friends. "God willing," he said ominously, "I will be back."

Taylor and his family will face little hardship in exile. While his country wallowed near the bottom of the UN index on infant mortality, life expectancy, education, and health care, Taylor, his family, and his business associates had hidden millions—and perhaps billions—of dollars in foreign bank accounts. An investigation by the London-based Global Witness, a nonprofit organization that focuses on natural resource exploitation and governments, found the Liberian government had stashed some $3.8 billion in Swiss bank accounts.

Taylor loves to put on a show for visiting U.S. officials and journalists. My interview with him at the Executive Mansion on January 19, 2001, was typical. First, I waited for several hours in a small dark downstairs office containing a desk, a worn-out sofa, and broken chairs. I was dozing on the couch when the door burst open and several burly men in ill-fitting suits with pistols stuck in their waistbands ushered me upstairs. Most of the lights were out, but a generator kept one elevator operational and one wing of the building well lit. As I entered a narrow wood-paneled room Taylor, dressed in a fine dark suit and matching tie, sat in a large wooden chair. My chair, opposite his, was straight-backed and austere, surrounded by TV lights that were not yet turned on. The room was crowded with several dozen officials and hangers-on, eager to see the day's entertainment. They milled around excitedly, trying to get close to Taylor or make a witty remark that would catch his attention, until television lights went on and the show began.

Taylor rose, shook my hand, and said he believed we had met before. I said I didn't think so or I would likely remember the event. In answering my first question he leaned toward me and called me Doug. Then he stopped himself, put his hand on my arm, and asked earnestly, "May I call you Doug?"

During the interview, Taylor, often speaking of himself in the third person, scoffed at the allegations of facilitating the trade of diamonds for weapons and said his government had severed all ties with the RUF. But mostly he wanted to talk about his love for the United States. He said he was baffled by the U.S. campaign to "demonize" him and "bring this government down, or maybe even assassinate the president."

"What has Liberia done that is so bad to deserve this?" Taylor asked. "We have been allies for 150 years, but they shut every door to us. So what else can we conclude but that this is what happens when they want to take a guy out? It is terrible."

Taylor, through the years, had made moves to ensure he was not the only one who benefited from the diamond wealth in neighboring Sierra Leone. He shared the wealth, through the purchase of weapons and war materiel, with the RUF. In fact, Taylor had helped found and train the RUF and let the Sierra Leonean rebels use Liberia for its resupply routes. In return for giving the RUF weapons, Taylor had for years gained a share of every diamond sale of the RUF, worth hundreds of millions of dollars.

The war Taylor sponsored in Sierra Leone was every bit as vicious as the war he waged in his own country. During the war in Sierra Leone, which began in 1991 and ended with the rebels' demobilization in 2002, much of the country was carved into terrorized fiefdoms run by rebel commanders with names like Mosquito, Superman, Poison, and Kill You Quick. Their foot soldiers were dead-eyed teenagers wielding AK-47 assault rifles and rocket-propelled grenades who were usually high on homemade gin and amphetamines. RUF camps were littered with what at first glance seemed to be large, used condoms. In fact the trash was the remains of empty PegaPacs, small plastic bags that contained raw gin. Combatants sucked on the bags all day to get a buzz. Following Taylor's model in Liberia, the RUF in Sierra Leone had abducted thousands of these young killers when they were children during the war. The kids were given guns and drugs and forced to kill, often starting with their own families. Because of their loyalty and fearlessness, the bodyguards of all the senior commanders, both in Liberia and Sierra Leone, were children seldom over the age of fifteen.

•

The RUF's diamonds were exchanged for the weapons, communications equipment, and other supplies that kept their ragtag army going in Sierra Leone. The cast of buyers—Americans, Belgians, Libyans, and Pakistanis—changed, but the dynamic did not. Taylor and the RUF entered partnerships with some of the world's most notorious arms dealers and mercenaries.

But the new buyers in 2001 were different. They desperately wanted to buy all the diamonds they could and were willing to pay above the market rate. I asked both in the diamond fields and among my diamond-buying contacts who was buying the stones. No one knew. It wasn't until months later, well after the tragic events of 9/11, that I discovered the overheated mining activity I had witnessed was tied to the suicide terrorist attacks. The buyers, the "bad Lebanese," were in fact senior operatives of Osama bin Laden's al Qaeda network. The purchase of millions of dollars' worth of diamonds was a desperate race against time to convert terrorist cash into a commodity that could survive U.S. retaliation. The tactic went undetected until long after it was too late to halt it.

•

Part of the problem in the CIA and elsewhere in the intelligence and policy-making community was that when al Qaeda was buying the stones, blood diamonds were barely on the radar screen as an issue. The CIA had one junior analyst assigned to the topic in 2001 and the State Department had one part-time employee. West Africa policy revolved mostly around how to contain Taylor and limit the violence in Sierra Leone, but, with few assets on the ground and no resources, U.S. policy was reduced to a few severely limited options.

Most of the groundbreaking research on how diamonds fueled

the conflicts of Sierra Leone, Angola, Liberia, and the Congo was done by nongovernmental organizations, not government intelligence services. Global Witness and Partnership Africa-Canada, two private groups that track the blood diamond trade, led the way. Gayle Smith, the NSC's Africa director in the last years of the Clinton administration, said the NGOs forced the administration's hand.

"We knew there was a problem and were trying to figure it out, but when Global Witness launched its campaign and had data, it coupled moral principles with good policy," Smith said. "By making it an issue of conscience, people who weren't going to talk about Sierra Leone were suddenly willing to do so. They made it an issue, rather than an African issue, and sadly, that gets it to a much larger constituency. They did an enormous service, they created a public constituency."

Smith knew the United States was not going to send troops into Liberia and Sierra Leone to bring stability or end the wars. Intelligence-gathering capabilities were almost nonexistent. The only option left to keep the entire region from imploding was nibbling at the edges, or "diet peacekeeping." This consisted of offering limited money and military training to West African countries like Nigeria, Ghana, and Senegal that were willing to try to tamp down the regional fires.

"It was a suboptimal option, that was true, but unless the UN was willing to put in a robust force, it was the only option," Smith said.

•

Al Qaeda's foray into the diamond fields of West Africa was not the first by a terrorist group. For years Lebanon's Hezbollah, or Army of God, and other Middle Eastern groups used diamond riches to finance their causes. Russian arms dealers, British and South African mercenaries, retired Israeli military officers, and American and European merchants of greed found their way to the diamond fields.

Such lawlessness and nihilism ruled Liberia and Sierra Leone because both nations top the list of what academics now call "soft states" or "pre-modern states." According to Robert Cooper, these are nations where:

> chaos is the norm and war is a way of life. Insofar as there is a government, it operates in a way similar to an organized crime syndicate. The pre-modern state may be too weak even to secure its home territory, let alone pose a threat internationally, but it can provide a base for non state actors who may represent a danger to the postmodern world . . . notably drug, crime and terrorist syndicates.

Both nations have turbulent histories. Liberia was founded in 1847 by freed slaves from the United States. Sierra Leone was a British colony created to harbor slaves freed by British warships intercepting Gold Coast slave traders. While the two nations were among the most prosperous and stable in Africa for decades, Sierra Leone had fallen into a spiral of political instability less than a decade after being granted independence from Great Britain in 1961. Liberia, which enjoyed a special relationship with the United States, was also slipping into a swamp of instability and massive corruption in the 1970s.

But the diamond trade did provide some blessings before it turned into the curse it became. One of the most striking things about the current destruction in both countries is that there was so much to destroy. Remnants of paved roads still crisscross both countries. Telephone poles still stand, rusting electrical transformers dot the countryside, and the signs designating burned-out buildings as the schools or clinics they once were are abundant.

By the 1980s, dictatorships in both countries became more brutal and the corruption more flagrant. This toxic combination opened the doors in both countries for continuous armed insurrection and the emergence of Taylor in Liberia and the RUF in Sierra Leone.

•

The modern history of diamonds began in 1869, with the discovery in South Africa of a huge, 83.5-carat stone. Cut down to a 47.75-carat gem, it became the famed Star of South Africa. Within twenty years the De Beers company, formed in 1880 by Cecil Rhodes, a British merchant who parlayed his single diamond concession into a virtual monopoly on the world's diamond sales, successfully harnessed the output of the rough-and-tumble industry. Today, while it no longer controls most of the world's diamond production, the company retains a chokehold on diamond sales, leaving the company's position in the $7 billion a year industry virtually unchallenged: Billions of dollars' worth of diamonds are bought up and hoarded in order to keep the price of the stones artificially high. De Beers can drive out unwanted competitors simply by flooding the market and causing prices to plummet.

While diamonds have been prized for their beauty for thirty-five hundred years, they are, as one diamond historian noted, "sublimely useless":

> Tradition, certainly, supports a diamond's value, but with hundreds of millions of individual diamond stones coming out of the ground each year, tradition is not enough. There have to be more reasons to buy diamonds, and there are: De Beers has invented them. The company spends $200 million a year advertising diamonds and it does the job so well that most advertising professionals judge De Beers ads to be among the most successful in history.

•

The first diamonds in Sierra Leone were discovered in 1930. Significant commercial production began in 1935, when the educational system and infrastructure of the British colony were the envy of West Africa. That same year the colonial authorities reached an agreement with De Beers, giving the company exclusive mining and prospecting rights in Sierra Leone for ninety-nine years, through the Sierra Leone Selection Trust. By 1937, Sierra Leone was producing

1 million carats a year, growing to 2 million carats by 1962. Even at peak production levels, Sierra Leone provided less than 4 percent of the world's diamonds. But the stones were highly valued for their quality and ease of extraction and attracted some notable literary attention. Graham Greene's novel *The Heart of the Matter* is about the diamond trade in Sierra Leone. Ian Fleming, the creator of James Bond, also wrote about West African diamonds in his nonfiction *Diamond Smugglers*.

Even before Sierra Leone's independence, the patterns that would ultimately pave the way for al Qaeda's involvement in the diamond trade were in place. By the late 1950s, the British moved to control rampant diamond smuggling in Sierra Leone's isolated and remote eastern regions abutting Liberia. Lebanese and local diamond dealers had already begun smuggling their goods over the border. De Beers, fearing a loss of market share, opened an office in the Liberian capital of Monrovia in 1954.

Seventeen years later President Siaka Stevens of Sierra Leone effectively nationalized the mining trust, renaming it the National Diamond Mining Company, an entity that became notorious for siphoning off the best diamonds for the personal enrichment of senior government officials. Legitimate diamond exports fell from 2 million carats in 1971 to 595,000 carats nine years later. By 1988 they had dwindled to 48,000 carats, or about 2 percent of the diamonds being mined. As the state's revenue plummeted, the once-thriving educational and health systems and the national transportation network fell into disrepair. Citizens watched their government shrivel into a kleptocracy. When the RUF mounted its insurrection, it justified the violence as necessary to rid the country of the massive official corruption. It was an argument that, in the early days of the revolution, resonated with many Sierra Leoneans.

Corruption remains a huge problem. On my frequent trips to Sierra Leone, I found it to be the most cheerfully and blatantly corrupt country I had ever visited. From the time I set foot in the country everyone, from the passport inspector to the person examining international vaccination cards at the airport to the official issuing press credentials, would ask for "dash," the slang request for cash. The amounts were small, usually less than $2. But virtually no contact with an official was free, and not paying could delay passage in and out of the country, or any other mundane act, for hours if not days.

As President Stevens built his personal fortune, he also played a crucial role in placing Shi'ite Muslims from the Lebanese community in Sierra Leone in key government positions, introducing radical Middle Eastern politics into the West African diamond trade. By the early 1980s all factions in Lebanon's civil war derived substantial funding from the Sierra Leonean diamond trade. Stevens's right-hand man was Jamil Said Mohamed, who played a key role in establishing the government's diamond monopoly. Mohamed was also a close childhood friend of Nabih Berri, a Lebanese born in Sierra Leone who went on to lead the Amal militia in Lebanon and become speaker of Lebanon's parliament. According to the *Middle East Intelligence Bulletin*, a respected regional newsletter, Berri has distinguished himself as "both one of the most reviled of Lebanon's militia elites (even among fellow Shi'ite Muslims) and the most loyal of Syria's Lebanese allies." Through Berri and Mohamed, Iran became interested in Sierra Leone and built a large cultural center in Freetown. In 1986, Mohamed and Berri prevailed on Sierra Leone's president, Joseph Momoh, to invite Yasser Arafat, leader of the Palestine Liberation Organization, for a visit. In Sierra Leone, Arafat offered several million dollars to Momoh in exchange for setting up a clandestine training base for the PLO on Banana Island, a speck of land off of the coast. However, negotiations broke down and the camp was never built.

•

At the same time another force was stirring in Africa. Libya's Mu'ammar Gadhafi, intent on spreading his vision of pan-African revolution, had established the World Revolutionary Headquarters in the Libyan desert. There, Libyan secret services trained thousands of would-be revolutionaries from across Africa, Latin America, and Asia. By the 1980s the headquarters had become "the Harvard and Yale of a whole generation of African revolutionaries." Among the West African students were those who became the core group that would plunge the region into the abyss of war and destruction over the next decade. Taylor from Liberia and Foday Sankoh from Sierra Leone both trained under Gadhafi in his camps. Blaise Compaore from Burkina Faso, another impoverished West African neighbor of Liberia and Sierra Leone, was also a key Gadhafi ally.

The trainer for the West African group was a Senegalese soldier of fortune named Ibrahim Bah, who is also known by a host of aliases. He was born on March 31, 1957. Soft-spoken and secretive, Bah speaks fluent French, Arabic, and English and several local dialects. By the late 1980s, he had already fought in a Senegalese revolt, studied Muslim theology in Egypt, trained in special warfare in Libya for four years, and served with the mujahideen in Afghanistan from 1982 to 1985. After a brief return to Libya, he joined Hezbollah in southern Lebanon and fought against Israel. Returning to Libya, Bah served as a bodyguard to Gadhafi and a trainer in his terrorist camps.

Bah met Taylor in 1988, when Taylor was introduced to Gadhafi. The introduction had been secured by Compaore, an ambitious officer in the army of Burkina Faso who was already close to the Libyan leader. Burkina Faso, previously known as Upper Volta, is a small, landlocked nation east of Liberia. Compaore had won regional notoriety the year before by ordering the murder of his best friend and mentor, Burkina Faso president Thomas Sankara. When Sankara was killed, Compaore assumed the nation's presidency, where he remains today.

In the Libyan camps Taylor also met Foday Sankoh, the almost illiterate former corporal in the army of Sierra Leone. Although not attending university, Sankoh had worked with student activists and earned a living as an itinerate photographer before traveling to Libya for revolutionary training. At least a decade older than most of his comrades, with an unkempt graying beard, he was known as Pap or Papa.

Destabilizing Liberia was of particular interest to Gadhafi because of that nation's long-standing close ties to the United States. Gadhafi was particularly incensed by the 1986 U.S. bombing of his home, which killed his young daughter and narrowly missed killing him. Gadhafi-supported forces in Chad had suffered a series of defeats by insurgents backed by the CIA. Liberia was a natural target for Gadhafi because it served as the main CIA and Pentagon base in sub-Saharan Africa throughout the Cold War.

The U.S. Embassy in Monrovia was one of the biggest in the world, housing regional communications and intelligence-gathering equipment. Just outside Monrovia, the United States had a satellite tracking station and the largest Voice of America transmitter on the African continent. In the 1940s, the Americans had built Roberts International Airport—an asphalt strip long enough to accommodate large transport aircraft—to help ferry troops to the North African and Italian campaigns of World War II.

With Gadhafi's support, Taylor launched his uprising against the Liberian government of Samuel Doe on Christmas Eve 1989. Ibrahim Bah was with Taylor as Gadhafi's special representative. Both Bah and Taylor were granted membership in the Massawa, Gadhafi's inner circle that has access to Libyan intelligence and wealth. Bah helped organize and train Taylor's forces. Mixed in with the new Liberian insurgents were the core members of Sankoh's newly formed RUF, training for their own insurrection in Sierra Leone.

By 1991 Taylor controlled a large swath of Liberia, but Nigeria was leading an African peacekeeping force that was blocking his advance into the capital of Monrovia. Gadhafi, Taylor, and Bah decided Taylor's chances of victory would be improved if a second front were opened in Sierra Leone. That way, the Nigerians would have to divide their forces. So in 1991, the RUF launched its first expedition from

Liberia into Sierra Leone and declared the revolution under way. Bah led an RUF unit into the fray and assumed the revolutionary rank of general. Sankoh also joined the raid. Both Taylor and Compaore in Burkina Faso sent troops with the RUF to help ensure the new force did not suffer a demoralizing defeat.

The outside world dismissed the insurrections in Sierra Leone and Liberia as minor inconveniences to their respective governments. However, both would turn their countries into killing fields.

The United States and European nations did little to stop the carnage that was ravaging Africa in the early 1990s. The disastrous results of October 1993 operations in Mogadishu, Somalia, where eighteen U.S. Special Forces troops were killed and their bodies dragged through the streets, left the Clinton administration skittish. The 1994 genocide in Rwanda, where hundreds of thousands of people were killed in ethnic strife, failed to move the international community to action. Liberia was left alone despite the ferocity of the violence.

The Liberian war was shown to the world in pictures of child soldiers, skulls mounted on sharpened sticks, and fighters dressed in women's wigs and masks and wearing magic charms. The amulets are to give them magical powers to defeat death. The outfits, so strange to Western eyes, were an expression of the fighters' belief that they were, as warriors, dangerous beings hovering between the male and female worlds.

By 1997, Taylor had fought several rival Liberian factions and the Nigerian peacekeeping forces to a stalemate. He ran in and won presidential elections blessed by an international community that was anxious to get Liberia off the menu of crisis spots in the world. Fear motivated many to vote for Taylor. At his rallies, young men would chant, "He killed my pa, he killed my ma, I'm going to vote for him."

To garner the international legitimacy he desperately wanted, Taylor courted several high-profile African-American politicians with influence in the Clinton administration. These representatives and lobbyists worked hard to protect the warlord from public condemnation of Liberia's abysmal human rights record. These included the Rev. Jesse Jackson and some members of the Congressional Black Caucus. Lobbying firms hired by Taylor worked hard to portray him as a pro-American democrat.

Taylor also courted the right. He allowed the Rev. Pat Robertson, the conservative televangelist and onetime Republican presidential candidate, to invest in Liberia. In 1998 Robertson's Freedom Gold Ltd. invested $8.5 million in a gold mining operation in Liberia. Taylor was to get a 10 percent stake in the operation when it went public. With the investment, Robertson and his organization became staunch defenders of Taylor's regime, often publicly praising Taylor as a fine, upstanding Christian man and fellow Baptist. Freedom Gold's manager, James Matthews, said that in the twelve trips he made to Liberia from 1998 to early 2002, he had not found "any reason to confirm the reports" of widespread human rights violations in Liberia.

While Taylor thrived in Liberia, in Sierra Leone the RUF had made little headway beyond a scattered rural base. Sankoh offered no vision or ideology and his meager forces barely eked out a subsistence living from the land. Isolated units moved randomly through the northern and eastern regions of the country, robbing and occasionally entering into combat, but there was no cohesion and little hope of victory until Taylor's electoral triumph in Liberia. Taylor's new position enabled him to use Liberia's state apparatus to offer more ambitious support to the RUF while solidifying his own tenuous hold on power.

Following Taylor's election in 1997, he and Bah wasted little time in harnessing the wealth and power of Taylor's newly legitimate position to shape the RUF into a greatly improved fighting force. For the first time, the rebels were able to buy radio communication equipment for rebel field commanders. Until then, messages had generally been sent by couriers who would often walk a day or more to deliver them. Now satellite telephones allowed Taylor, Bah, and senior RUF commanders to stay in immediate contact. Mercenaries from South Africa, Libya, and the former Soviet bloc were brought in to train RUF units at special camps in Liberia. New weapons were shipped to the RUF combatants, including rocket-propelled grenades and antiaircraft guns.

Sankoh had been arrested and jailed in Nigeria in March 1997 while trying to carry a concealed weapon onto an airplane. As a result, the RUF was under the leadership of the notorious hairdresser-turned-commander Sam Bockerie, known as General Mosquito. His nickname came, he once told me, because he sucked the life out of his enemies. Bockerie organized the RUF into something more closely resembling an army. He instituted the use of defined ranks, formed cohesive units, and for the first time began to focus on intelligence gathering. In short order the RUF took control of more than half of Sierra Leone.

Bockerie, revered by his men for both his ferocity in combat and his reputed magical powers that stopped bullets, often said he viewed Taylor as his father. Bockerie ensured the diamonds flowed from Sierra Leone to Liberia in an orderly manner.

One RUF combatant described being in combat and watching a bullet hit Bockerie in the mouth. The bullet fell to the ground, leaving the commander with only a bloody lip. Another bullet bounced off Bockerie's arm. "He was very strong, and he had strong, strong magic," the soldiers said. "He never stayed in the back, like Sankoh did. He loved to hear the guns." The roar of the guns would finally catch up with Bockerie. On May 6, 2003, he was executed by Taylor's security forces. Taylor feared Bockerie was about to turn himself in to a special United Nations court to testify against the Liberian leader. After executing Bockerie, Taylor's men killed his wife and at least three of his children.

Bockerie and other commanders would request weapons by

calling Bah or other senior officials in Monrovia on a satellite telephone. The requests were passed on to Taylor's security chiefs, who made sure the orders were filled. The materiel moved by truck from a bunker hidden behind black steel doors, under the tennis courts at Taylor's heavily guarded private mansion in the Congo Town neighborhood of Monrovia. While most of Monrovia has no electricity or running water, Taylor's home was brightly lit day and night. After the trucks were loaded, they were driven by night across the rutted trails through the jungle to eastern Sierra Leone, about a ten-hour drive if heavy rains didn't slow travel. Some supplies were also flown directly to the RUF by helicopter.

The effects of the improved weapons and training were visible within weeks: The RUF gained ground across Sierra Leone against the demoralized and corrupt government army. Many government soldiers hadn't been paid for months. Officers refused to spend time in the bush, preferring to stay in Freetown. Discipline was nonexistent. At the first sound of shooting the troops would often throw down their weapons and flee.

Bockerie launched Operation No Living Thing a few months after taking command of the RUF. It was a gruesome rampage across the eastern and central part of the country that razed scores of villages to the ground and, as the name promised, left little alive in its wake. The offensive signaled the arrival of the newly energized RUF. For the first time, the rebels took control of the rich Kono diamond fields in eastern Sierra Leone, near the Liberian border. This gave Taylor and the RUF sustained access to the diamond fields and their wealth.

The military success of the RUF also brought the first reports of widespread atrocities: amputations, rapes, and mass abductions. In May 1997, as the government's military situation deteriorated, rebellious army troops seized power in Freetown. Many of the soldiers in the field had already been cooperating with the RUF in looting civilian towns, earning the pejorative label "sobel," meaning soldier-rebel.

Maj. Johnny Paul Koroma, in prison for plotting a coup, was freed by the mutineers and named chairman of the Armed Forces Revolutionary Council. He immediately asked the RUF to join the new junta, which it did. It was a logical culmination of years of co-operation between the totally corrupted elements of the army and the rebels they were supposed to be fighting.

Hundreds of RUF combatants, many of whom had never seen electricity or running water, flooded the seaside capital and engaged in a spree of looting and murder.

In Freetown, on the southwestern edge of the country, the presidential palace and the houses of the wealthy sit high on the slopes of Signal Hill, far above the teeming slums along the oceanfront. The mansions are reachable by narrow, paved roads that wind up the hillside. Here the junta sat for nine months. The rule of the council was "characterized by systematic murder, torture, looting, rape, and the shutdown of all formal banking and commerce throughout the country." To make ends meet, the rebels mounted Operation Pay Yourself across the country. It was an unprecedented exercise in systematic looting that stripped thousands of people of all their earthly possessions.

In February 1998 a Nigerian-led West African force retook Freetown and restored the elected government. But the RUF had what it most wanted: control of eastern Sierra Leone, bordering Liberia and containing the diamond fields. A safe passageway to Monrovia was opened.

•

With the unimpeded access to the diamond mines lying on the border with Liberia came the explosion in brutality that made Sierra Leone notorious.

In April 2000, in front of her battered plastic tent at the Amputees and War Wounded Camp in Freetown, Kadia Tu Fafanah, a forty-one-year-old mother of nine, described how two preteen boys of the RUF used an ax to hack her legs off above the knees, leaving only two stumps. The camp sits on a barren, dusty dirt strip just off one of Freetown's main highways and is home to several thousand people. Raw sewage trickles through the ditches that bisect the rows of huts and tents that are filled with the war's mutilated. There is no privacy in the small tents that share common walls. Flies buzz through the dust and garbage where children play or help tend to the maimed.

"It was Wednesday, January 20, 1999," Fafanah said as she sat fanning a small cooking fire, recalling the days when the RUF stormed the capital in one of the war's grisliest chapters. "They put us in a house to burn, about one hundred of us, but it wouldn't light. So they put the men in one line and shot them. I tried to run away, but I fell in a gutter. The children caught me. They amputated five others, but I was punished more for trying to run away. They took both my legs. They were small boys and they held me down while one cut me off."

Many children, after a few years in rebel hands, could no longer remember their real names. Instead, they assumed the names given them by their commanders. Psychologists have said that many children survived by adopting a new identity, becoming some of the most prolific killers in the war. The deep trauma could be seen in boys like Ernest Vanboi, who was seven years old when the RUF abducted him from his home and burned his house to the ground. Short, shy, and smiling, he said he did not think he had amputated anyone's arms or legs but he did recall witnessing such atrocities.

When I visited with him in the eastern city of Kenema in April 2000, Vanboi had been recently freed by the RUF. While he at times played with those around him like the child he was, Vanboi could not answer numerous questions about his life, his family, or his village. Psychologists have said such memory loss is common among child soldiers. It is often the product of witnessing their own parents' murders, and sometimes of having been forced to carry out the executions. That initial shock was almost always compounded by being forced to witness the execution of other children who refused to join the rebels or who tried to escape. Those who joined, like Vanboi, often had the initials RUF carved into their thin chests, both as a forced initiation and as a way of ensuring they could not slip back, unrecognized, into civilian life.

While in that initial state of shock and fear, the children were taught that their commanders were their true fathers and RUF commander in chief Foday Sankoh was the supreme father and had magical powers. Their new fathers gave them AK-47 assault rifles, taught them how to lock and load, and sent them out to kill. Gradually, the children said, the killing became easier.

"The commander told me when I was captured, 'Your father is gone. Now I am your father,'" said Siamba, abducted when he was eight years old. "In the bush we committed a lot of atrocities. We did many evil things." Like most of the children, Siamba barely spoke above a whisper. Their eyes shifted constantly while speaking.

One thing the children do remember vividly is the preparation for what they called "mayhem days," sprees of killing and raping that lasted until the participants collapsed from exhaustion. They said they were given colored pills, most likely amphetamines, and razor blade slits near their temples, where cocaine was put directly into their bloodstreams. The ensuing days would be a blur; the children often remembered only the feeling of being invincible, before the drugs wore off.

Musu Burah, a kindly woman of seemingly infinite patience who runs a community-based child-care center in Kenema, said it was unfair to blame the children. "A child is a child," she said, looking at her young charges milling about the overcrowded, tin-roofed house where a shifting group of a dozen or so child combatants were recuperating. "But whoever led the children astray is responsible and is a monster."

•

As the weapons from Liberia flowed in, the diamonds from Sierra Leone flowed out. Usually wrapped in rough bits of plastic or stuffed in glass bottles, the stones were brought out in small bundles by the handful of trusted couriers who had driven the weapons in. The rough, unpolished stones were either taken directly to the Executive Mansion and hand-delivered to Taylor or given to Bah, who split his time between Monrovia and Ouagadougou, Burkina Faso. While the RUF hand-recorded their shipments in primary school notebooks, they never learned how to appraise the value of the gems. Taylor and Bah handled the business side. A UN report said that:

> Estimates of the volume of RUF diamonds vary widely, from as little as $25 million per annum to as much as $125 million. Whatever the total, it represents a major and primary source of income for the RUF, and is more than enough to sustain its military activities . . . The bulk of the diamonds leave Sierra Leone through Liberia . . . Such trade cannot be conducted without the permission and the involvement of Liberian government officials at the highest level.

Taylor's cut was usually one-third of the price that the stone brought when sold. Bah's cut was about half of that. Middlemen, business costs, and weapons purchases took the rest. Thus, RUF commanders and diamond traffickers said, Taylor and Bah reaped enormous profits, exchanging diamonds worth millions of dollars for weapons and equipment worth far less.

The risk of trafficking in "blood diamonds" was virtually nonexistent. It is a point of honor among diamond buyers to ask no questions about the provenance of the stones they buy. In the diamond fields of Sierra Leone, the Democratic Republic of Congo, and Angola, Hezbollah and Israeli buyers work side by side, competing and cooperating.

"If anyone ever tells you they ask or care about where stones come from or who is selling them, they are not a real diamond merchant," a beefy Lebanese diamond dealer in Kinshasa, Democratic Republic of Congo, told me after admitting to funding Hezbollah while also doing business with Israelis. "They are lying. A real diamond dealer will never ask." An Israeli diamond dealer, who regularly did business with buyers he knew were Hezbollah and some he suspected were al Qaeda, agreed. "Here, it is a business," he said. "The wars are over there. Here we do business, there they do war."

So, despite a UN-mandated embargo on diamonds from Sierra Leone and Liberia, the stones are openly smuggled into Antwerp, Belgium, and other diamond centers, where they enter the diamond chain. "You could come to Antwerp with a suitcase of diamonds, dancing and shouting you had stones, and no one would pay any attention to you," said one diamond merchant who made the trip many times with illegal stones. "The fact is that no one there cared at all where the stones came from, as long as they came."

Once it is in the gemstone chain, it is almost impossible to tell where a diamond originated. About 80 percent of the world's polished diamonds pass through Antwerp, where the trade is concentrated in a maze of buildings and shops that line the narrow Hoveniersstraat district. Although the diamond district covers just a few city blocks, it stores, cuts, and polishes billions of dollars of stones every year.

The person chosen by Taylor and the RUF to handle the diamond sales was Ibrahim Bah. He was widely viewed within the RUF as a near deity because he was worldly and multilingual, comfortable in a world most of them could not even imagine. Because he was low key, reliable, and trustworthy, Bah soon "handled much of the financial, diamond and weapon transactions among the RUF, Liberia and Burkina Faso." He relied on a changing cast of diamond merchants to help him navigate Antwerp's treacherous diamond community. Occasionally, he traveled there himself to sell stones.

The diamonds were usually sold in a secret bidding process. In

January 1999, Bah and a trusted assistant flew to Brussels with a parcel of diamonds that eventually sold for $3.6 million. After spending two days in a luxury hotel, Bah and his aide were informed by their Belgian contact that arrangements had been made for the bidding to take place in Antwerp. There, in the contact's office, the packet of stones was carefully laid on a table. Nine trusted diamond buyers had been summoned to bid. They arrived at thirty-minute intervals, examined the stones, wrote a bid on a small piece of paper, put the paper in a sealed envelope, and left. At a prearranged time only the winner was called back. If he could not produce the cash within thirty minutes his bid was forfeit and the next-highest bidder was called.

But the diamonds' ultimate value to Taylor and the RUF was their purchasing power. Despite the end to its civil war in 1997, Liberia remained under an international arms embargo. In order to obtain the weapons he needed, Taylor turned to those in the world's vast underground weapons market who specialized in embargo-busting. Many were part of other organized criminal networks.

Victor Bout, short, stocky, and usually sporting a bushy mustache, doesn't look the part of a swashbuckling adventurer in Africa. Born in Tajikistan in 1967, he graduated from Moscow's prestigious Military Institute of Foreign Languages, where he became fluent in six languages. His English is flawless and his French near perfect. He talks often of his love for the environment and the need to preserve Africa's rain forests.

Nicknamed the Lone Wolf by associates, he went into business for himself when his air force regiment was demobilized as the Cold War ended. In a few short years Bout acquired multiple passports and identities, along with one of the world's largest private fleets of aircraft. Most of his airplanes were aging, Soviet-built Antonovs. With the aircraft, he illegally moved hundreds of tons of sophisticated weapons to rogue armies across Africa, including shipments to Taylor in Liberia and the RUF in Sierra Leone.

In 1996 the operational base of his fleet of fifty to sixty aircraft was Belgium. After his activities came under scrutiny there, he moved to Sharjah, one of the seven tiny emirates that make up the United Arab Emirates. However, most of his aircraft were registered in Liberia under the company name of Air Cess Liberia. The reason, according to a UN report, is that an airline company incorporated in Liberia

> can locate its executive offices anywhere in the world and conduct business activities anywhere in the world. Names of corporate officers or shareholders need not be filed or listed and there is no minimum capital requirement. A corporate legal existence can be obtained in one day.

Known to law enforcement officials around the world as Victor B. because of his multiple passports and aliases, Bout—also known as Butt, Boutov, Budd, or Bulakin—kept his aircraft in Sharjah in part because of the emirate's lax control of its sprawling free trade zone. In the zone almost anything could be shipped in or out with only a cursory inspection at best. To hide his ownership of the aircraft, Bout constantly shifted the registrations among different African states that, like Liberia, promised no hassles. When UN panels investigating his dealing noted Bout's Liberian registrations, he moved them first to Equatorial Guinea, then to Swaziland, and then the Central African Republic. His welter of companies with overlapping directorships and headquarters listed at P.O. boxes made it virtually impossible to trace his businesses.

In Africa, Bout specialized in breaking international weapons embargoes. He quickly delivered entire, customized weapons systems to his clients, something none of his competitors could do.

"There are a lot of people who can deliver arms to Africa or Afghanistan, but you can count on one hand those who can deliver major weapons systems rapidly," said Lee S. Wolosky, a former

National Security Council official who led an interagency effort to shut down Bout's operations during the last two years of the Clinton administration. "Victor Bout is at the top of that list."

Bout delivered other things as well, earning a reputation as someone who could fly virtually anything anywhere in Africa. His airplanes ferried UN peacekeepers around central Africa, helped deliver food for U.S.-led famine relief efforts in Somalia, and flew crayfish and vegetables from South Africa to Europe. Along the way he became a supplier of air freight services for Gadhafi in Libya. In May 1997, when rebel troops under the command of Laurent Kabila were about to take Zaire's capital, Kinshasa, Bout supplied the airplane that flew dictator Mobutu Sese Seko into exile. The rebels got close enough to shoot at the plane, but not to down it. "Bout would fly for anyone who paid," said a former associate. "He is good because he takes the chances."

By the late 1990s, Bout was dealing weapons to several sides of the war in the Democratic Republic of Congo, as the victorious Kabila renamed Zaire. He was also supplying rebels of the Uniao Nacional Para a Independencia Total de Angola (UNITA), in Angola, Taylor, and the RUF. All of these clients were under international arms embargoes.

Between July 1997 and October 1998, UN investigators documented thirty-seven flights by Bout aircraft between Burgas, a Bulgarian city on the Black Sea, and Lomé, Togo, in West Africa. From there the goods were shipped to the UNITA rebels in Angola, under the leadership of Jonas Savimbi. The shipments included 15 million rounds of ammunition, 20,000 82mm mortars, 100 antiaircraft missiles, 20 missile launchers, and 6,300 antitank rockets. Bout obtained forged end-user certificates, the document required whenever weapons of war are bought to ensure the transaction is legal, from Togo. The certificate requires the purchasing government to swear the weapons will not be passed on to a third party. He used a Gibralter-registered company called KAS Engineering to make the shipments. Bout personally sent some of the forged certificates to KAS by express mail from Dubai.

Peter Hain, the British Foreign Office minister for Europe, called Bout "Africa's chief merchant of death" and added, "The murder and mayhem of UNITA in Angola, the RUF in Sierra Leone and groups in the Congo would not have been so terrible without Bout's operations."

•

Bout's entrée into Liberia was provided by Sanjivan Ruprah, a Kenyan who had become a part of Taylor's inner circle after moving to Monrovia in 1999. Ruprah, well known to international authorities as a weapons merchant and diamond dealer, was given at least two Liberian diplomatic passports. One was in his own name and another under the name of Samir M. Nasr. The passport with his real name listed his position as deputy commissioner of the Bureau of Maritime Affairs. The other authorized him to act as a "Global Civil Aviation Agent worldwide."

One of Ruprah's highest priorities in 2000 was to find Taylor a reliable conduit for sophisticated weapons. Another war was brewing in the region, one that posed a significant threat to Taylor and eventually drove him from power.

Backed and hosted by the government of Guinea and with the at least tacit support of the United States and Great Britain, a new group of rebels calling itself Liberians United for Reconciliation and Democracy (LURD) was preparing an offensive that would eventually deprive Taylor of control of the entire country except Monrovia. In August 2003, after Taylor went into exile, LURD agreed to participate in an interim government that pledged to hold elections within two years.

Taylor desperately wanted attack helicopters to beat back the LURD challenge. Bout, now Ruprah's business partner, was the man for the job. At least in partial payment for his services, Ruprah and through him Bout, were granted ownership of some diamond mines in Liberia. In early 2000 Bout arranged for Ruprah to buy two Soviet bloc attack-capable helicopters, an Mi-2 and an Mi-17, along with spare rotors, antitank and antiaircraft systems, missiles, armored vehicles, machine guns, and almost 1 million rounds of ammunition. The helicopters and weapons were routed from Bulgaria through Uganda and Ivory Coast. The shipment arrived in Monrovia on four flights on July 4, July 27, August 1, and August 23, 2000. The helicopters were flown on one of Bout's Ilyushin 76s, one of the world's largest transport aircraft. Ruprah set up a ghost company called Abidjan Freight in the Ivory Coast to conceal the fact that the aircraft and its cargo were bound for Liberia in violation of the UN arms embargo. A UN investigation noted:

> It is difficult to conceal something the size of an Mi-17 military helicopter, and the supply of such items to Liberia cannot go undetected by customs authorities in originating countries unless there are false flight plans and end user certificates, or unless customs officials at points of exit are paid to look the other way. The constant involvement of Bout's aircraft in arms shipments from eastern Europe into African war zones suggests the latter.

It is not clear how many other shipments Bout managed to deliver. But operating through a front company called New Millennium in the tiny country of the Gambia, several other large shipments arrived, along with spare parts and rotors for the helicopters.

Bout was happy to take diamonds in payment for his lethal loads to Liberia, as he was for his work in the Congo and Angola. He had even tried to set up a diamond export business in the Congo. With easy access to the Russian diamond exchange, Bout had no problem selling the diamonds. Investigators believe he packed away millions in African stones.

•

If Bout had stuck to supplying obscure African wars, he might well have escaped international scrutiny. But by the late 1990s U.S. intelligence officials had discovered another Bout tie that troubled them far more: possible weapons supplies to the Taliban and al Qaeda in Afghanistan.

Lee Wolosky, the NSC director for transnational threats, led a largely unsuccessful interagency effort to shut Bout down. The effort began when Wolosky noticed that Bout's name popped up in almost every conflict the NSC was tracking, from the African wars to the Philippines. "Bout, as the largest player in the world in the illicit air logistics business, is a critical aider and abettor to criminal and terrorist organizations, rogue heads of state and insurgencies—whoever is able to pay," Wolosky said.

But Bout didn't become a high priority until late 1999, when intelligence agencies became intrigued with Bout's operations in his base of the United Arab Emirates. The UAE was one of only three countries, along with Saudi Arabia and Pakistan, to extend diplomatic recognition to Afghanistan's Taliban government.

When the Taliban took over Afghanistan in 1996, the UAE, a tiny and enormously wealthy desert kingdom, became their favorite shopping ground. At the UAE's sprawling malls, gold markets, and duty-free zones, the Taliban and al Qaeda could purchase everything from medicine to chemicals to satellite telephones.

Bout already had a long history of dealing in Afghanistan. From 1992 to 1995, he was one of the main weapons providers for the Northern Alliance, which governed the country during that time and fought the Taliban. Former alliance officials said Bout's prices were steep, $60 for a single shell for a tank, but that he was one of the few reliable suppliers they had. So whenever supplies of guns or ammunition ran low the officials would bring suitcases stuffed with cash to Bout.

As in the African wars, Bout seemed to have a knack for surviv-

ing by playing all sides. On August 3, 1995, the Taliban downed a
Bout-owned aircraft near Kandahar, Afghanistan. The plane was carrying almost 4 million rounds of ammunition. The Taliban kept the
ammunition and took the seven crew members hostage. They were
freed a year later after Bout, with the Taliban now in control of Kabul,
abruptly switched sides.

"He was working for us," said Abdul Latif, Bout's main arms
contact in the Northern Alliance. "And then he was working for the
Taliban." A 1998 Belgian intelligence report said that Bout made $50
million in Afghanistan, "selling heavy ordnance of former Soviet
stock to the Taliban." Bout's pilots, mostly Russians and Ukrainians,
were paid $10,000 per trip.

In addition to the weapons flights, Bout appears to have negotiated other lucrative deals with the Taliban. One was to supply
maintenance and parts for Ariana Airways, Afghanistan's national
airline, and the Taliban air force. Another was to provide charter
flights from the UAE to Kandahar.

Ariana's international flights were banned in 1999 by order of
the UN. The charter service, which operated with UN authorization
from November 2000 through January 2001, was provided by the
Flying Dolphin airline, owned by Sheikh Abdullah bin Zayed bin
Saqr al Nayhan, a member of the UAE's ruling family. Flying Dolphin
was registered in Liberia but had its operations in Dubai. A UN report
called Zayed a "close business associate of Bout."

There was another joint business venture. Between 1998 and
2001, Mullah Farid Ahmed, acting on behalf of the Taliban, bought
five airplanes from each of two companies—Air Cess and Vial—controlled by Bout. Five of the airplanes, all Antonov 12s, were turned
over to the Taliban air force, and some were repainted and camou-
flaged in the colors of Ariana Airways. The planes were used to fly
tons of heavy artillery and BM-21 Hurricane rocket batteries into
Afghanistan. The Taliban left records of the ten aircraft purchased
from Bout and Zayed's companies in Afghanistan.

In 2000, with mounting evidence of Bout's involvement with the Taliban and al Qaeda, U.S. and British intelligence began a secret operation to disrupt Bout's activities. The United States also began a diplomatic campaign to get the UAE to expel Bout. But the Americans could take little direct action because Bout had violated no U.S. laws. In late 2000 the Clinton administration asked the UAE, at a very senior level, to shut Bout's operations down. UAE officials responded that they had no evidence of any criminal wrongdoing.

But UAE officials did agree to take incremental measures aimed at forcing Bout to move on. These included requiring aircraft based in its territory to be equipped with new modern radar systems and other equipment that would have cost Bout hundreds of thousands of dollars to install. Still, Bout's fleet continued to fly. When the Bush administration entered the White House in January 2001 the Bout operation suddenly dropped off the list of priorities—until the September 11 attacks. "Suddenly, he was back on our radar screen in a very significant way," a senior Bush administration official said. "His importance suddenly loomed very large."

In late 2001, Sanjivan Ruprah, Bout's Kenyan partner in Liberia, who landed on the United Nations travel ban list issued in February 2001 along with Taylor and scores of other senior Liberian officials, was anxious to cut a deal with U.S. officials that would get him off the blacklist. What he had to offer was information on Bout's empire. He quietly made contact with the FBI and CIA and began telling them what he knew. However, he was unable to reach an agreement with U.S. authorities and was arrested in Belgium in February 2002 on charges of criminal association and using a false passport.

Bout was next. On February 25, 2002, the Belgian government, through Interpol, the international police organization, issued a warrant for Bout on charges of illegal weapons trafficking. Known as a "red notice," the international arrest warrant was immediately transmitted to Moscow, where Bout spends part of each year. U.S. officials confidently predicted the Russians would turn Bout over to the

Belgians for trial or at least arrest him. But the Russians insisted Bout was not there.

Three days after the warrant was issued, Igor Tsyryulnikov of Russia's Interpol office told the Interfax news agency that "we can say for sure Bout is not in Russia." As the official statement was sent out over the news service in Moscow, Bout was in the middle of a two-hour interview in the studios of Echo Moskvy Radio, a local Moscow radio station, protesting his innocence and calling the allegations "outrageous."

"What have I done to be afraid of?" he said. "I haven't done anything in my life to make me run or hide." While acknowledging making flights to Afghanistan until the 1996 Taliban victory, he said he stopped flying there after that.

"First [the Russians] say they don't know who he is, then they say they don't know where to find him," said one angry U.S. official. "He was on the air for two hours. He must be very hard to locate." Three days later Bout appeared on CNN and angrily denied that he traded guns for diamonds. "I have never touched diamonds in my life and I'm not a diamond guy, and I don't want to go into that business," Bout said.

Just as suddenly as the case against Bout had accelerated, it dissipated. When President Bush prepared to travel to Moscow for a summit with Russian president Vladimir Putin a few weeks later, National Security Adviser Condoleezza Rice was asked if Bush would demand action on Bout. She said no.

European intelligence sources say the sudden backing off on the case was part of a deal Bout cut with U.S. authorities when the war in Afghanistan began, following the 9/11 attacks. With some of the only aircraft available in the region, he may have simply switched sides again. Intelligence officials say Bout flew U.S. clandestine operatives into Afghanistan and badly needed ammunition and other supplies to the Northern Alliance. In exchange, they said, his past activities would be ignored. So, instead of facing trial and risking the loss of his fleet or financial empire, Bout is regularly seen around Moscow's tonier restaurants, often with a large entourage. Those who know him say his favorite food is sushi.

Bout's partner Ruprah also seems to have escaped trial. In May he skipped bail in Belgium and illegally slipped into Italy, using a false passport. He was arrested there but allowed to return to Belgium, where he is supposed to report to the police on a weekly basis. In early 2003 he had failed to show up for several weeks.

•

Bout was not the only world-class weapons dealer who found his way to Taylor's Liberia to trade arms for diamonds. Leonid Menin, an Israeli businessman originally from Odessa, Ukraine, was arrested on August 5, 2000, in Italy, on charges of cocaine possession and weapons trafficking. Menin engineered the sale of hundreds of tons of sophisticated weapons to the RUF while operating the Exotic Tropical Timber Enterprise, a logging company under Taylor's protection in Liberia. When he was arrested at the Europa Hotel in the company of several high-priced call girls, he had a $1,500-a-day cocaine habit, $3 million in his bank accounts, and diamonds worth $500,000 in his possession. Menin was carrying passports from the former Soviet Union, Russia, Germany, and Bolivia, each identifying him by a different name.

While dealing extensively with Taylor's notorious son, Chucky Taylor, Menin delivered sixty-eight tons of weapons to the RUF in 1999. To get the weapons, Menin bought a forged end-user certificate from Burkina Faso. The shipment, including surface-to-air missiles and antitank weapons, arrived in Ouagadougou on March 13, 1999. The weapons were transshipped in a matter of days to Liberia on a BAC-111 aircraft owned by Menin. The airplane had previously been the team airplane of the Seattle Supersonics of the NBA.

When he was arrested, Menin was also carrying an end-user certificate from the Ivory Coast. The document was dated May 26, 1999, and authenticated by the Ivory Coast's embassy in Moscow. It authorized the purchase of 113 tons of weapons, including 5 million rounds of AK-47 ammunition, 50 M-93 30mm grenade launchers, 10,000 munitions for the launchers, and 20 night-vision binoculars. The weapons had been delivered in the middle of 2000.

Menin was freed on bail in 2002 and disappeared.

CHAPTER THREE: The al Qaeda Connection

A few days after 9/11, I was having lunch with one of my best sources, who happened to be traveling through Abidjan, Ivory Coast, while I was at home between trips. For a journalist, Cindor Reeves, known as CR, was a dream source. Not only was he smart, articulate, and accurate, he was also the younger brother of Charles Taylor's first wife, Agnes, and grew up in Taylor's inner circle. Because of this, he was entrusted with sensitive missions that ranged from making weapons deliveries to the RUF to transporting diamonds to Antwerp to escorting VIPs. About six foot two, slender with close-cropped hair, CR was usually dressed in baggy jeans, running shoes, and at least one heavy gold chain. In recent years he had served as aide-de-camp to Taylor's friend and diamond man, Ibrahim Bah. CR manned Bah's satellite phone and fax and sat in on many important meetings. He was used to being seen and not heard.

Unlike most players in West Africa's deadly sports of war and profiteering, CR could read and write at a high school level and had an uncanny memory for names and dates. Relaxed, soft-spoken, and confident, he seldom drank alcohol and didn't smoke, two other things that set him apart.

On that September day, we sat under a ceiling fan in the California Barbeque, an American-owned restaurant that I retreated to when I wanted a good rack of ribs. After ordering, we chatted about the wars and weapons shipments, diamonds, and mercenaries. I knew CR well enough by this time to ask him almost anything, and there was one thing I wanted to know.

"Do fighters in the bush really offer human sacrifices and eat the hearts of their victims to gain their strength?" I asked. I felt embarrassed asking the question but had heard graphic descriptions of the practice, and wanted to know if it was true or one of many myths that hang over Africa.

CR didn't bat an eye. Yes, he said, looking up from his plate slowly, it was true. Only a few "really big men" like Taylor, RUF leader Foday Sankoh, and their senior commanders carried out the practice because it was such powerful magic. The main organ that gave one spiritual power was the heart, he said. So it was often roasted and eaten. While he had witnessed the practice, he said he had never participated in it. Suddenly, I lost my appetite for the ribs.

Then CR posed an unexpected question of his own, a question that would change both our lives.

•

Due to recent fighting in Liberia's perpetual civil wars, security at Roberts International Airport was unusually heavy the morning in early March 1999 when Ibrahim Bah dispatched CR to meet two special passengers arriving on the Weasua airlines flight from Abidjan, Ivory Coast. The turboprop aircraft was an aging Antonov 28 with a Ukrainian crew. Ukrainians are the only ones willing to fly the decrepit, cockroach-infested planes with bald tires that constitute Liberia's most reliable link to the outside world. Roberts is the country's only international airport. Yet in a region where flights are routinely delayed for hours and often for days, Weasua was almost always on time. And so the flights were almost always packed.

With his official ID card from the First Family, CR had access to the inner sanctums of Taylor's military and security apparatus. He walked past the guards armed with AK-47 assault rifles to the tarmac. Among the last passengers to climb down the rusting metal staircase jammed up against the airplane's small back door were two wiry young men. "Are you Ben Ali and Ali Ben?" CR asked in French. He told them General Bah had sent him. In fact, the two men were Khalfan Ghailani and Fazul Abdullah Mohammed, identified by the FBI as two senior al Qaeda operatives who had participated in the August 1998 bombings of the U.S. embassies in Dar es Salaam, Tanzania, and Nairobi, Kenya. It was their first trip to Liberia, but they both were experienced al Qaeda hands. Mohammed was from the Comoros Islands and had been the head of al Qaeda's Kenyan cell. Ghailani was Tanzanian and had helped buy the truck for the attack in Dar es Salaam.

Bypassing immigration and customs in the new airport, recently built by Taiwan as payment for diplomatic recognition, CR took the men to his black Toyota Hilux. They drove thirty-two miles on one of the country's few paved roads through the gently rolling hills covered with lush jungle. They passed the gutted remains of the old airport, bombed to rubble by all sides in the war, and through the battle-scarred countryside. Overgrown trees from the Firestone rubber plantation, one of the largest in the world before Liberia's descent into chaos, could be seen just after leaving the airport.

They pulled into the city, which has no running water or electricity, and headed straight to room 104 of the Boulevard Hotel. The hotel, with its faded, dark lobby, usually filled with hookers in garish miniskirts, served as Bah's Monrovia home. With Bah to receive the guests was Gen. Benjamin Yeaten, Taylor's most trusted confidant and gatekeeper. Yeaten, beefy and perpetually scowling, was also the commander of Taylor's feared Special Security Service, with power to disappear political enemies or arbitrarily collect "taxes" from the few businesses that were still open.

The two new arrivals spoke with Bah in Arabic for a while, then discussed plans for flying to the remote northern town of Foya, near the border with Sierra Leone, to see about the diamond deal that had enticed the newcomers to Liberia. Yeaten said he would have a helicopter ready just after daybreak.

Right on time, the guests, along with CR, Yeaten, and Bah, were taken to James Spriggs Payne Airport, a small airport inside Monrovia, where they waited in a ramshackle VIP lounge littered with empty beer bottles and pungent with the stench of stale urine. The helicopter lifted them over the country's dense jungle and misbegotten roads. Less than an hour later they landed in Foya, a dirt-poor jungle town despite the millions of dollars in diamonds that pass through its muddy, rutted streets every year. Only five miles from the border with Guinea and nine miles from Sierra Leone, Foya was the commercial center and trading post for the RUF. The diamonds flowed out and weapons, ammunition, food, medicine, and cash for the rebels flowed in to this motley collection of huts and bombed-out homes.

The visitors stepped off the chopper and were swarmed by heavily armed child combatants dressed in ratty T-shirts and flip-flops. These were the bodyguards of the RUF high command and they led the delegation to the waiting commanders. All the leaders were under thirty years old. They were led by Sam Bockerie, Commander Mosquito, the RUF's acting commander; Dennis Mingo, known as Superman, whose abduction of children made his reputation for savagery; Eddie Kanneh, the RUF's money man; Col. Morris Kallon, a battle-hardened field commander responsible for razing villages across the country; and Brig. Gen. Issa Sesay, the RUF's deputy commander, whose daily consumption of alcohol, marijuana, and cocaine rendered him incoherent most days by early afternoon.

The group went to a nearby house to talk business. Bah introduced the visitors and said that from now on all RUF diamonds would be sold to them. It was not the first time Bah had brought diamond buyers to meet the RUF. Over the previous two years Bah had cut numerous deals with a variety of purchasers whose identities were of little concern to the rebels. All they wanted were guarantees that, in exchange for their diamonds they would get the weapons, ammunition, satellite telephones, vehicles, and medicine vital to fueling their war.

The visitors gave Bockerie $50,000 as a goodwill gesture. Bockerie brought out about 300 carats worth of diamonds and handed them to the visitors, to prove he could deliver. With business done, the visitors set up a satellite phone and made two calls, one to Belgium and one to Pakistan. Bah spoke briefly on the phone to Pakistan. With everything in order, the group flew back to Monrovia.

At 2:30 A.M., the two visitors, Bah, Yeaten, CR, and other senior security officials were summoned to the Congo Town residence of Taylor. A nocturnal creature, Taylor holds most of his important meetings in the wee hours of the morning. Guards from the Anti-Terrorist Unit, trained by South African mercenaries and armed with AK-47s, stood guard in front of the well-lit walls, which were topped with rows of concertina wire. They walked past the manicured courtyard where peacocks and ostriches roamed, to the second-floor living room. A Boyz II Men CD was playing. The two men brought along the payment that had been counted earlier in Bah's hotel room. When Taylor arrived and bade everyone be seated, they handed him a brown leather pouch containing $500,000 in cash. It was the standard amount for doing diamond deals in Liberia. Often the payments were called "advance taxes." But the money went straight to Taylor's pocket.

Both sides would benefit enormously from the budding relationship. Thirty days later a large shipment of arms and ammunition for the RUF arrived, sent through the Gambia. The rebels used the cash from al Qaeda to buy the weapons. The stones gave al Qaeda a fail-safe way to hide its assets outside banks and other financial institutions. Belgian investigators later traced $20 million through a single account they believe was used by al Qaeda to purchase diamonds.

•

I met CR on my first trip to Monrovia in April 2000, shortly after I began my African tour. Steve Coll, the *Washington Post*'s managing editor, had met CR in 1999 when Coll and photographer Michel duCille did a Sunday magazine piece on the RUF. Trips with the rebels were rare and dangerous, and Taylor had personally approved their trek.

John Caldwell, an American businessman with years of experience pushing the limits of legal activities in Africa, arranged the trip because he was buying diamonds and attempting to set up other business deals with the RUF. He hoped the trip could garner some good press for the rebels. Coll wanted to write about the atrocities in Sierra Leone, which had occurred at the same time as the Bosnian conflict and had received almost no international coverage. Taylor asked Ibrahim Bah to work out the logistics of the visit. CR was assigned as their driver and bodyguard for the two-week journey. The three hit it off and Coll suggested I get in touch with CR when I hit the ground there.

The magazine piece, far from the public relations coup Caldwell hoped for, was the first definitive account of the RUF's brutality in the American press. Still, CR agreed to talk to me when I first visited Monrovia. We got along well and stayed in regular contact. Because Bah and Taylor had established his relationship with the *Washington Post*, CR and I met openly. We almost always met late at night at the Mamba Point Hotel, one of the few functioning establishments in the battle-scarred, sweltering seaside capital. Five years after the civil war ended, only the few in the capital who could afford their own generators had lights. Entire city blocks, reduced to rubble in the fighting, have never been rebuilt. Tens of thousands of people live in bombed-out buildings that frequently collapse in the rainy season. Unemployed young men, many of whom fought on one or more of the myriad sides of the war, line the cracked and cratered streets. At night the downtown avenues are filled with the smoke of charcoal fires as women cook meager meals outdoors.

Just down the road from the sprawling but almost empty U.S. Embassy, the Mamba Point had a massive generator, providing satellite TV and air-conditioning when it was working. The bar had cold beer and a Chinese cook who could produce an eclectic menu including excellent pizzas, Chinese food, pancakes, and pastries. These amenities made the Mamba Point a favorite hangout for the few in the town who could afford the steep prices, all payable only in U.S. dollars: visiting journalists, relief workers, missionaries, and the elite of Taylor's regime.

CR and the RUF leaders he brought in tow insisted on dining on pizza on the hotel verandah overlooking the pounding surf rolling onto a beautiful white sand beach. Because of CR's standing and contacts, I had exceptional access to the RUF and the happenings in Taylor's inner circle. During the first meetings I was terrified the RUF would want to exact revenge for Coll's article. But with no Internet access, cut off from the outside world and mostly illiterate, they had never seen the piece. In their minds any representative of the *Washington Post* was a friend because its reporters had gone into the bush with them.

Through CR I met a who's who of the RUF: Bockerie, the former hairdresser; Gibril Massaquoi, the chief spokesman; Kallon, the notorious child abductor. I also met one of RUF leader Foday Sankoh's wives, several of his bodyguards, and other field commanders. After our meals, the RUF leaders would shake my hand and assure me that "the *Washington Post* and the RUF are brothers." It was clear they never read what I wrote using the information they gave me. I wrote stories on Taylor's role in supplying weapons for diamonds, the internal divisions within the RUF, and their decision not to disarm despite their public promises to do so. I also wrote about the RUF's victims, child soldiers and amputees. I wrote about Taylor's inner circle and dealings with mercenaries and how he sold sections of the nation's prized forest reserve to timber companies.

In July 2001 Taylor, under increasing international pressure to halt his alliance with the RUF and to stop the trade in blood diamonds, began looking for my sources. Unlike the illiterate RUF leaders, Taylor kept a close eye on what was written about the region, and especially about him. His wife owned the sole Internet provider in the country. Taylor was especially angry about stories detailing the role of the Oriental Timber Corporation, a Malaysian logging company that shipped tons of weapons into the Liberian port of Buchanan in 2001 and 2002. It was not hard to track some of the information to CR. Taylor had CR and his pregnant wife arrested. They sat in jail for several weeks, until CR could get together enough money to bribe his way out. Badly shaken because his usual impunity had evaporated, CR called me. He said he was just out of prison and told me to never call him again. He hung up before I could answer.

I was stunned and felt guilty, although I didn't know exactly what had happened. So I was surprised in early September when CR called me from Ouagadougou, Burkina Faso, where he was visiting his old friend and boss Ibrahim Bah. CR had gone there from prison to see if Bah could patch up the rift with Taylor. But Bah and Taylor had just had a falling out over money and Bah had said there was little he could do. CR headed for Abidjan shortly after 9/11, where he borrowed $500 from a friend to pay the bribe for his wife's freedom. We met there and, while waiting for her to arrive, spent several days in extensive conversations eating and drinking coffee in the comparative luxury of Abidjan's restaurants. During these meetings CR regaled me with stories of the wars he had witnessed and people he had met. He told me of treks through the jungle and Taylor's life.

He also told stories of a mysterious Pakistani woman visiting a safe house in Monrovia and picking up large quantities of diamonds. Bah, he said, had rented a spacious house with a generator for his new Arab clients. He said there was a new weapons pipeline set up by a Lebanese named Aziz Nassour and the Arab buyers.

When CR's wife arrived about a week later, she had to be hospitalized for a few days because of vaginal bleeding. I shuttled them back and forth to the hospital and helped pay the medical bills. Then they set off for Accra, Ghana, to start a new life.

It was during one of our last meetings in Abidjan, in mid-September 2001, our lunch at the California Barbeque, that CR asked me the question: "What is Hezbollah?"

•

Why, I wondered, would someone who spent most of his time in the West African bush be interested in Hezbollah? CR explained that the group of Bah's Arab diamond clients at the safe house often asked him to join them in watching videos of Hezbollah suicide bombings. "I don't think they like the Israelis very much," CR said. He added that there were pictures of "the man with the beard that is on television all the time"—bin Laden—on the walls of the house.

CR had noticed something else amiss. The Arabs were paying more than the going rates for stones, and were furiously buying as many as they could. In July there had been a high-level meeting between Aziz Nassour, the new weapons supplier, and the RUF high command. Nassour asked the RUF to double its diamond production and promised to pay premium rates for whatever was produced. Longtime RUF clients were being turned away to meet Nassour's requests.

I filed the Hezbollah information away. A few days later I heard from a European intelligence source that Imad Fayez Mugniyah, a senior Hezbollah leader, had recently been spotted in West Africa on a fund-raising mission among the tens of thousands of Lebanese who live in the region. As part of its terrorism coverage, *Newsweek* magazine that week carried a two-page spread of mug shots of the FBI's Most Wanted Terrorists, including a picture of Mugniyah.

Immediately after 9/11 there was little space in the newspaper for stories unrelated to terrorism. I thought maybe these leads would allow me to get into the action, breaking off an unexpected though minor piece of the terrorism puzzle with an African angle. So when I met CR the next week in Accra, where I was traveling for other stories, I took along the *Newsweek*, thinking there was a slight possibility he would recognize Mugniyah as a visitor to the safe house in Monrovia. CR looked at Mugniyah's mug shot, said he had never seen the man, and we ate our meal by the swimming pool of the Novotel.

As I prepared to pay the bill, CR continued chatting while leafing through the magazine. He stopped in mid-sentence and pointed to the mug shots on the adjoining, folded-back page of the magazine. "I know these people," he said after scrutinizing three pictures in the row of mug shots of al Qaeda operatives. "They have been in Liberia," CR said. "I myself met them at the airport and took them to the diamond fields. We even stayed together in the bush. They bought many, many diamonds."

One of the pictures was of Abdullah Ahmed Abdullah, described by the FBI as a "top bin Laden adviser." The two others were Khalfan Ghailani and Fazul Abdullah Mohammed, the two who had arrived in Monrovia together. The FBI described all three as key al Qaeda operatives.

I asked CR to look at the pictures again to make sure, and then to tell me everything he could remember about them. I asked when they had been there, and he said two of them had been in Sierra Leone and Liberia earlier in 2001. I had started out thinking there might be a Hezbollah tie to Taylor's diamonds. Now suddenly CR was linking the diamond trade to al Qaeda. I told CR that, although I had never known him to lie, I was deeply skeptical.

"I know these people, my brother," CR said, staring at the pictures. "They changed their names but they can't change their faces."

After CR's initial identification of the al Qaeda operatives, I started seeing other pieces of the puzzle. CR, during my visits to Monrovia, used to kid me all the time that I didn't really know who Bah was. He had also mentioned several times that Bah had been to Afghanistan in the early 1980s, before heading to Lebanon to fight with Hezbollah. The RUF was mining more diamonds than any time in history. Strange new Arab men were paying premium prices for the stones. It all seemed to fit.

My U.S. and European intelligence contacts had no information on West African diamond sales to al Qaeda. Confirming the information meant sitting down face-to-face with the commanders of the RUF who dealt with the al Qaeda men. Because the al Qaeda leaders were reportedly there only a few months earlier, I knew if these people didn't recognize the men, then CR was mistaken.

•

I asked an intermediary to set up a meeting in Freetown, Sierra Leone, where many of the RUF commanders were spending time as a halting, UN-brokered peace deal was gradually implemented. I stressed the meeting was tremendously important. He said he would see what he could do. Thinking it was unlikely the trip would yield much, my wife, Leslie Bumstead, five months' pregnant with our second child, and I decided she and our two-year-old son, Jonas, would accompany me and visit friends in Freetown. Jonas especially loved the ten-minute helicopter ride from Lungi International Airport to Freetown. The ride, in an aging Soviet chopper, is required because going by land can take hours.

Good to his word, the intermediary said we could meet at 9 P.M. for a secret, off-the-record session at the Cape Sierra, a once-proud tourist hotel now decaying from the corrosive tropical heat, the sea air, and an obvious lack of guests and maintenance. Six RUF commanders were already seated silently on the one ratty sofa and the few chairs in the small suite. Teenage boys with AK-47s stood guard in the dark, vacant hallway, smoking and listening to music blasting from a tinny radio.

I introduced myself to those I had not already met. After some brief chitchat I started laying out everything I knew and thought I knew about the deals with al Qaeda. I tried my best to bluff and cajole the sullen young men into telling me about their diamond deals and their relationship with the al Qaeda operatives. I passed around pictures of the al Qaeda leaders CR said had been there. The RUF men slouched in their seats nursing warm beers and wearing wraparound sunglasses despite the fact it was close to midnight. A few pulled out cheap, filterless cigarettes and smoked while I plowed ahead. After a while the electricity went out. The hotel's generator was not working. We continued our rather one-sided dialogue by candlelight. With the stifling heat we opened the window to catch the cool ocean breeze but were immediately invaded by mosquitoes.

Sweaty, tense, and tired, I had no idea if I was getting through to them. While sometimes agitated by what I said, they mostly stared at me and talked rapidly among themselves in Krio, the local dialect. Like the vast majority of RUF members, most of those at the meeting could not read or write and had lived much of their lives in the bush. Finally, around 11 P.M., I was exhausted and ready to give up and go to bed. Then one of the men excused himself and went into the hallway for some air. I followed. The surf was pounding and the humidity stifling as the tropical lightning storm played across Aberdeen Bay.

"We do know those people," the young man said, referring to the al Qaeda operatives. "It is true they were here. It is true they bought diamonds." He confirmed details of some of the meetings I had asked about, the location of the safe house in Monrovia, and the time frame. "We all know the house," he said. "We have all been there."

Another commander emerged and described how the al Qaeda operatives constantly talked on the satellite telephone to their main contact, whom they called Alpha Zulu. I knew from CR that Alpha Zulu was Aziz Nassour's code name but I hadn't mentioned it because, in the tension, that detail had slipped my mind. The two commanders described the July meeting in Monrovia that CR had talked about, where Alpha Zulu had asked the RUF to double its production. They also described Nassour's man on the ground, known by the code name Sierra Oscar, as the person who handled most of the money. Sierra Oscar was Samih Osailly, Nassour's cousin.

When we rejoined the main group, it was clear something in our earlier conversation had made them angry. I had told them Nassour was buying the RUF a batch of new pickup trucks and motorcycles in exchange for the diamonds. Now they demanded to know if Nassour was Alpha Zulu. I said yes. While I was out of the room the commanders had been discussing what to do if this were the case: Issa Sesay, the RUF field commander, had indeed received new vehicles, but was hoarding them. They had been at a loss to explain where the new merchandise came from and were planning how to get revenge for not getting their cut. Their anger led to more confirmations of the al Qaeda deals.

The next day the RUF leaders I had met with flew by UN helicopter to the RUF headquarters in Makeni for an emergency meeting with the high command. They met RUF chief Sesay and other top leaders and explained my story to them. Sesay, already well into his daily spree of alcohol and drugs, was terrified and "sweating like a pig," one participant said. The two al Qaeda operatives were widely recognized as having been sent by Alpha Zulu. Alpha Zulu was known to all of them. The high command decided to promise a full investigation while admitting nothing if I wrote my story.

I wrote a draft of the story and flew home, anxious to get the family out of Freetown before the story ran. It ran on the front page of the *Washington Post* on Friday, November 2, 2001, and was picked up by wire services and radio reports around the world. The story named Aziz Nassour, Samih Osailly, and Ibrahim Bah as the keys to the al Qaeda connection and described the safe house in Monrovia. It explained why the terrorist group wanted to put millions of dollars into precious stones and how the Taylor government had protected the operation. Accompanying the story were pictures of Bah, taken by *Post* photographer Michel duCille on his trip. During their last day together Bah, who had refused to allow his picture to be taken, relented. Until then, Bah had prided himself on avoiding being photographed. The CIA and British and French intelligence had long tried unsuccessfully to get a picture of him. Now he was on the front page.

As I expected, the U.S. government said it had no information on any al Qaeda ties to diamonds in West Africa. Taylor issued denials and attacked me as an alcoholic seeking to defame his government because Liberia would not pay me hundreds of thousands of dollars to write nice stories about Taylor. Bah said he was a used car salesman in Ouagadougou, Burkina Faso, with no connection at all to diamonds. The RUF announced an "internal investigation," one that would go nowhere. It seemed the storm would blow over quickly.

But on the next Saturday afternoon, when I arrived home in Abidjan, Ivory Coast, after a trip, there was an urgent message waiting for me from the U.S. Embassy's Regional Security Officer. My stomach knotted. I knew it was important when he insisted I come to the embassy at 9 A.M. Sunday. It was a short meeting in the basement of the heavily fortified building. I already had a pretty good idea of what this was about. There was no small talk. He showed me two lines of a classified cable saying there were "credible threats" of "retribution" against me for the story. The officer said he had no more information or any way to evaluate the seriousness of the threat, but was required by U.S. law to inform me of the potential danger.

Shaken and unsure of what to do, I talked to my wife and the senior editors of the *Post*. We agreed I should travel somewhere else in Africa until things cooled off. With a pregnant wife and two-year-old son I didn't want to take unnecessary risks, but a real threat seemed unlikely. At least that's what I told myself. The last thing I wanted to do was get myself or my family hurt. But I had a visceral objection to giving Taylor and Bah the satisfaction of driving me off the continent.

On Monday Phil Bennett, the *Post*'s assistant managing editor for foreign news, called to tell me the intelligence service of another country had warned the paper there was a plan to "take care of the *Washington Post* reporter." Bennett ordered us to leave immediately.

The next available flight was Thursday so we settled into a tense four days of tedious waiting. We were so deeply in denial about the seriousness of the situation that, at the time, it seemed reasonable to think we could return in a few weeks. We made no arrangements to ship our belongings or to close the bureau.

While we had daytime and nighttime watchmen, as most people living in the upper-class sections of Abidjan do, they were not armed and provided little security. We didn't want them to leave, but felt it was unfair to ask them to stay. We said they were free to quit if they wanted to, given the increased risk. Both stayed on.

CR, who was still in touch with Bah, warned me Bah was planning to plant drugs on me in order to have me arrested at the airport. Then, he said, they could beat me and scare me, but not kill me. Given the extensive contacts of Bah and Taylor in the army and police of Ivory Coast, I declined an offer of local police protection. But CR's story seemed credible, and I had no desire to spend several years in an Ivorian jail. For protection, I asked that an embassy official escort us through customs and immigration and wait until we boarded the flight, which was scheduled to depart at 11 P.M. The embassy agreed, and two imposing security officers stuck with us every step of the way. Everyone from ticket agents to customs and immigration officials seemed to realize it was not a good idea to bother us that night. Even though the flight was delayed several hours, the officers waited with us until we were seated on the airplane. We were deeply grateful. In the week before Thanksgiving, we found ourselves unexpectedly back in Washington for the holidays.

CHAPTER FOUR: Roots of the al Qaeda Connection

A l Qaeda's interest in diamonds and other pre-
cious stones did not begin with the venture in West Africa. But prior
indications of their interest were largely ignored by U.S. intelligence.
The most compelling evidence was provided in the trial of Wadih el
Hage, a Lebanese and naturalized U.S. citizen who worked for several
years as bin Laden's personal secretary. He was arrested on September 20, 1998, and charged in the U.S. Embassy bombings in Nairobi,
Kenya, and Dar es Salaam, Tanzania, which had occurred six weeks
earlier. He was convicted and sentenced to life in prison without pa-
role. While plotting the bombing, el Hage shared a room in Nairobi
with Fazul Abdullah Mohammed, one of those who then went on to
Liberia and Sierra Leone to buy diamonds.

During the trial, government witnesses who had defected from
al Qaeda made repeated references to diamonds. The testimony
shows al Qaeda was entering into commercial diamond ventures in
its early days. However, the prosecutors in the case, focusing on el

Hage's direct link to bin Laden, asked few follow-up questions about the stones.

El Hage's file of business cards, his personal telephone directory, and a notebook full of numbers and notes were also introduced as evidence. The most intriguing note is on a page where he wrote "Liberia," followed by a list of four names and four phone numbers there. It also lists the cost of certain pieces of mining equipment, and offers a sort of primer on buying diamonds, written in Arabic: "When buying uncut stones, we need to look at their shape, color and size," one entry says. "No two stones are the same, nor do they cost the same amount." Another says: "The bright white color is the one that is most sought after and is more expensive." The note had to have been made prior to el Hage's September 1998 arrest, indicating contacts stretching back several years. The documents had largely been overlooked by intelligence officials and investigators. Alex Yearsley of Global Witness combed the trial records and found it in March 2003.

Other el Hage documents contain numerous references and contact numbers for diamond dealers. One handwritten note in his telephone directory, dated April 4, 1995, says: "Called few jewelry stores, visited rooms, but either not interested or want different kinds." El Hage kept the names, phone numbers, and addresses of jewelers, mostly specializing in diamonds, in the United States, Antwerp, London, and Cyprus. In some cases he had their home telephone numbers.

The link between el Hage and diamonds also surfaced in the German interrogation of Mamoun Darkazanli, who is charged with being part of the al Qaeda Hamburg cell that planned the 9/11 attacks. Four days after 9/11, Darkazanli was asked by police if he knew el Hage. Darkazanli responded: "Yes, el Hage wanted to make a deal in uncut diamonds. The deal did not come about because there was no trust between el Hage and the diamond dealers in Germany." Darkazanli indicated the deal was attempted in 1993.

From the time el Hage's documents were confiscated in 1998

until December 2002—fifteen months after 9/11—no U.S. government agencies had contacted any of the jewelers listed, not even those in the United States, to investigate leads that could lead to al Qaeda.

•

Al Qaeda's interest in diamonds and precious stones is not unusual. Throughout much of the 1990s the Taliban and Northern Alliance fought over and profited from emerald fields in the Panjsher Valley, north of Kabul. The decade before that, the mujahideen, with whom bin Laden first gained notoriety, mined the emeralds in the Hindu Kush mountains to finance their war against the Soviets. Before the Taliban was routed in 2001, the emerald fields were controlled by the legendary warlord Ahmad Shah Masood, providing a significant portion of his war chest to fight the Taliban.

Al Qaeda also made inroads into the tanzanite industry. Tanzanite is a rare gem, found only in one five-square-mile patch in northeastern Tanzania. El Hage's diary makes clear his interest in dealing in the stone, whose popularity soared after being featured in the movie *Titanic*. In one undated notation beside the name and address of an Antwerp jeweler he wrote, "The tanzanite are not identical. He wants to make a pair of earrings, a ring and necklace. It has to have same color." Next to the name of a jeweler in San Francisco, el Hage wrote "will buy rough [stones]. Is willing to come over to Nairobi. Any amount of raw, $60, $80, up to $100/gram."

An extensive November 2001 *Wall Street Journal* investigation found an openly radical Muslim presence in the heart of the tanzanite mining district. Buyers tied to bin Laden were purchasing the gems from miners and middlemen and smuggling them to Dubai and Hong Kong. It is not clear whether, like diamonds, the tanzanite was being bought primarily as a way of hiding money or whether it was a money-making venture.

Alex Magyane, a Tanzanian official investigating the trade, said he has traced bin Laden–linked smuggling of rough tanzanite through Kenya to bazaars in the Middle East. "Beyond any doubt I am 100 percent sure these Muslim gem traders are connected to Osama bin Laden," he said. Musa Abdallah, a tanzanite miner for six years, said bin Laden was popular among Muslim tanzanite diggers, and that Muslim fundamentalists had formed "a mafia to dominate the trade." "Yes, people here are trading for Osama," Abdallah said. "Just look around and you will find serous Muslims who believe in him and work for him."

At the center of the trade is the Taqwa mosque, where the imam, Sheik Omari, issued edicts saying Muslim miners should sell their stones only to fellow Muslims. He also preached on the virtues of suicide bombings. Asked if he worked with or belonged to al Qaeda, Sheik Omari answered vaguely that "al Qaeda means 'base.' I don't know any base. But Islam says we must support our brothers and sisters and those who defend Islam from its enemies."

Like diamonds, emeralds and tanzanite are often sold for cash, leaving no paper trail and falling outside the traditional banking system. They are another way of slipping through the cracks of the world's new economic order.

•

El Hage's diaries show bin Laden was interested in operations in Liberia at least as far back as 1998. The group already knew Ibrahim Bah, Taylor's diamond man, who had fought in Afghanistan. Bah could be trusted and was already well positioned in the diamond trade. The terrorists knew they would also be operating where Western intelligence services were not looking for them.

Since his time in Afghanistan and Lebanon, Bah had maintained contact with diamond buyers across the Arab world. He had escorted diamond merchants from Dubai to Monrovia in early 1998. Lebanese merchants affiliated with Hezbollah regularly purchased diamonds with his blessing.

The first known West African contact with al Qaeda came on September 23, 1998, when Abdullah Ahmed Abdullah arrived in

Monrovia. It was just six weeks after al Qaeda's bombings of the U.S. embassies. The FBI lists Abdullah, an Egyptian, among the planners of the attacks. He joined the Egyptian Islamic Jihad and traveled to Afghanistan in the late 1980s, where he trained the mujahideen in the use of explosives. He later went to Somalia to train the militias that attacked U.S. forces there, and in 1998 moved to Kenya to help plan the attack on the U.S. Embassy in Nairobi. He had left Nairobi two days before the bombs went off. The FBI is offering a $25 million reward for information leading to his capture.

The day before Abdullah arrived in Monrovia, Bah called CR to ask him to make the necessary arrangements for a special visitor. Bah said he would be arriving the following day at 11 A.M. on a special Air Burkina flight authorized by the president of Burkina Faso. The next day Bah and Abdullah were met at the airport by senior Liberian security officers. Bah introduced Abdullah as Mustafa and ordered CR to drive them straight to the African Palace Hotel, where they stayed the rest of the day.

At 1 A.M. CR was awakened by a courier and told to drive Bah, Abdullah, and a few others to the Executive Mansion, where Taylor had a residence. Abdullah brought no cash for Taylor, something that seemed to upset the president. After a brief conversation, Bah assured Taylor that, if all went well with the RUF, another delegation of Abdullah's people would soon return with cash to begin doing business. Later that day, after a few hours' sleep, Abdullah, Bah, and a security detail boarded a chartered helicopter and flew to Foya. Abdullah, who was desperate for Marlboro cigarettes, tried to buy a pack but only had a $100 bill. No one in the town had enough change to help him out, so others bought the cigarettes for him. The group boarded a Toyota pickup truck and drove forty-five miles to the RUF headquarters in Koidu. Because the road was so bad, the drive took nearly three hours. In Foya, Abdullah met the RUF's hairdresser-turned-commander, Sam Bockerie, and other leaders, and examined several hundred carats of stones. Appearing satisfied, he again promised that another group would come and finalize the dealings. That same afternoon they returned to Monrovia, and Abdullah left the next day.

•

Al Qaeda's dealings with the RUF and Taylor were not always smooth after the initial introductions were made. While investigators believe al Qaeda bought stones regularly, the group did not have a monopoly on the RUF's diamonds. In July 1999, the government of Sierra Leone and the RUF signed a peace agreement that led to a tentative cease-fire. As part of the agreement, RUF leader Foday Sankoh was not only freed from prison but given the rank of vice president and placed in charge of the nation's diamond resources.

Feeling unconstrained by deals made by Bockerie in his absence, Sankoh set about auctioning off the nation's wealth to whomever was willing to pay him the most. From a luxurious home hidden behind high walls and protected by his own RUF security, Sankoh conducted business by satellite phone, often dressed only in his underwear. He granted American businessman John Caldwell and his Belgian partner Michel Desaedeleer a monopoly on the sale of all of Sierra Leone's diamonds and gold in exchange for 50 percent of the commissions they generated. Caldwell set up an offshore company called Beca Group Ltd., based in the British Virgin Islands, for the venture. Desaedeleer later told me he was stunned at how little Sankoh knew of the outside world. When Desaedeleer presented Sankoh with a check in payment for a deal, Sankoh looked at the paper blankly and asked, "What is this?" Despite such naiveté, Sankoh knew how to double deal. While dealing with Caldwell, Sankoh signed similar diamond monopoly deals with South African merchants and was negotiating still others.

Under the cease-fire agreement, the RUF was to suspend all diamond mining. Instead, activity slowly picked up. Sankoh's feared Black Guards, ruthless even by the standards of the RUF, exercised an iron grip over the trade, executing anyone suspected of keeping diamonds for themselves. Sankoh's appetite for diamonds caused deep splits in the RUF. His efforts to bypass Taylor in order to keep more money for himself incurred Taylor's wrath. By October 1999 Taylor asked Sam Bockerie, the RUF's top field commander, to assassinate Sankoh. But Sankoh was tipped off and Bockerie fled to Liberia with a large cache of diamonds and several hundred battle-hardened combatants.

Sankoh soon caused other problems. In late April 2000, RUF troops took more than five hundred UN peacekeepers hostage to protest UN efforts to control the diamond fields. Sankoh claimed the UN troops were simply "lost in the bush." When the RUF appeared to be marching on Freetown, Britain, the former colonial power, rushed more than one thousand elite troops to halt the rebel advance.

As the hostage story gained world attention, Taylor, hoping to win the goodwill of the international community, offered to mediate the release of the prisoners. But Taylor's offer had unforeseen repercussions. With the lives of the UN officials at stake and the world media focusing on a tiny nation again teetering on the edge of chaos, both Britain and the United States took more decisive action than they had in the past. The British, concerned for the safety of their troops in Sierra Leone, poured electronic and satellite intelligence-gathering resources into the region. Intelligence agencies monitored Taylor's communications and traced his frequent calls to senior RUF commanders. Satellites were deployed to monitor the movements of troops and weapons. "Suddenly," one senior U.S. intelligence source told me, "we were looking up Taylor's ass in ways he couldn't imagine."

What they found alarmed them. Satellite photographs showed caravans of trucks bearing rifles, ammunition, and medicine flowing from Liberia to the RUF, despite RUF public promises to disarm.

Taylor's direct control of the RUF was established through intercepts of his satellite phone conversations with senior RUF commanders, directing the movements of the hostages and their choreographed release to win maximum media exposure. The extensive ties between the inner circle of Taylor's security establishment and the RUF were laid bare.

On May 8, 2000, the crisis in Sierra Leone boiled over. Several thousand angry protesters marched through the sweltering streets of Freetown to Sankoh's villa, which was protected by UN forces as well as RUF security. The mob hurled stones and bottles, then someone began shooting at the main gate. The UN troops fled and the RUF guards opened fire on the crowd, killing about a dozen people. Enraged, the crowd stormed the house. Sankoh took a briefcase he thought was full of diamonds and fled over the back wall with two aides. They headed up the footpaths into the hills behind Freetown. Aging and overweight, Sankoh could not keep up with his security detail. When they stopped to rest, Sankoh opened the briefcase, only to find he had grabbed the wrong valise. He ordered one of his guards to go back and get the one filled with diamonds. The guard was too scared to obey. Sankoh's greed undid him within a few days.

At dawn on May 17, Sankoh and a bodyguard crept out of their hideout and tried to find their way back to Sankoh's villa, which they didn't know had been thoroughly ransacked. Journalists and authorities had collected piles of Sankoh's documents, including notebooks detailing his diamond sales and payments to Taylor. Someone, it was never known who, picked up the diamond-filled briefcase and became instantly wealthy.

Local residents recognized Sankoh and alerted a militia commander known as Black Scorpion, who laid an impromptu ambush and nabbed the rebel leader. A crowd gathered. They beat Sankoh's bodyguard to death and stripped Sankoh naked. Handcuffed and naked, he was turned over to British officers and whisked off to a secret prison hideaway. Sankoh died in prison on July 29, 2003. He was being held on charges of crimes against humanity.

•

With Sankoh's imprisonment, control of the diamond trade shifted back to Ibrahim Bah, and the al Qaeda representatives re-emerged as key players. By July 2000, Bah was looking for someone who could handle large quantities of diamonds on their behalf. Allie Darwish, a small-time diamond dealer in Antwerp, heard of the action. Through a relative, Darwish contacted Bah. Short, wiry, and nervous, Darwish, a naturalized U.S. citizen, now works at a gas station near Boston.

Darwish quickly realized he was out of his league in the deals Bah wanted. But he knew someone who could play with the sharks, someone with years of experience in selling massive amounts of diamonds from Africa who was intimately familiar with the diamond trade in Sierra Leone and Liberia. Enter Aziz Nassour, the man CR and the RUF would later identify as Alpha Zulu, the principal diamond buyer for the al Qaeda operatives.

Broad-shouldered and beefy, the five-foot-eight Nassour was born on April 30, 1961, in Sierra Leone. He lived for years in Zaire and was one of the chief diamond handlers for longtime dictator Mobutu Sese Seko. In Kinshasa he was known as Aziz Mobutu because of his close ties to the dictator.

Nassour boasted of smuggling $25 million of diamonds a week from Zaire to Europe. Even after Laurent Kabila toppled Mobutu's regime in 1997 and changed the country's name to the Democratic Republic of Congo, Nassour continued to operate there. He also began to buy RUF diamonds through Liberia.

Nassour's young cousin, Samih Osailly, also wanted in on the deal. Nervous, edgy, and perpetually strapped for cash, Osailly was a decade younger than Nassour. Osailly had appeared on the diamond scene in Sierra Leone in 1997, selling military uniforms and weapons in exchange for diamonds. By the time I met him in December 2001, Osailly was involved in a nasty divorce case in Belgium and given to bouts of deep self-pity and depression. The Nassour-Osailly families ran a welter of joint businesses in both Sierra Leone and Antwerp. The boards of directors were almost exclusively family members.

Nassour is also a power broker in Lebanon, where he supports the Amal militia, a radical Shi'ite Muslim group founded in 1975. In 1982 a faction broke off from Amal and called itself Hezbollah, or the Party of God. Both Amal and Hezbollah have elected members in the Lebanese parliament. Although Nassour's name is on the UN list of persons banned from international travel, he travels extensively, using different names and passports. When in Beirut, he spends much of his time at the luxurious Sheraton Hotel, where he is under the protection of Nabih Berri, the Amal leader who is the speaker of the Lebanese parliament.

Nassour always took my calls and was unfailingly polite in our telephone interviews, even when I told him I had evidence linking his illicit diamond deals to al Qaeda. While offering differing interpretations of the evidence, he would neatly adapt his story to whatever new information I presented him. He invited me to Lebanon as his guest. He even sent me an electronic New Year's card.

•

With his contacts in Africa and experience in smuggling diamonds, Nassour recognized the potential for a big score when Allie Darwish approached him in the early summer of 2000. By July 2000, Darwish had introduced Ibrahim Bah, Taylor's diamond man, to Nassour. Darwish received a $50,000 commission for making the introduction. Nassour put his cousin Samih Osailly in charge of operations on the ground.

In November 2000, Osailly set up shop in Monrovia. Nassour guaranteed a favorable business climate by paying Bah $6,000 a month for his services and promising the RUF sophisticated weapons in exchange for diamonds. The RUF knew what it wanted. The rebels demanded surface-to-air missiles and four-barrel antiaircraft cannons.

Business looked promising. Anxious for a cut of the action, Allie Darwish flew to Monrovia on December 9. By December 23 Bah and the two al Qaeda operatives, Ghailani and Mohammed, had arrived. To cement the relationship, they decided to visit the diamond fields in Sierra Leone. On December 26, a convoy of five pickup trucks carrying Osailly, Darwish, the two al Qaeda representatives, and much of the RUF high command set out to tour the diamond fields. Nassour didn't make the trip, but bought a great deal of goodwill by donating several expensive new satellite phones to the rebels. CR drove one of the trucks loaded with RUF leaders and weapons.

But the time with the rebels was uncomfortable. The presence of the al Qaeda men, foreigners who kept to themselves, rankled because they were often on the satellite phone speaking a language no one understood. Osailly was nervous and demanded an AK-47 to protect himself. Darwish hated the bush because he was not used to being out of the city. Things came to a head around New Year's Eve, when Osailly wanted to take several thousand carats of high-quality diamonds back to Monrovia without paying for them. Nassour, by satellite phone, promised the RUF leaders payment for the stones would arrive in Monrovia in a few days. One faction of the RUF wanted to keep either Osailly or Darwish hostage until the cash was in hand. Finally both men were allowed to leave, but were ordered to report immediately to Liberian security upon arriving in Monrovia. To the dismay of Darwish and Osailly, the money was not there when they arrived in Monrovia in the first days of January 2001. The courier was delayed because of an attempted military coup in neighboring Ivory Coast, where flights from Europe landed. The airport there had been closed for five days. When the courier finally arrived, he was carrying $300,000 and the tension dissipated.

About ten days after Darwish and Osailly returned to Monrovia, the al Qaeda operatives returned too. There was a series of conversations among RUF leaders, Bah, and Osailly regarding the purchase of sophisticated arms. Nassour used a satellite cell phone registered to ASA Diam, one of his many companies, to try to broker a deal. Nassour briefly visited West Africa in January 2001 for talks and called dozens of times a day for the next eight months. Couriers arrived every week on the Thursday Sabena Airlines flights from Brussels to Monrovia, usually carrying around $500,000. The RUF began making weekly delivery of high-quality stones.

With the two al Qaeda operatives established in Monrovia, Bah and Nassour were anxious for a more permanent setup outside of the hotel. They rented a large safe house, tucked in between two houses belonging to Libyan security forces.

In early February, Darwish was going out to buy some fruit when Bah asked him to take the two al Qaeda men with him because they did not have proper shoes to return to the bush. Darwish spent the afternoon with them, taking them around to different shops. He was amazed that both remained virtually silent throughout.

Nassour, meanwhile, was busy arranging a large weapons shipment for the RUF from Bulgaria. He also began to badger Bah to get the RUF to step up the diamond mining.

The two al Qaeda operatives, Mohammed and Ghailani, settled into the new house in April. Mohammed spent most of his time in the bush, organizing and transporting the stones. Ghailani remained at the house, receiving the money and ensuring the stones got safely delivered to the couriers. In April, Abdullah, the senior al Qaeda officer who set up the initial contact in 1998, returned and stayed at the house for at least a week.

But things were occasionally tense. In late March 2001, Nassour fired his cousin, Osailly, who had taken his teenage girlfriend to Monrovia and was drawing a lot of unnecessary attention. The girlfriend wore extremely short shorts and paraded around town with a monkey on her shoulder. Osailly was drinking heavily and Nassour suspected him of siphoning off some the diamond money to pay for his parties and casino visits, where he ran up large gambling debts.

Tensions were also building with Bah, Taylor's initial broker in the deal. Nassour and Osailly came to rely more and more on Taylor's top aide, Benjamin Yeaten, for protection and access. They were paying Yeaten $6,000 a month for protection and, with that muscle, slowly squeezed Bah out of the diamond deals. Bah, who had set the whole operation up, was no longer necessary.

A bitter Osailly left Monrovia in early April. He later told friends he recognized the al Qaeda operatives as the men he dealt with in Monrovia. He said he was afraid because Nassour kept sending money, hundreds of thousands of dollars at a time, with orders to deliver it to the men, yet refused to say what he was up to.

With Osailly gone, Nassour stopped shipping the RUF diamonds to Antwerp. Instead, he sent the diamonds straight to Lebanon, where al Qaeda took direct custody of them.

•

On May 2, 2001, bin Laden's chief deputy and main strategist, Ayman Zawahiri, wrote a memo to Abdullah, the al Qaeda operative active in West Africa, describing a "project" whose success "may well be a way out of the bottleneck and transfer our activities to the stage of multinationals and bring joint profit." The memo was found in a computer purchased by the *Wall Street Journal* after the fall of the Taliban in Kabul. The computer contains hundreds of internal al Qaeda communications. The project, intelligence analysts say, could have been the West African diamonds, where the mining in the summer of 2001 was about to reach unprecedented levels.

Around the same time, numerous calls were being placed from Nassour's ASA Diam office and satellite telephone to Afghanistan and Pakistan, where Nassour later told me he had no business dealings. The last call to Afghanistan was made on September 10, 2001. Nassour claimed he did not know who placed the calls from his office satellite telephone.

On June 16, 2001, a woman using the name Feriel Shahin arrived in Monrovia from Quetta, Pakistan. CR had faxed her a visa that allowed her to bypass normal immigration procedures. On it she listed herself as a guest of "Abrahima Bah" and her address in Monrovia as that of the safe house. CR and others were told to take especially good care of her because she was a partner of Nassour. The woman, who kept her head covered, seldom ventured out of the house. After about a week she received a large parcel of diamonds from the RUF and left the country with the two al Qaeda operatives. The three arrived in Karachi, Pakistan, in late June. There they stayed several nights at the Shaharah-e-Faisal hotel before continuing on to Quetta, where their trail was lost.

In July 2001, as his business was accelerating, Nassour made two brief trips to Liberia. On July 9, he met with Taylor. But Nassour stayed only a couple of days because the RUF commanders who were supposed to meet him had been unable to get to Monrovia. Nassour left and, according European intelligence reports, went to Dubai, al Qaeda's financial center, where he picked up $1 million for Taylor. The money was to pay for protection for the two al Qaeda men, Mohammed and Ghailani, and to guarantee their ability to buy diamonds.

On July 16, Nassour met with the RUF high command in Monrovia and again asked the rebels to increase production, promising to buy all the stones they could mine. He also promised to deliver large numbers of Toyota Land Cruisers and Yamaha 250 motorcycles, vehicles that the RUF could use either in the war or for political campaigns if the peace process led, as promised, to the RUF's participation in presidential and parliamentary elections. Immediately after the meeting, the RUF leaders faxed Taylor a letter stating:

> Sir, we write to inform you of our present dealings with Mr. Aziz Nassour, that was introduced to us by Gen. Abrahima Bah, upon your recommendation. Sir, we agree to sell all of our diamonds to Mr. Aziz Nassour through your offices.

Sir, General Abrahim will buy these and other items for the movement from funds that will come from the sale of diamonds.

1- Drugs for our wounded soldiers and their families.

2- Fuel and gasoline, engine oil and some new tyres for the operations of the movement.

3- Military uniforms and boots for our high ranking officers.

4- Some cash that will keep us moving until General Abrahim come from Belgium.

5- One 4 x 4 truck.

May the Almighty richly bless you. Thanks.

•

By this time, the summer of 2001, local diamond merchants in Sierra Leone knew something was seriously amiss. Just as the rainy season began in earnest and diamond production should have been increasing, no stones were available to buy. Word filtered to Bo and Kenema in eastern Sierra Leone that every ten days or so a handful of Lebanese diamond merchants were receiving $500,000 from mysterious sources in Monrovia, with orders to buy up all the diamonds they could. The usual sellers told of being paid premiums of up to 30 percent for their stones.

Bo and Kenema are the traditional diamond purchasing centers, where the RUF and anyone else can sell their stones with no questions asked. The chaotic, bustling streets of both towns are jammed with cars, motorcycles, and pedestrians and lined with gaudy signs advertising diamond offices with names like Best Buy and Diamonds Forever. Most of the businesses are small, dark rooms that are virtually empty except for scales and other rudimentary diamond-analyzing equipment. The Lebanese buyers sit all day looking at the stones brought in by poor miners. Usually the purchaser also owns a small store crammed with cheap radios and stereos, rubber boots, and other mining necessities in case the seller needs somewhere to spend his money. But in the summer of 2001, those stores were un-usually empty. "At the prices they were paying, it was clear they were not buying to make a profit," said one major dealer trying to buy stones during that time.

Joseph H. Melrose, the rumpled, heavyset U.S. ambassador to Sierra Leone, monitored the diamond trade even though his embassy had less than a dozen diplomats. Melrose wrote a cable to Washing-ton about persistent reports that "bad Lebanese" were cornering the diamond market and the concerns this was raising locally. Given to wearing Mickey Mouse ties and perpetually smoking a pipe or cigar, Melrose loved hopping on UN choppers and touring as much of the country as he could, often to the consternation of his lone security officer.

Melrose was alarmed when he overflew the diamond mining re-gions, the same ones I drove to, and saw the swarm of activity. A frag-ile cease-fire with the RUF had held for several months and the rebels slowly surrendered their weapons to the UN. But instead of going home, the RUF units that disarmed usually just moved as a unit into mining. Despite the mining activity, Melrose found the country's ex-port figures for diamonds were plummeting. Where were the dia-monds going?

•

The answer came a year later, when Belgian investigators were tipped off by officials of the Artesia Bank that there were serious ir-regularities in Aziz Nassour's ASA Diam account. ASA Diam was owned by Nassour's cousin but used by Nassour for his Africa busi-ness. From 1997 until early 2000, ASA Diam registered no transac-tions at all, according to corporate records. Suddenly, from early 2000 through April 2001 the ASA Diam account in the Artesia Bank in Antwerp turned over about $70 million. While the company was declaring the diamonds as originating in the Congo, investigators found the stones were, in fact, coming through Monrovia.

Beginning in April 2001, while the ASA Diam account continued to receive large deposits, the company no longer reported any diamond sales in Antwerp. The diamonds were simply disappearing. Al Qaeda had begun taking direct custody of the stones rather than routing them through the traditional diamond center.

•

On April 12, 2002, the Belgian police arrested Samih Osailly in Antwerp on charges of diamond smuggling and illegal weapons sales. Belgian police analyzing bank records and information garnered from Osailly's computer, believe that $20 to $50 million passing through the ASA Diam account was the money that al Qaeda operatives paid for diamonds.

Osailly's computer and documents also produced evidence that he and Aziz Nassour, possibly on behalf of al Qaeda, were seeking to buy sophisticated surface-to-air missile systems and powerful rockets from half a world away. The proposed deal shows just how global the black market for sophisticated weapons has become.

The weapons were to be purchased in Central America, from the Nicaraguan army, with the aid of an Israeli arms dealer based in Panama and a Russian based in Guatemala. Investigators do not know if the deal ever resulted in weapons being transferred. But it was being planned in January 2001, just as the alliance between the diamond purchasers and al Qaeda was being cemented.

The first link between the West African buyers and the Latin American arms stockpiles was unknowingly provided by CR. After fleeing Liberia he had given me faxes and other documents he had kept. One was a fax received by Ibrahim Bah on January 16, 2001. It was handwritten in Spanish and was from Guatemala. It appeared to be a sample form of an end-user certificate, the document that shows weapons sellers that the weapons have been purchased by a legitimate government. Without a valid certificate, such sales are illegal.

The handwritten document CR gave me was addressed to "Sergey Ladigin, Director for Latin America of the firm Rosobonoron Export," the Russian state weapons sales company. CR said the paper

was related to a weapons deal, but he didn't know any more. I kept
the papers without realizing how important they would be.

•

In December 2002, I received a call from an acquaintance investigating a massive illegal weapons shipment in my old stomping
grounds, Latin America, where I had been a reporter for fifteen years.
Morris Busby, the former U.S. ambassador to Colombia, acting on behalf of the Western Hemisphere alliance known as the Organization
of American States, was investigating an illegal arms deal that sent
thousands of assault rifles to Colombia's vicious right-wing paramil-
itary organization. The United States has designated the group, the
United Self-Defense Forces of Colombia, a terrorist organization and
documented its leaders' extensive trafficking in cocaine and heroin.

Busby said the weapons sale was orchestrated by Shimon
Yelinek, an Israeli arms dealer based in Panama. Among the documents uncovered were references to weapons sales to Liberia. Busby
asked if I knew anything about it.

Just days before, I had been told by European investigators that
among the papers found in Osailly's possession were faxes of
weapons requests and an end-user certificate, sent to a "Mr. Simon"
in early January 2001. The investigators had identified "Mr. Simon"
as Yelinek. Osailly's notes showed he was trying to purchase Draganov rifles, among the most accurate sniper rifles in the world. But
what was most alarming was an apparently authentic end-user certificate from the government of the Ivory Coast, dated January 8,
2001, authorizing the purchase of many of the goods Yelinek was
seeking. The certificate, signed by the Ivory Coast's minister of defense, authorized a Bulgarian company to sell more than 10 million
rounds of ammunition, 10,000 Dragonav sniper rifles, night-vision
equipment, and grenade launchers.

Busby showed me some of the documents that had surfaced in
his Yelinek investigation. One stopped me cold. It was an exact copy,

neatly typed, of the handwritten paper CR had given me a year before. The story unfolded on three continents.

On January 2, 2001, Yelinek sent an e-mail to the representative of a Russian weapons firm based in Guatemala, discussing an "order that our friend in Africa need [sic]. They need it very urgent [sic]." The e-mail asked for quotes on prices "with and without an end-user certificate. Destination Liberia." Attached was a list of requested items that included the usual rifles and ammunition, but also included 20 SA-8 missiles with a trainer, 200 rockets for BM-21 multiple rocket launchers, and thousands of Draganov sniper rifles. The weapons were to be obtained from the government of Nicaragua. In the exchange of e-mails and faxes, Nicaragua even provided a price list for the goods, including cost differentials if the equipment was left over from the 1970s or of newer vintage. On January 16, Bah received the fax of the draft for creating an end-user certificate. He apparently typed it up and sent it back to Yelinek.

The SA-8 system, which requires three people to operate, is not used in West Africa and the BM-21 is also a rarity there. The sniper rifles as well are unusual because the forested, hilly terrain is not suited to their use. In addition, the RUF had no discipline for sharpshooting. They tended to spray as much fire as they could at any given target.

"The likelihood these types of weapons were going to the RUF rebels in the bush is very hard to believe," said one European intelligence analyst. "[They] almost certainly had to be destined for somewhere else." One place where all those weapons commanded premium prices was Afghanistan, investigators said. The Taliban and al Qaeda, fighting against the Northern Alliance, routinely sought the rocket launchers and sniper rifles.

Nassour passed the weapons list and end-user certificate on to Yelinek while Yelinek was in a hotel in Miami, Florida.

The partnership of Nassour and Yelinek seemed odd. But it

turned out that the radical Shi'ite Muslim and the former Israeli military officer were old friends. When Nassour was selling diamonds for Mobutu in Zaire in the early 1990s, Yelinek was providing security to the despot. The two, while on opposite sides of the Middle Eastern conflict, remained in contact through the years. Nassour said he got involved in the deal because he thought it was a legitimate sale and that he could make a large commission. But, Nassour said, the deal was never consummated. Yelinek was imprisoned in Panama in November 2002 on charges of illegal weapons smuggling.

•

It is not clear how long after 9/11 the West African diamond pipeline to al Qaeda stayed open, but the money to protect the two operatives, Fazul Abdullah Mohammed and Khalfan Ghailani, was well spent as they moved around the region. The two spent a good part of the summer of 2001 "in the presidential complex [in Ouagadougou] in the district Zone du Bois. The complex is called Maison des Hotes," according to a European intelligence report. After Nassour's payment of $1 million, the report says, the two moved to Camp Gbatala in Liberia. The military camp, located next to Taylor's sprawling private farm, is the base of the Anti-Terrorist Unit and the South African mercenaries who train them.

In late November 2001, a few weeks after my initial story on al Qaeda's West Africa operation ran, the Pentagon's Defense Intelligence Agency began receiving reports that four Arabs linked to al Qaeda—Mohammed, Ghailani, and two others—were still residing in Gbatala. The DIA, which has more people on the ground in West Africa than the CIA, took the reports seriously. The CIA did not. A small team of U.S. Special Forces, on a training exercise in neighboring Guinea, was put on standby to snatch the four. However, because the troops were mostly white and none spoke Krio, it was impossible to put together a team to infiltrate the camp for final reconnaissance. "We had multiple-source, reliable intelligence reports that those two and two others were in Gbatala and we stood up a team to do the snatch," said a military officer with direct knowledge of events. "But in the end we couldn't get the 100 percent identification we needed to pull the trigger and cause a possible international incident. After about a week the group stood down."

Ghailani apparently returned to Afghanistan to fight and may have been killed there. His personal papers were found near Kandahar. Mohammed is presumed to be alive. Abdullah has assumed operational control of al Qaeda's finances.

On my return to Washington in late November 2001, at the request of the CIA, I agreed to brief a group of analysts on how I obtained the story of al Qaeda's ties to diamonds. My primary concern was for them to understand the unique conditions under which I developed the story and why I believed it to be true.

The initial meeting with about a dozen analysts was somewhat confrontational, as I had expected. I began by saying I couldn't identify my sources or tell them much more than was in the story. Professional ethics demanded that I protect my sources and not divulge confidential information. But I could tell them the story of the story. They agreed.

We met around a small wooden table in a conference room of the CIA headquarters in Langley, Virginia. Lemonade and water were provided. The agents introduced themselves, using first names only. Most had notebooks, and one woman held a folded map of Monrovia. I wasn't sure what to say. As a journalist, I was uncomfortable briefing government officials. Yet I felt I had a duty to in this case, where the information could stop a terrorist attack or save lives.

I had dealt with the CIA for years, and the relationship was professional if not cordial. In El Salvador and Colombia I had reported extensively on some of the unsavory aspects of the agency's relationship with members of death squads and drug traffickers. There were occasional clashes, but I felt we had a mutual respect.

So I told my story, from CR's initial recognition of the al Qaeda men to my meeting with the RUF to getting on the plane from Abidjan. My throat was dry and I drank glass after glass of water. I was trying very hard not to cross over the line of what I, as a journalist, could say.

The analysts asked a barrage of questions. There were requests for clarification and sometimes dismissive remarks. With the map of Monrovia, they asked me to identify the safe house the al Qaeda operatives used. I did.

One agent in particular was unconvinced. He suggested the RUF had set me up in an elaborate scheme to discredit Taylor. Or perhaps, he said, one faction of the RUF was trying to set up another faction. I responded that if he had spent any time with the RUF he would know the leaders there, even if clean and sober, couldn't plan that. They had no knowledge or understanding of the international media or the ability to create Machiavellian schemes on an international scale.

It was clear from the questions that some of the agents were concerned I was going to write that there had been a massive intelligence failure in their not detecting the diamond trail. Knowing that the intelligence and law enforcement agencies were already reeling from the criticisms leveled at them for failing to stop 9/11, I addressed the issue head on. I said I didn't view this as a result of either carelessness or stupidity. The CIA had lost more assets in West Africa than almost anywhere else in the world after the Cold War. Many stations around the continent, which had been used primarily as recruiting grounds for Soviet bloc agents, were closed or cut to the bone. With the Cold War over, the stations were deemed redundant.

I knew some of the station chiefs in West Africa. Often they covered more than one country with virtually no staff. Out of necessity their reporting was limited to basic political and military problems. They didn't have the time or the resources to monitor what went on in the bush of Liberia or Sierra Leone. Even the most energetic field officers found that their reports had a low priority back home, where West Africa was considered a backwater.

After almost two hours, the meeting drew to a close. The most antagonistic agent stood up to leave. "If this had been happening, we would have known about it," he said. "There may be ties to Hezbollah or someone there, but not al Qaeda." I had assumed that the CIA had no prior knowledge of what I was talking about and would be primarily interested in verifying the information. I was wrong.

•

Almost two years after my initial publication on al Qaeda's foray into the diamond trade, the CIA still maintained there was no link, despite corroborating evidence found by others. Instead, in our dealings, the officers became more and more defensive and antagonistic.

I was baffled and prodded my sources for an explanation. I requested several times, in writing, comment from the CIA for this book and my stories. There was no response, not even a formal rejection of my requests. The only comment I got was in a brief December 2002 telephone conversation with Bill Harlow, chief CIA spokesman, when I asked for comment on my second, more detailed story on al Qaeda's ties to the diamond trade. He told me the story was a "pile of horseshit."

Another source who worked with the CIA said that, after each diamond story I wrote, congressional representatives would demand answers, often asking why a newspaper reporter seemed to know more about al Qaeda finances than the government. "It just really pissed them off," my friend said. "They were not about to investigate a story that they had no stake in. So they just kept saying it wasn't true."

But it was more than that. It turned out the CIA believed I had information I would publish that would be even more embarrassing than the diamond stories. I didn't know it at the first briefing, but I soon dug up what the CIA really feared and thought I already had: The CIA had twice ignored compelling information that would have shed light on the diamond trade between Liberia's Taylor and those close to al Qaeda. Nothing their agents could have known would have stopped 9/11, but they were terrified of new intelligence failures being exposed.

"What you have to understand is that following 9/11, the CIA got hammered," said one of my sources who worked extensively with the CIA. "Their first, and sometimes only, reaction to new revelations, revelations that made it appear they didn't know what was going on, is to cover their collective ass." It turned out there was something there to try to cover.

•

The CIA's position was becoming untenable to Congress and the few government investigators who were paying attention. The BBC did a documentary, using none of my primary sources, and found and filmed former RUF fighters who knew and did business with the al Qaeda diamond buyers. On camera, the diamond miners identified the two al Qaeda operatives out of rows of photographs and said the two had bought large amounts of diamonds. When the BBC reporters asked the CIA for comment, a spokesperson "strongly urged" the station not to run the story, saying it would be a disservice to its viewers. The BBC, having corroborated the information on the ground, with confirmation from British intelligence, ran the story as a thirty-minute special in February 2003, inaugurating its new digital channel, BBC 3.

Global Witness, the London-based organization investigating the ties between the exploitation of natural resources and dictatorships, also carried out an extensive investigation that corroborated my findings through documents and interviews. But the most telling new evidence supporting the story was in the findings of the UN-backed Special Court investigating and prosecuting the massive human rights violations and crimes against humanity of Sierra Leone's civil war.

David Crane, the respected American former military prosecutor who was named the court's lead prosecutor, told me he had verified about 80 percent of my findings from completely different sources. Crane, a slight, soft-spoken former inspector general at the Pentagon and assistant general counsel for the Defense Intelligence Agency, handled many high-profile investigations during his career. With a reputation for being hard-nosed but fair, Crane has a mandate to prosecute those most responsible for the crimes against humanity committed during Sierra Leone's civil war. Investigating the connection to al Qaeda did not directly fall under that purview, but Crane said his investigators kept running into terrorist ties as they looked into other crimes.

"Al Qaeda is using diamonds to wash its funds and [Sierra Leone] is the place where they are doing it," Crane told me in an interview in his sparsely furnished office in Freetown. "It is very specific evidence of al Qaeda's ties to the blood diamonds of West Africa. There being no rule of law here, there was a vacuum where people could operate with impunity, and they did that in Sierra Leone, including al Qaeda."

Specifically, the court investigators, led by Alan White, corroborated the presence of the al Qaeda operatives Mohammed, Ghailani, and Abdullah in Monrovia at the time CR, my Liberian source, had specified. Court investigators identified a fourth al Qaeda leader,

Sheikh Ahmed Salim Swedan, as visiting Liberia in June 2001 to buy diamonds. Like the others, he is on the FBI's Most Wanted Terrorists list, and, like the others, he participated in the 1998 U.S. Embassy bombings in East Africa.

Court investigators also verified the existence of the safe house and the connections to Ibrahim Bah and his Lebanese contact, Aziz Nassour. "Diamonds fuel [the Sierra Leonean] conflict and diamonds fuel terrorism," Crane said. "Charles Taylor is harboring terrorists from the Middle East, including al Qaeda and Hezbollah, and has been for years. It is time for the world to know this and who Charles Taylor really is. He is not just a regional troublemaker, he is a player in the world of terror and what he does affects lives in the United States and Europe."

On June 4, 2003, the court unsealed its indictment of Taylor for crimes against humanity and issued an international warrant for his arrest. He was only the second sitting head of state, after Slobodan Milosevic, to be so indicted.

The indictment was unsealed while Taylor was in Accra, Ghana, for peace talks. After briefly attending the opening ceremony, where he sat alongside the presidents of Nigeria, South Africa, Ivory Coast, and Sierra Leone, Taylor fled to the airport. Rather than arrest him, the government of Ghana flew him home on an official jet. Taylor technically remains an international fugitive, but in fact is being hosted by the Nigerian government in a luxurious villa.

Crane went public with his statements linking al Qaeda to the West African diamond trade several times, and his comments were much harder to dismiss than my newspaper stories. But the CIA quietly put out the word that I was using Crane for my own purposes, and stuck to their statements that al Qaeda's presence in Liberia and Sierra Leone was a fiction.

The UN Special Court was not alone in pursuing the investigations. A year after my initial story ran, European intelligence agencies, pooling their resources, knowledge of the diamond trade, and growing expertise in terrorism, believed the connection between al Qaeda and the West African diamond trade to be real and threatening. With voluminous documentary evidence accumulated in Belgium—telephone records showing calls from the satellite telephone of Aziz Nassour to Afghanistan right up until September 10, 2001, bank records for ASA Diam company, and travel records—the intelligence agencies felt they had documented the ties. So they were stunned that the CIA dismissed their information out of hand. European intelligence officers felt the CIA was treating its sister services as third-rate operations.

In a highly classified report prepared in February 2003 to brief congressional questioners, the CIA held to the line that there was no evidence of an al Qaeda tie to the diamond trade. While saying it was probable that Hezbollah profited from the deals I described, the agency still falsely stated that Hezbollah and al Qaeda did not work together because of religious differences, according to two sources familiar with the report.

I was not the only journalist whose reporting was dismissed by the CIA and other intelligence services. The intelligence community reacted much the same way to the *Wall Street Journal* report on al Qaeda's use of tanzanite. Robert Block, an old colleague and friend from my days in Central America, had written the story carefully and thoroughly with the late Daniel Pearl. A veteran correspondent with almost a decade-long track record in Africa, Block was no stranger to conflict zones or on-the-ground investigations. With a stringer, he infiltrated the tanzanite-mining area. His stringer, who did not want his name used for fear of retaliation, visited the radical mosque, taped interviews nailing down the al Qaeda connection, and helped put the story together.

After our stories ran, Block and I compared notes. He, too, was named in classified cables as a "fabricator" of his story. He was called a "liar." The CIA and other agencies not only put out the word not to talk to him after the story ran, but came up with some absurd reasons as to why the story couldn't be true. Despite the extensive writings by al Qaeda's own operatives, including bin Laden's personal secretary, Wadih el Hage, on the terrorist group's use of tanzanite, every effort was made to dismiss the story.

"They didn't know what tanzanite was when I first approached them [the U.S. Embassy] in Nairobi," Block said. "Their reaction was 'tanza-what? Should we know about this?' No one had read the court transcripts. They didn't have a clue." The irony is that both Block and I talked to the CIA and other intelligence agencies not only because we wanted to corroborate the information but because, in the chaos following 9/11, we both felt we could make a contribution to cutting off terrorist funding. "It was," Block noted, "our patriotic instincts that got us into this mess."

•

What I didn't know when I first met with the CIA was that they had, in fact, already missed several opportunities to dig into the diamond story. There were indeed footprints to try to cover.

Their first chance came in February 2001.

Shortly after arriving back in Antwerp from Monrovia, Allie Darwish, the Lebanese-American diamond dealer who had initiated the diamond deals that eventually led to al Qaeda, didn't know what to do. He had just returned from Liberia and had an end-user certificate for the purchase of tons of weapons. He was supposed to deliver the document to Aziz Nassour, the Lebanese diamond merchant he had enticed into the dealings. The weapons were to go to the RUF. But Darwish had been shocked by the child soldiers, the amputees, and the slavery he had seen on his trip into Sierra Leone with the al Qaeda operatives. He had no interest in helping the rebels get more weapons.

Darwish also sensed an opportunity. He had an outstanding arrest warrant for check fraud in Miami. He decided to call the U.S. Embassy, hand over the end-user certificate, and report on the diamonds-for-weapons deals he had witnessed. He thought that, in exchange for the information, he could get his Florida warrant erased. But no one at the embassy in Brussels would take his call. Instead, the three times he called he was told someone would get back in touch with him. After waiting several days each time for a response, he called again. What Darwish didn't know was that his calls had set off a furious debate in Washington over how to handle him.

Finally, a political officer from the U.S. Embassy in Brussels was instructed by Washington to hear Darwish out. The meeting lasted four hours. Darwish, nervous, hesitant, and talking in his usual scattershot fashion, showed the officer the original certificate and told his story.

Darwish did not talk about the al Qaeda connection because he did not know about it at the time. But he told them about the smuggling of weapons in exchange for diamonds by the RUF, Taylor, and the rest of those involved. He offered to leave the original end-user certificate, but the officer refused to take it, making a photocopy instead. After telling the story, he asked if the Florida warrant could be waived. The answer was inconclusive. A few days later he met with two other embassy officers who described themselves as "law enforcement officers." He retold the story. Again his inquiries about his warrant were met with equivocation.

The embassy officials sent a cable on Darwish to Washington within a few days and requested further instructions. The report included the satellite phone numbers Darwish had given them for Nassour, Bah, and others involved in the illicit diamond and weapons deals. No one in Washington had those numbers at the time. It detailed the safe house in Monrovia, diamonds-for-weapons deals, and the roles of the key players. "The cable asked for guidance," said Lee Wolosky at the NSC, and "knocked the socks off officials at the National Security Council."

When the cable arrived, Wolosky's office was just starting to focus on the Russian arms merchant Victor Bout, who was active in Liberia, and Bout's ties to al Qaeda and the Taliban. "Given the broader information we were looking at, it was an outrageous but potentially credible story," Wolosky said. "There were very few people in the government who were connecting the dots at that time."

Backed by his superiors at the NSC and senior State Department officials, Wolosky pushed for a formal deal with Darwish that would include forgiving his arrest warrant. But Justice balked, saying the NSC was interfering in law enforcement matters. The CIA, whose opinion carried the most weight, said it had no interest in Darwish's information.

In fact, at that time, the CIA had no resources allotted to investigate the blood diamond trade because it was not viewed as a threat to national security. In the end, no guidance was sent. The days turned into weeks. The initial cable from Brussels was not even forwarded to the U.S. embassies in Freetown or Monrovia, where the information could have been followed up.

Tired of waiting, Darwish went to Portugal, where he had a business buying used cars. While there he got an angry telephone call from Ibrahim Bah, demanding the end-user certificate for the weapons be returned. Darwish called the American Embassy in Brussels and asked what to do. He was told to return the certificate and stop calling.

Wolosky, convinced nothing would be done with Darwish's information, passed the intelligence on to the British out of concern for the British troops deployed in Sierra Leone. "It was a dramatic failure of the United States government to take action," Wolosky said. "If we had gotten our act together then, we might have had a better picture of al Qaeda's African and diamond operations in the crucial months prior to 9/11."

It was not the last missed opportunity.

•

On September 5, 2001, CR, my Liberian source, was with Ibrahim Bah at Bah's home on the outskirts of Ouagadougou, Burkina Faso. Having bought his way out of Taylor's prison in Monrovia, CR was hoping Bah could broker a reconciliation with the Liberian leader. CR, as he often did, answered Bah's phone. Bah was expecting a call from Belgium and did not want to talk to the person. But the caller spoke in Arabic, so CR passed the phone to Bah. After a brief conversation Bah hung up. He told CR to wait and see what would happen to the United States, which thought it was the world's police, in the next few days. CR, fearing the threat was aimed at UN peace-keepers in Sierra Leone, called the U.S. Embassy and asked to speak to someone about a matter of great importance. CR's motives were not entirely altruistic. He wanted to get back at Taylor for imprison-ing him and his wife and he was also hoping for a ticket out of his current uncertain and dangerous situation. He was given an ap-pointment with a political officer on the following afternoon.

After a brief meeting, the officer, who was new to Burkina Faso, asked CR to return Monday, September 10, at 2:30 P.M. By then, the officer said, someone who really knew the region would be available. The person who flew to Ouagadougou for the meeting was the re-gional CIA station chief from Abidjan, who had also just begun a new assignment.

The September 10 meeting was not overly cordial. CR explained a little bit about who he was, and said that he thought something se-rious was going to happen to Americans and that Bah had received a warning. He said he was afraid there would be an attack, either in Liberia or Sierra Leone. After about an hour the station chief dis-missed CR and told CR that if he were ever in Abidjan, he could drop by the embassy for a chat. That was the end of the conversation.

U.S. officials won't comment on the meeting.

•

Because few knew the full story behind the CIA's reluctance to investigate the diamond story, the agency's attitude was puzzling even inside U.S. intelligence circles. Other intelligence agencies found the evidence convincing. In a highly classified, limited circu-lation report, another intelligence group that monitors West Africa found the West African diamonds–al Qaeda link probable. The report found no smoking gun, but outlined why the transactions were "probable" and logical. "The CIA won't believe this happened unless you show them a receipt for diamonds signed by bin Laden," said an official who saw both reports. "Even then, they would probably say it didn't prove anything."

•

On November 29, 2001, at 8:40 A.M., two American officials walked into the dingy, sweltering Ministry of Security in Ouagadougou to meet with Ibrahim Bah. Blaise Compaore, the president of Burkina Faso, had initiated the meeting, telling the U.S. Embassy that his government could make Bah available for questioning in light of the allegations in my story. The Americans were initially undecided about whether to take up the offer, but eventually accepted. Bah, in the aftermath of the story, had proclaimed his innocence and said he was simply a used car salesman. To prove his innocence, he agreed to the meeting. The strategy of the U.S. officials going to the meeting, suggested by senior officials in Washington, was simply to prompt Bah to tell them what he knew, rather than to ask him specific questions. This was because the Americans realized they knew virtually nothing about Bah or his dealings, and they did not want the meeting to reveal just how weak their position was.

According to the official minutes kept by the Burkina Faso security forces, the meeting lasted until 10:25 A.M. During that time the American officials, including one from the CIA, asked Bah about allegations of his ties to al Qaeda. It was just eleven days after intelligence intercepts indicated that Taylor and Bah were possibly trying to kill me. No mention of that was made during the meeting.

Bah blamed CR for the allegations of his ties to al Qaeda, saying CR wanted a U.S. visa for the information he was providing. While denying any role with al Qaeda, Bah acknowledged doing business with the Lebanese diamond merchants who sold diamonds to the terrorists, Aziz Nassour and Samih Osailly. He said he had been introduced to Nassour by Allie Darwish. He acknowledged renting the house in Monrovia to be the headquarters of his commercial activities, but said that "business disagreements" had forced him to give up the house.

The meeting ended cordially, with the Americans requesting and receiving permission to photograph Bah to verify his identity. They even photographed one of the U.S. officials posing with Bah, smiling.

But that was not the end of the relationship. A separate report dated April 8, 2002, by the government of Burkina Faso, in response to requests from the UN panel of experts, said that "since Nov. 29, 2001, American investigators have met many times with Mr. Ibrahim Bah about his presumed implication in the diamond trade of Sierra Leone and the benefit of that trade to Osama bin Laden. At the end of the various audiences requested by the Americans, who followed the correct procedure for investigating, the security forces of Burkina Faso put Mr. Bah on an Air Burkina flight to Abidjan on Dec. 23, 2001." This showed that Bah not only met with the Americans, but that he was allowed to travel to Abidjan, Ivory Coast, in violation of the UN travel ban.

•

The meetings with Bah in Ouagadougou were with the Defense Intelligence Agency and CIA officials. What the letter did not say was that, during the meetings, the CIA gave Bah several thousand dollars and attempted to recruit him in a more permanent manner.

Several sources subsequently told me there was a growing feeling in the CIA, due to congressional pressure to act on blood diamonds and investigate a story in the press, that information they did not generate and could not track down was causing too much trouble. Rather than investigating in the field, they wanted a deal with Bah, who simply denied the story. The CIA, said one knowledgeable source, fell for Bah's line "hook, line, and sinker." But for Bah to be taken seriously, CR's credibility had to be destroyed.

The decision to pay Bah and try to get him on the payroll was controversial inside the CIA. Veteran Africa hands warned that Bah, after years of living by his wits and outside the law, had no real incentive to collaborate. Those opposed to the move wanted concrete evidence that Bah would help in dismantling the diamond and weapons networks he had pioneered. And they argued that having someone responsible for the brutality committed in the wars in Liberia and Sierra Leone on the payroll was problematic at best, especially if the relationship ever became public. But they lost the debate.

In my early reporting I was unaware of the Darwish walk-in in Belgium. I also chose not to report CR's contact with the embassy in Ouagadougou because I felt the information could not have prevented 9/11. While I thought it was bad judgment for the CIA to dismiss him, it was not part of the story. But I had underestimated the fear among some in the CIA that they might be blamed for ignoring potential warning signs of 9/11.

I did not learn of the CIA's ongoing contacts with Bah until early in the summer of 2002, when CR called me again. He had a new baby, financial difficulty, and Taylor's goons looking for him in Ghana. Two of the people he worked with closely in Liberia had been summarily executed by Taylor's security guards. CR said he wanted out of his old life completely and asked if I could help. CIA officials had told me that if any of my good sources ever wanted to talk, they would be interested. I knew the CIA station chief had already dealt with CR in Ouagadougou, but I assumed the agency had rethought its position.

I asked CR if he would be willing to talk to the agency, stressing there was no guarantee that he would get anything in return for his information. If it worked out, I wanted to know nothing about any arrangement. I told him that if he were ordered to break contact with me, he had to respect that.

CR said he understood. So, through an intermediary, I approached the CIA, which seemed very interested. The agency flew a two-man team to Africa to talk to CR and possibly polygraph him. In extensive phone calls, I explained to CR that he might be subject to a lie-detector test and stressed the importance of telling only things he knew for certain. I wished him luck, unsure if I would ever hear from him again.

But on the day of his initial meeting with the CIA I received a phone call from CR, who is not easily rattled. He was angry, scared, and screaming. When he finally settled down and told me the story, the magnitude of my mistake became clear. The agents, both un-known white men, had taken CR to a hotel, without allowing him to disclose the location to his wife. With little preamble, they took his cell phone away, strapped him to the polygraph machine, and began to aggressively question him. They asked why he had lied to me. They asked why he claimed to be married. They asked why he lied about the al Qaeda connection. With each question, and subsequent accusation that he was lying, CR panicked. He yelled back that he was not lying. The needle movements were off the charts. After seven hours, having received no food or water, he was told to leave, that he had lied on every single answer and the agency wanted nothing to do with him. A few days later an agent told the intermediary that CR had failed all sixteen questions, including his name. One thing was strange, the intermediary said: His contacts at the agency seemed very happy with the result. From then on, when they were ques-tioned, the CIA would say that one of my main sources had failed a polygraph test, a perfect way to discredit both of us.

I knew the results were preposterous. I had passed on to Euro-pean and U.S. intelligence sources over the course of two years reams of information given to me by CR, in an attempt to verify it, find out more, and report on it. Everything he had said had checked out, from his insistence that Bah was Senegalese when the Americans and British were insisting he was Gambian, to the names of the ships de-livering weapons to Taylor and the address and rent paid at the safe house in Monrovia. He was the first to talk about Nigerian shipments of weapons to Liberia in late 2001, first dismissed by the CIA but later verified. He was the first to name Nassour, Osailly, and Darwish in the diamond deals. There were other eyewitnesses to the presence of the al Qaeda operatives and their deals. I was baffled and angry.

On September 13, 2002, about a month after the polygraph fiasco, a reliable European intelligence source e-mailed me that Ibrahim Bah made a deal with the Americans and was "being debriefed for some days now." All of a sudden, it dawned on me what the CIA had done, but I still couldn't believe it. After discreet inquiries, a knowledgeable senior U.S. official confirmed my suspicions. The whole meeting with CR, he said, was "a setup. It was meant to show your source as being unreliable for two reasons: to be able to discredit him if his meetings with the embassy personnel ever became public; and to clear the way for dealing with Bah, who can now be portrayed as reputable."

He was right. A congressional source showed me several letters from the CIA in response to inquiries about the ties between the West African diamond trade and al Qaeda. They all contained the line that the "reporting was circular in nature," and that the source of the initial information was unreliable because he had "failed a polygraph exam."

The contacts with Bah continued into 2003. Reliable sources said the CIA offered him $1 million for his information, and that Bah turned them down. He was getting offers from other intelligence services that were even more lucrative.

Bah pulled off one final coup. After extensive dealings with investigators for the UN special court and promises of cooperation with them, the court decided not to indict him. It was a controversial decision that court officials said was justified because Bah primarily acted as an intermediary, providing introductions and safe passage to diamond dealers and weapons merchants. But, they said, they found little evidence that he was personally responsible for the crimes committed in Sierra Leone. Bah is currently living quietly in Ouagadougou, enjoying the fruits of his years in the diamond trade.

•

When Joe Melrose planned his departure from Sierra Leone for early September 2001 after three tumultuous years as the American ambassador, he was looking forward to retirement and life in academia. After thirty-two years in government service, he had secured a teaching job at his alma mater, Ursinus College, in southeastern Pennsylvania. He bought a house less than a mile from campus. The pipe-smoking Melrose looked the part of the rumpled professor.

Blunt and not given to formalities, Melrose had served in Pakistan, Nigeria, and other trouble spots before landing in Sierra Leone as ambassador. There, he won the respect of nongovernment agencies doing humanitarian work by meeting regularly with them and working to stretch the minuscule U.S. aid package as far as possible. He would frequently hop on helicopters or into his heavily armored jeep with his security officer and survey projects, visit refugee camps, or pop in on demobilized rebels. He worked hard to bring international attention to the plight of the amputees and the women who were raped by the RUF and other militias.

Melrose was one of the few ambassadors I have known who welcomed drop-in visits from journalists. He hosted dinners for diverse groups at his residence, sitting in fading splendor on Signal Hill, above the Freetown harbor.

On my first trip to Freetown in April 2000, I had dropped by the embassy to set up an interview with him. With telephone service virtually nonexistent, personal visits were the only way to get anything done. I was ushered into his office on the spot. He ended up putting me in touch with Kelly MacDonald, the head of the International Rescue Committee, a group working with child soldiers and rape victims. MacDonald arranged for me to visit the IRC's facilities in the eastern cities of Bo and Kenema. While I had covered numerous other conflicts, that trip was an eye-opener to the levels of violence that separated the Latin American insurgencies of the 1980s from the wars in Sierra Leone and Liberia. This trip gave me my first glimpse of the cost of this conflict: the systematic rape of women, the gut-wrenching meetings with child combatants, the destroyed infra-structure. Few ambassadors would have recommended or helped set up such a trip.

Working with a small staff because of security constraints, Melrose also managed the small amounts of U.S. military aid chan-neled to the peacekeeping forces in Sierra Leone. Evacuated during the bloody RUF assault on the capital in 1999, Melrose was deter-mined not to be evacuated again in April 2000, when the RUF took the UN hostages.

Because the RUF appeared poised to attack Freetown again, for-eigners were evacuated in droves. But Melrose and his British coun-terpart, Alan Jones, agreed that their governments needed to keep at least token staffs in the country. The closure of the two most high-profile embassies, they knew, would cause panic and be a huge psy-chological victory for the rebels. Despite some reluctance in Washington and London, the two prevailed and helped keep a bad situation from spinning into chaos.

However, Melrose's time as ambassador was not without con-troversy, mostly centered on his role in the peace agreement between the RUF and the government, negotiated in Lomé, Togo. Signed in July 1999, the accord granted the RUF amnesty for the atrocities committed and gave the rebels senior government positions in a power-sharing arrangement that would lead to elections. That in-cluded giving RUF leader Foday Sankoh the cermonial rank of vice president and placing him in charge of an advisory board studying the development of the nation's diamond fields and other mineral wealth. In exchange, the RUF agreed to a cease-fire and a demobi-lization plan. Support for the negotiations was Clinton administration policy. Secretary of State Madeleine Albright visited Freetown on October 17, 1999, and personally met with Sankoh and other rebel leaders to help cement the deal.

Melrose and others familiar with the process argued that there was no other way to bring peace to Sierra Leone. The amnesty, which was harshly criticized by human rights groups, had already been agreed to in previous talks. The agreement did not bar prosecution by international bodies, such as the special court, which as of June 2003 had indicted thirteen people for crimes against humanity. "Unless you kept the amnesty in at Lomé, the RUF would give nothing," Melrose said. "And the cease-fire held pretty well for eleven months, until things fell apart in April 2000."

After a round of farewell parties, Melrose was scheduled to leave his post in Freetown on September 9, 2001. However, on the eve of his departure, thieves broke into his residence and stole his passport and money. Getting a new passport meant traveling to Guinea, as his own embassy had no passport facilities. Melrose arrived in Conakry, Guinea, on September 11, where he heard about the attacks. Over the summer Melrose, who was a veteran at crisis management, had already been placed on standby assist in terrorist-related emergencies. He had been dispatched to Kenya in 1998 to help investigate the U.S. Embassy bombing and had also been sent to deal with the aftermath of the 1986 Beirut bombings. Communication with his State Department superiors was impossible, so Melrose decided to head on to Washington. When he arrived he was immediately put in charge of one of the eight-hour shifts of the newly formed emergency terrorist task force.

It was there that I tracked him down in October 2001 as I began to work on the story of terrorist ties to the diamond trade. I called again when the story led to al Qaeda. Melrose immediately grasped why a terrorist organization would want to use diamonds and was familiar with the Hezbollah connection in Sierra Leone and across West Africa. He also knew the diamond industry well and had helped draft the certification procedures for Sierra Leone's diamond exports. After my initial story ran, he wrote a memo explaining why it could not be dismissed out of hand, as people in both the State Department and intelligence community were scrambling to do.

"My position was that the story was possible," Melrose told me later. "I knew the journalist fairly well and trusted his reporting, but more importantly, it was feasible. It fit with a lot of other stuff I knew was going on in Sierra Leone. My argument was that you had to look at the story that way."

In Melrose's discussions, someone in the State Department asked him if my story might be connected to the "cable about the walk-in" in Brussels, referring to the report written on Allie Darwish's visit to the embassy there to discuss the weapons-for-diamond deals. Melrose didn't know what they were talking about because the Darwish cable had never been forwarded to him. When he found it in the files, he was furious. The information from Darwish could have been of great value in Sierra Leone at the time it was first obtained. Now it was several months old. With his assignment on active duty extended for ninety days because of the attacks, Melrose continued to investigate the diamond issue, traveling to Brussels and elsewhere, gathering more information that supported the story. Through the end of 2001, there were joint meetings with the CIA, Treasury, and State Department counterterrorism colleagues to discuss the issue of diamonds and what steps to take. Melrose became more convinced the link between al Qaeda and the West African diamond trade existed, but no action was taken. The biggest roadblock was the CIA.

"The basis for skepticism was twofold," Melrose said. "First, it was unconventional, so it was dismissed. People were not willing to think or look outside the box. If it is unconventional, they are not interested." The second factor, Melrose said, was that there was little corroborating evidence in the U.S. intelligence community. "But my position was that, factually, nothing contradicts what is being said either," Melrose said. "They took the lack of corroborating evidence in hand and said it meant there was nothing there. Some of us took it to mean it was something we needed to find out about. And I am pretty convinced the link existed."

•

Rep. Frank Wolf, a conservative white Republican from Virginia, does not fit the mold of an activist on African affairs. But since 1999, the twelve-term congressman has been one of the congressional leaders in the fight to clean up the world trade in blood diamonds. He was introduced to Sierra Leone by his longtime friend, Rep. Tony Hall, a liberal Democrat from Ohio. The two had developed a deep friendship through years of attending the same small prayer group on Capitol Hill. Hall urged Wolf to travel to Africa with him, to see firsthand the pain and suffering of the continent. By the 1990s the two were taking one or two trips a year together, a traveling odd couple that mystified colleagues and turned Wolf into an unlikely champion of humanitarian issues on a continent that has never been near the top of the agenda of presidents or Congress.

In July 1999, unable to get the Clinton administration's attention on blood diamonds, Hall and Wolf introduced legislation to force diamond merchants to disclose the origin of their stones. Although it went nowhere, it was the first time such a thing had been contemplated, and the bill got the attention of the diamond industry.

In December 1999, Hall invited Wolf to visit Sierra Leone with him. The RUF had ransacked the capital earlier that year in one of the war's bloodiest periods, and the amputations of arms and legs had reached an all-time high. "I didn't want to go to Sierra Leone," Wolf told me. "I went as a kind of favor to Tony, but then I got pulled into it." Wolf's report on the trip was filled with pictures of amputees and their stories. Horrified by their visits to the amputee camps and the brutality of the diamond wars, the two redoubled their efforts to take legislative action. Their efforts were opposed by the diamond industry, which hired high-powered lobbyists to fight back.

In July 2000 Hall further roiled the waters. Speaking at the World Diamond Congress, he urged the diamond industry to act against blood diamonds, and likened the suffering created by the trade to that of the Holocaust. He also suggested that the industry contribute $60 million a year, the amount estimated to be lost to African nations because of diamond smuggling, to UNICEF or other humanitarian organizations to help reconstruct war zones. Finally, he proposed the diamond industry give according to the same formula that diamond merchants recommend to grooms buying diamonds for their brides: invest two months' salary. Two months of diamond earnings, or about $1 billion, could be used to start a revolving fund for microcredit in areas devastated by war. In the ensuing uproar, all regular business at the meeting was scrapped. Eventually the industry founded and funded the World Diamond Council to deal with the issues, but little of substance has been done.

The efforts of Hall and Wolf roughly paralleled international efforts, in the face of the growing outrage, to bring some form of accountability to the diamond industry. Known as the Kimberley Process, a group of thirty countries, led by South Africa, worked for two years to hash out minimal international guidelines for the sale of unpolished diamonds. Ultimately, much of the compliance would rely on the industry policing itself.

In June 2001, Hall, Wolf, and a handful of Senate allies introduced new legislation to make it illegal to buy blood diamonds, or diamonds that came from rebel-controlled areas in Africa. However, advocacy groups were deeply divided over the process. Should they go for a deal that would pass but would be weak? Or should they go for a strong bill that would likely never pass? The main sticking point was an "automatic trigger" provision in the bill. Advocacy groups wanted a country to be automatically punished if it was caught trafficking in blood diamonds. The administration refused to go along with that, wanting more flexibility in handling individual cases.

At the same time, the diamond industry was turning up the heat on the issue, which was of little import to most in Congress. In all, the diamond industry spent some $2 million in lobbying fees in 2001.

Hall and Wolf's bill went nowhere until my November 2001 story in the *Washington Post,* outlining the al Qaeda ties to diamonds, forced action. Some of the advocacy groups wanted to use the story to try to force the Bush administration into more concessions, but Wolf and Hall felt they had gone as far as they could. With a groundswell building, the administration agreed to watered-down language on Hall and Wolf's diamond bill. The diamond industry supported the bill, in part for fear of appearing to support terrorism. The House passed the Clean Diamond Trade Act on November 28, 2001, by a vote of 408 to 6. Hall hailed the vote as "an historic step to introduce transparency to the diamond trade and take the profits away from people responsible for the carnage in Africa."

But the measure was not brought to a vote in the Senate. The Bush administration didn't push it, and, when public pressure faded, so did the sense of urgency.

On November 5, 2002, the Kimberley Process culminated with forty-seven nations, including the United States, agreeing to a certification system aimed at eliminating blood diamonds from the marketplace. In essence, each parcel of diamonds must have a certificate of origin to show if it was legally mined. In practice, diamonds are easily smuggled and conflict diamonds can still enter the system. But the certification process at least establishes an international norm that makes it possible to detect violators.

The Bush administration released a statement saying the "United States is committed to ending the use of rough diamonds by rebel groups to fund insurrections against internationally recognized governments, and atrocities against civilian populations." It promised Bush would work "expeditiously" with Congress to pass the legislation necessary for compliance with the Kimberly Process. On April 8, 2003, the House passed the necessary legislation by a vote of 419 to 2. Two days later it unanimously passed the Senate and was signed into law on April 25.

For some, the victory was mostly hollow. "The bill doesn't really do anything," Wolf acknowledged ruefully. "It was pretty weakened in the end. I think the lobbying efforts of the diamond industry were very effective."

Wolf, Hall, and others have said they now believe that only a widespread boycott of all diamonds would force the diamond industry and legislative bodies to take serious measures. "Until there is an economic boycott, something that will bring pain to the diamond industry, nothing significant will be done," Wolf said. "Until then, whatever [legislation] passes will be insignificant and will serve to give them a fig leaf to hide behind. If you brought business to its knees, you could then legislate."

On October 16, 2001, nine days after the United States began its campaign of bombing Afghanistan in retaliation for 9/11, a senior aide to Taliban leader Mullah Omar entered the central bank office in Kandahar. Using his political and religious clout, he bullied the manager into allowing him to withdraw $5 million in U.S. currency and Pakistani rupees. He stuffed the money into a large burlap sack, loaded it into a waiting Toyota Land Cruiser with the help of two men, and sped away.

On November 12, Taliban leaders collected $6 million from the central bank in Kabul. The scene was repeated across the country. "They took all the money from the other branches, but we don't know the details," said Allah Hashmee, manager of the Kabul bank. "No check, no receipt, they just came and took it." In addition to the millions of dollars known to have been taken from official government accounts, millions more were held privately, outside of official banking channels. Much of the Taliban's budget, in fact, came from bin Laden and his al Qaeda cohorts, usually not in the form of cash. Gold, a favorite currency of the Taliban and al Qaeda, was stored in ingots in the central bank and in the homes of prominent leaders. It, too, was collected. In the waning days of Taliban control of Afghanistan, Omar and bin Laden sent waves of couriers carrying gold bars and bundles of dollars—the treasury of the country and the terrorist movement—across the porous border of Afghanistan into Pakistan.

While al Qaeda and the Taliban were routed on the battlefield, they achieved an important tactical victory in their last days of power. Tens of millions of dollars were saved, enough to ensure that the financial infrastructure of the terrorist enterprise would survive.

From the Afghan-Pakistan border area, where sympathy for al Qaeda ran high, the money and gold were consolidated and taken by trusted couriers to the port city of Karachi, Pakistan. There, the Taliban consul general Kaka Zada oversaw the movement of the wealth to the desert sheikdom of Dubai, United Arab Emirates. The transfer to Dubai relied on couriers and *hawala*s, the virtually untraceable money transfer systems widely used across the Middle East, North Africa, and Asia. Zada also personally acted as a courier at least once, taking $600,000 in a diplomatic pouch to Dubai in late November 2001.

Such money movements are not unusual. Pakistani officials estimate that $2 to $3 million a day are hand carried from Karachi to Dubai, a flight of less than an hour. But in the three weeks from the end of November to mid-December 2001 there was a large spike in the amount of money traveling that route, reaching $6 to $7 million a day. Once in Dubai, much of the wealth of the Taliban and al Qaeda was converted to gold bullion and scattered around the world. Gold, unlike cash, is exempt from almost all reporting requirements that govern currencies, making it much harder to trace.

In Dubai, the gold transactions went undetected at the time. Questions are rare in one of the gold capitals of the world and a traditional smuggling center for the region. "Gold is a huge factor in the moving of terrorist money because you can melt it, smelt it, or deposit it on account with no questions asked," said a senior U.S. official. "Why did it move through Dubai? Because there is a willful blindness there."

The United States had one tool, initially developed for the drug war, that was quickly adapted to use in the war on terror: the Numerically Integrated Profiling System or NIPS, a vast, sophisticated U.S. Customs database that tracks the import and export of commodities into and out of the United States. Using that program, customs agents noted a spike in gold imports into the United States in late 2001 by companies suspected of laundering money for al Qaeda.

As with the diamond trade, tantalizing clues to al Qaeda's use of gold were available from public testimony, transcripts that were largely ignored by Western intelligence services. In the 1998 embassy bombings case, prosecution witness Tamara Ratemo, a Kenyan, told the court she rented her 10-room house on the outskirts of Nairobi to Fazul Abdullah Mohammed, who later handled the diamonds for al Qaeda in Sierra Leone and Liberia. Asked if Abdullah had said why he needed such a large house, Ratemo responded: "Yes . . . he had some business people who would be coming to visit frequently . . . He said the kind of people that [he would be] dealing with, they are trading gold and they would come from Dubai."

•

The gold souk in Dubai, dozens of city blocks of gleaming buildings rising out of the desert, is one of the world's largest gold centers. It makes no effort at subtlety. Dubai is an ultramodern city of paved highways, enormous malls that draw millions of shoppers a year, luxury hotels, dry desert heat, and sand. It sits on a small peninsula that is the strategic crossroads of the Arabian Gulf, South Asia, and Africa. The gold market, in the heart of the old city, advertises itself with gaudy electric lights that make the White House Christmas displays seem like candlelight affairs. Hundreds of stores that sell nothing but gold jewelry, gold bars, and gold powder compete for buyers and bathe the downtown in a perpetual golden glow. Other sectors sell acres of duty-free electronic goods. Buyers and gawkers stroll the narrow streets of the market, often lugging suitcases stuffed with cash. Robberies are almost unheard of in the strict Muslim emirate.

Thriving since 1947, the market has long played a vital role in the economies of India and Pakistan. One of the seven emirates that make up the United Arab Emirates, Dubai was the financial center of the Taliban and al Qaeda. The UAE was one of only three countries to recognize the Taliban regime—along with Saudi Arabia and Pakistan—and Dubai was vital to the survival of the militant Islamic revolution. Gold was one of the main reasons.

Demand for gold in India and Pakistan is extremely high for religious, cultural, and legal reasons. Gold is used in ceremonial rites for Hindus, and for dowries in marriages. But for centuries gold has also been the preferred medium of exchange for businessmen and traders on the Indian subcontinent. Gold is a traditional hedge against inflation, hoarded as security against times of high inflation or hardship. The annual demand for gold in India is estimated by Interpol, the international police agency, to be an astonishing eight hundred metric tons, almost triple that of the United States.

"A person in the hinterland here can tell you what their house or farm animal is worth in gold, but has to think about the value in rupees or dollars," said one Pakistani financial expert. "Gold is part of our being."

Because gold imports into both Pakistan and India have traditionally been restricted and subject to high tariffs, gold smuggling from Dubai, where the gold trade is unregulated, has been enormously profitable for decades. Dubai's location is ideal, making it a nexus of myriad smuggling networks that flow through Iran, India, Pakistan, and the Arab world to Afghanistan and Central Asia. A study of gold smuggling in the mid-1990s by Interpol found that $4.2 billion in gold was smuggled into India in 1991. In the late 1980s and early 1990s the price of gold in India was 65 percent higher than in other countries, making gold smuggling an enormously profitable, multibillion dollar industry.

Tariffs have since come down, but remain high enough to make smuggling profitable, though less ubiquitous. Dubai imported three hundred metric tons of raw gold in 2002, down from eight hundred metric tons in 1996. Most of the gold comes into Dubai from large Swiss banks or precious metal dealers in London. Following the collapse of the Soviet Union, tons of stolen gold came through the former Soviet bloc to Dubai. From Dubai, the gold is smuggled out to the Indian subcontinent in the form of 10-tola bars. A tola, the standard weight used in the region, equals 11.7 grams. Much of the gold is smuggled aboard the thousands of dhows, the traditional Arab sailboats made of wood that ply the waters between Pakistan, India, and Iran. Many are now outfitted with high-powered engines to outmaneuver law enforcement vessels. Because the smuggling benefits all sides, enforcement is generally lax.

Gold was also a familiar currency to the leadership of both the Taliban and al Qaeda, who preferred it to dollars and other currencies. On the Arab peninsula gold has a commercial, rather than religious significance. In Afghanistan, gold was preferred to the almost worthless and unstable currencies in the surrounding countries. Those selling opium and heroin in the lush Afghan valleys demanded payment in gold. Smugglers of televisions, generators, medicines, and other contraband demanded payment in either gold or opium. During the war for control of Afghanistan, the Taliban was broadly backed by Pakistani and Indian businessmen who wanted a single authority to guarantee their merchandise could be trucked across Afghanistan. In the years between the withdrawal of the Soviet forces and the Taliban's conquest, any small-time warlord could set up a roadblock and extort a tax, killing business.

The Taliban promised to end the practice, and in exchange received substantial financial backing from the transportation syndicates. Much of the aid was in gold. Opium growers operating in areas under Taliban control were assessed taxes in gold. Donations to the Taliban and al Qaeda from wealthy Saudi backers were also often made in gold. In the early days of the Taliban regime the national airline, Ariana Airlines, flew gold bullion directly from Dubai to the Taliban's unofficial capital in Kandahar. When U.S.-led forces occupied Afghanistan they found al Qaeda training manuals that included not only chapters on how to build explosives and clean weapons, but sections on how to smuggle gold either on small boats or concealed on the body. Using specially made vests, gold smugglers can carry up to eighty pounds, worth up to $500,000, on their person. Cash is far bulkier.

"The Taliban took gold into Afghanistan because there was nothing else they could take there," said Patrick Jost, a gold specialist who worked for eight years as an analyst at the Treasury Department's Financial Crimes Enforcement Network (FinCEN). "The local money was worthless and foreign currency would bring suspicion. But if you show up with gold, people know exactly what it is worth." Gold has an added role as the engine of the region's subterranean financial system, the official currency of the network known as *hawala*.

•

Unknown to most people in the Western hemisphere, *hawala*s have operated for centuries in the Arab world and Asia, predating the modern banking system. The system is almost entirely built on trust, family relationships, and regional affiliations. While unregulated by governments and nominally illegal, *hawala*s flourish because they are a vital link in economies across Asia and the Arab world. The money that flows through it often never actually moves at all. The word *hawala* means to change or transform, and also carries a connotation of trust. Rather than using force to make sure deals are honored, *hawala* relies on social pressure. If a family member cannot or will not honor a *hawala* deal, the rest of the family will often pitch in to make good on the payment. If the family cannot, other *hawal-*

*adar*s, even those in competition with the defaulter, will meet the obligations. They understand that if trust is lost, the system will crumble. The offender becomes an outcast in his clan and community, a fate that is deemed worse than physical punishment.

The *hawala* system is an integral part of the economies of India, Pakistan, Afghanistan, Somalia, and Yemen, all countries that have millions of nationals living and working abroad who want to remit money home to their families. This explains why there has traditionally been little effort to clamp down on the practice, even though it is supposed to be illegal. Many of the expatriates work in the Arab world—less that 20 percent of the UAE's population of 3 million are citizens—and in the United States. These people, sending small amounts every month, make up the vast majority of *hawala* users. The stream of money is vital to the economies of many nations.

*Hawala*s handle hundreds of billions of dollars a year. In 1998, the amount of money in India's *hawala* system was $680 billion, equal to about 40 percent of the nation's gross national product and roughly equal to the size of Canada's entire economy. In countries where there is no functioning banking system—Afghanistan under the Taliban, Somalia, and Yemen—the economy lives by *hawala*.

Here is how it works:

A Pakistani laborer in Dubai needs to send $500 to his family in rural Pakistan. Banks charge high fees, often don't have branches outside the major cities, and take weeks to deliver. Banks offer only the official rate of exchange for hard currency, often far below the black market rate. A bank transaction leaves a paper trail so the money can be taxed.

So the laborer takes his money to a *hawala* broker who can deliver it within forty-eight hours for a flat 2 percent fee. The *hawaladar* usually operates an ancillary business that generates a large amount of cash, such as a travel agency or retail business. The *hawaladar* also has an extended network of trusted family or friends, including someone near the laborer's home village. He calls or e-mails his cousin there and tells him to deliver $500 to the laborer's wife. The *hawaladar* may give the laborer a code or some sort of receipt to hold on to until the money is delivered. If that particular *hawaladar* does not have connections in the town, he will find someone in the *hawala* network who does and pass the business on to them. When the money is delivered, the records are often destroyed. The *hawaladar's* bookkeeping reflects what he owes his cousin or the other *hawaladar*, not the names of the sender or the recipient of the money.

Two weeks later, when the cousin needs a $500 order of powdered milk, he e-mails Dubai, where the goods are purchased and sent to him. The *hawaladar* in Dubai will bundle that order along with other orders that come in from other clients, and ship the goods across to his partners in Pakistan for distribution. The books balance on each side of the transaction, yet no money has ever actually moved. Few records are kept, and the few that may exist are usually destroyed when the books are balanced. To attract business, *hawala*s rely on word of mouth and advertisements placed in newspapers that cater to expatriate communities across the Arab peninsula, Asia, and the United States.

Law enforcement officials distinguish between "white *hawala*," the vast bulk of the transactions, usually migrant workers sending money home, and "black *hawala*," transactions that involve criminal intent, terrorist financing, or money laundering. But white is frequently intertwined with black, so trying to shut down even part of the system would devastate the economies of several key U.S. allies, including Pakistan and India. Ending *hawala* would also badly hurt the millions of migrant workers who do most of the labor in the Arab world.

This was demonstrated to me in Karachi, Pakistan, in January 2002. I sat sipping tea with a businessman who runs a clothing business and a *hawala* on the side. It allows him to get better exchange rates and helps him keep his costs down by avoiding taxes, he explained. Like many *hawaladar*s, he was not a wealthy man. His small, dark office off a crowded alley in the center of the city had not a hint of luxury. But he scoffed at the idea of going after *hawala*s to stop terrorist financing. "Maybe one out of every one thousand or two thousand transactions is dirty," he said with a shrug. "Trying to find terrorist funds here is not like trying to find a needle in a haystack. It is trying to find a needle in a needle stack."

Dubai, the trader added, "only exists because of currency controls in Pakistan and India" and the trading system that allows a few people to get rich on all sides. "Greed has no borders and no enemies," he said.

*Hawala*s have many friends and customers: terrorists, tax cheats, ordinary gangsters, as well as politicians and government officials looking to hide bribes and other proceeds of corruption.

Because of volatile currency exchange rates, *hawala* accounts are often kept in gold, which has a standard value across the globe. The daily price in New York will be the same as the price in Zurich or Dubai. It is not open to discussion or negotiation. Thus, gold is the lifeblood of the system. A 1998 study of money laundering and smuggling by countries of the British Commonwealth found that "if gold and silver smuggling were stopped, 80 percent to 90 percent of the *hawala* transactions would automatically cease."

Patrick Jost, the former Treasury analyst, explained the added attraction of the *hawala*-gold link in countries where bin Laden operated.

"There are no traditional banking systems in Afghanistan or Somalia," Jost said. "Everything is done through *hawala* and gold is the fuel *hawala* runs on."

•

After 9/11, *hawala*s became the focus of Operation Green Quest, the U.S. Customs–led initiative to cut off terrorist financing. But in the months and years leading up to the attacks only a small but persistent group of investigators—Jost and a handful of others who remain in government service and asked not to be identified—had seen the system as an integral part of the terrorist financial network. Those who did make the linkage also understood the role of gold in terrorist finances.

Despite repeated efforts by individual agents in Customs and Treasury's FinCEN to draw attention and resources to the twin problems, little was done. FinCEN was set up in the 1990s as a place to centralize information and databases on financial crimes, especially related to drug trafficking, but gradually turned its focus to monitoring the compliance of banks with different reporting requirements.

Part of the reason so little progress was made in tracking *hawala* was that the concept of *hawala* and its use of gold was so foreign to most of those involved in tracking illicit finances. Almost all efforts to track criminal financial networks were focused on tracing the billions of dollars in drug money that flows mostly to Latin America. The relatively small amounts of money moved by terrorists, tens of millions instead of billions, complicated the task.

"We were talking about a different culture and a completely different way of doing business than what we are used to," one of the officials said. "It was complicated and went right over their heads. We are so ethnocentric we couldn't conceive of doing something different ways."

There was another setback. In the late 1990s FinCEN had attracted a group of analysts from different agencies to study "alternative remittance systems," or the use of commodities such as gold and systems such as *hawala*, in illegal activities. Much of the work focused on methods used by drug traffickers, but with experts in other fields, the effort soon broadened out.

Alvin James, who worked at FinCEN with Jost and other analysts, said the group found that there were great similarities among informal money-moving organizations, from the Black Market Peso Exchange for Colombian drug money to *hawala*s to systems used by the Chinese. The group began to analyze data and to meet on a regular basis.

"We began to understand underground systems. We hit the tip of the iceberg," said James, who left the center in frustration in April 2000. "We were seeing these systems, by their nature, were opaque and done without paper. They are efficient and move a hell of a lot of money, not all of it bad money. But if you want a system to move bad money, these systems were tailor-made to do so."

The group began looking at different databases to see what patterns emerged. One of those chosen for analysis was passport entry and exit. The first group studied was Somalis, because an unusually high number of illegal cash transfers were tied to people with Somali passports. Agents from the Drug Enforcement Administration, Customs, and other investigative agencies had run into the same phenomenon. But the FinCEN analysis was shut down because leaders of the financial war on crime worried that it smacked of racial profiling.

With new leadership at FinCEN in 1999, the whole idea of looking at systemic methods of moving money was shelved. Instead, FinCEN leaders decided to concentrate their efforts on gathering banking information and looking at suspicious banking activities. The center not only stopped all operational enterprises, but removed all the information gathered on the FinCEN database to track drug money and other systems. In an effort to salvage the data, James copied it onto computer disks and gave it to the U.S. Customs Service, where it was seldom used.

By 1999 the working group, after writing what now prove to be prophetic papers on *hawala*, gold, black-market money movements, and other commodity transfer systems, was disbanded and the work was shelved. Officials explained the move as being part of an internal reorganization to better focus FinCEN's limited resources on its core mission of bank monitoring.

But most of those who participated in the enterprise left government service in dismay. "If it wasn't *Miami Vice* money laundering, our bosses didn't want to know about it," Jost said. "There was a time when communication was encouraged, when thinking outside the box was encouraged, but suddenly that stopped. Analysis stopped. That's not what I'm about, that's not what the other guys were about. So we all drifted away."

Those involved in the group believe that, had the effort been allowed to go forward, U.S. law enforcement would have been much better positioned after 9/11 to attack terrorist financing. "It really is a shame," said James. "We could have been a world leader in this, but we stuck our head under a rock. Instead of going ahead and learning, we did completely the opposite. It is just a shame."

Jost said that, while he doubted 9/11 could have been prevented, "we wouldn't be scrambling around like this if our work had continued. We wouldn't have this flailing around and we wouldn't have the sense of 'what the hell is this' when they looked at *hawala* and gold."

A few officials stayed on, trying, as one said, to get senior money-laundering analysts and policy-makers to "forget all the Western notions about how money moves. We were getting all kinds of law enforcement cases where they couldn't figure out how the money was moving. The answer was *hawala* but no one understood that." Before 9/11, the official said, "no one would listen to us. If there is ever a serious postmortem, there will be a lot of people with a lot of egg on their faces. Now we have people popping up all over the place, 'discovering' *hawala*, when really it is stuff we already know."

Immediately after 9/11, as terrorist financing investigations kicked into high gear, one of the first groups discovered and shut down was a massive *hawala* run by Somalis. Attorney General John Ashcroft said the group, al-Barakat, had direct ties to al Qaeda.

The one place where gold and its connection to *hawala* was taken somewhat more seriously was in the National Security Council in the waning days of the Clinton administration and the early days of the Bush administration. But even that interest yielded few results until after 9/11 because the NSC had to rely on other agencies, such as the FBI, the CIA, and Treasury to provide it with information. The agencies were often reluctant to devote the necessary resources.

"There were people who knew about gold and *hawala* in general and wanted to pursue it," said one senior counterterrorism official who served in the NSC at the time. "But the truth is we really knew virtually nothing and still know virtually nothing. We don't know where the *hawala*s are or even the real order of magnitude on how much money they move. The NSC was begging for attention to this from the law enforcement community long before 9/11, but we got nowhere." After the attacks it became painfully clear just how far behind the curve U.S. officials were.

•

In January 2002 Abdul Razzak sat in his cramped office above one of his jewelry stores in the heart of Dubai's gold market and thumbed his worry beads in frustration as I asked questions about his company's alleged ties to the finances of the Taliban, which was hosting bin Laden. His operation, I was told by sources in Karachi, served as both a *hawala* and gold broker for the Taliban government, an activity that was not illegal since the UAE recognized the Taliban regime. It was the third time in two days I had interviewed Razzak, a Pakistani merchant who did not look or act like one of the most powerful men in the Indian subcontinent. Friend and bankroller of several governments in his homeland, Razzak is also close to the royal family in his adopted home, the UAE. Razzak's gold empire, called ARY (the initials standing for his full name, Abdul Razzak Yaqoob) Traders, stretches from the Arabian Peninsula and the Indian subcontinent to Great Britain and the United States. ARY is synonymous with the gold trade, and Razzak is known as one of the giants in the business. The conglomerate includes a refinery, money exchange houses, a satellite TV station based in London, one of the biggest gold outlets in Dubai, and several enormous jewelry stores in prime Dubai locations. For years Razzak was the only foreigner in the UAE allowed to own his own building, a sign of his closeness to the UAE's ruling family.

With his thick salt-and-pepper hair and beard, smudged white robe, thick, dark glasses, and fractured English, Razzak looks and sounds more like the small-time cigarette and rice importer that he was than the magnate worth hundreds of millions of dollars that he has become. Well known throughout the region, Razzak has a host of legal problems and could not return to Pakistan without facing arrest. His most famous misadventure came in 1993.

Shortly after Benazir Bhutto was elected to a second term as Pakistan's prime minister, Razzak struck a deal with her and her husband. In exchange for a monopoly on the hugely lucrative business of importing gold into Pakistan, Razzak would help the government eradicate gold smuggling. Bank records show that ARY deposited $10 million in the account of the prime minister's husband for the two-year monopoly on gold imports, a business he thought would yield an even higher return for him. Razzak denies doing anything illegal.

Razzak was often featured in the local press, almost entirely in puff pieces praising his community service or charitable donations. So the questions about terrorism, the Taliban, and al Qaeda slowly brought him to a boil. As he had with previous allegations, he denied any wrongdoing and said the stories were the work of unnamed enemies who were jealous of his success and wanted to destroy him.

I was there because sources who had helped move money for the Taliban, along with U.S. and British investigators, said Razzak had been instrumental after 9/11 in helping the Taliban spirit millions of dollars, converted into gold, out of Afghanistan. My Pakistani sources said Razzak and other prominent gold traders in Dubai had ties to Ibrahim Dawood, India's most wanted criminal kingpin, alleged to be involved in drug trafficking, prostitution, and extortion. In October 2003, Dawood was designated a terrorist financier by the U.S. and UN. Dawood is also a prolific financier of Indian movies.

A Muslim born in India, Dawood is accused of masterminding a series of bomb blasts that tore apart the city of Mumbai on March 12, 1993. The bombs targeted Hindus and left 257 people dead and 713 wounded. Dawood fled to Karachi, Pakistan, and maintains strong ties to Pakistani intelligence services. He lives openly in a heavily guarded mansion in Karachi and shuttles between Karachi and Dubai. For a decade Dawood has mysteriously managed to avoid arrest in either place. Most important to me, my sources said he was deeply involved in gold smuggling, particularly during the late 1990s, when the Pakistani intelligence services openly supported the Taliban and al Qaeda. He also had strong ties, through the gold trade, with the massive jewelry business on the subcontinent, an industry that buys huge quantities of diamonds. It was through Dawood's enterprises and network that al Qaeda was able to move diamonds and turn them into cash when necessary.

Halfway through our initial interview, Razzak called in a television crew from ARY Digital, his satellite TV station based in London that is broadcast throughout Southeast Asia and the Arab world, to tape the event. He brought out gold bars, bragged he was able to move any amount of gold to virtually anywhere in the world within twenty-four hours, and said he sold more than three tons of gold, worth about $27 million, a month. He denied any association with terrorist activities, but said it was not his job to know where the gold went after he sold it. "Dubai is an open market, a good market and I import everything legally and sell it legally," Razzak said. "You say you want one hundred kilos and I can give you that. What you do with it is your business." At times Razzak downplayed his own importance in the region. Then he boasted that every major political figure in Pakistan still called him regularly for consultations.

In the end, realizing I was not there to do another fluff piece, he dismissed me and his crew. "I am a God-fearing person but all my life I have been afraid of religious people like the Taliban," Razzak said. "I don't like to deal with Taliban people and we don't like Taliban people." He also denied any dealings with Dawood.

Unsatisfied with the meeting, I asked if I could come by again the next day. I didn't expect him to agree, but, reluctantly, he did. As I approached his office the next afternoon, up a dark stairwell and past a row of traders working quietly at laptop computers, I could see Razzak had brought in reinforcements. One was a sharply dressed Canadian lawyer. The lawyer began explaining the company's separate but interlocking businesses. Without my asking, he launched into the operation of the gold business, then talked about ARY's money exchange house and their hopes of expanding into the U.S. gold market. Razzak was nervous as the man talked, and finally exploded.

"You are answering questions he is not even asking," Razzak said. "If he asks a question he can be answered, but why are you telling him things he did not even ask to know? It is none of his business." With that, he dismissed both of us.

Sensing it was a story worth exploring, I talked to other gold dealers and sources recommended to me by my Pakistani friends. I also arranged to see the economics officer at the U.S. Embassy. The officer, I was told, monitored the gold market and knew all the major players. The next day I drove an hour on a perfectly flat, paved road through the desert to the U.S. Embassy in Abu Dhabi, another of the emirates of the UAE. After a few initial pleasantries I launched into questions about Razzak and ARY. After listening to me for a few minutes with a look of puzzlement, the officer interrupted me.

"What is ARY and who is Razzak?" he asked. "I don't know what you're talking about."

I returned to Washington stunned that no one in the embassy had even heard of one of the largest companies in the gold business. I asked for a meeting with officers of Operation Green Quest, Treasury's unit leading the hunt for terrorist money. Part of the presentation was a demonstration of the NIPS supercomputer program used to track the import and export of commodities. After the official presentation, I asked an intelligence officer to use NIPS to run a check on ARY.

I had been told in Pakistan and Dubai that some of the gold moved out by the Taliban and al Qaeda was eventually shipped to the United States. My Customs source said he couldn't run the check with me there, because the program was classified. But he promised to do it later.

"You hit the jackpot," he said excitedly in a phone call the next day. "You wouldn't believe what we are finding about ARY."

I asked what it was. "I can't tell you," he said. "The investigation is now classified. We wouldn't have started it without your information, but now we can't talk to you about it."

But Customs officials did want to know how I had managed to track down Razzak. I told them I had looked in the telephone book and then called the ARY office for an appointment.

The Green Quest investigation, handed to the New York office, quickly grew into an international affair involving at least seven countries. U.S. officials said they found unusual spikes in gold imports from Dubai in December 2001, just as my Pakistani sources had said there would be. British officials launched the most aggressive search and slowly began unraveling the ties between ARY and Indian crime boss Ibrahim Dawood. Investigators said they found that in addition to its gold business, ARY runs a large *hawala* operation. For years, intelligence officials said, Razzak had helped the Taliban and al Qaeda money flow around the world, undetected.

In November 2002, a group of several hundred family members of the victims of 9/11 amended their federal class action lawsuit filed against the perpetrators of the attacks, to include ARY Ltd., one of Razzak's companies. They are represented by Ness, Motley, P.A., the same law firm that successfully sued tobacco companies for billions of dollars. The suit alleges that:

> ARY Gold, a branch of ARY Group, is involved in terrorist financing according to several investigations around the world . . . ARY Gold engaged in gold transactions on behalf of the Taliban and al Qaeda.
>
> Gold trading was usual between ARY and the Taliban. This "gold trail" was described by intelligence officers, law enforcement officials, gold brokers and sources that have direct knowledge of some of al Qaeda's financial movements . . . Defendant ARY Gold is an aider, abettor and/or material sponsor to international terrorism.

•

In the summer of 2002, elite European intelligence units monitoring al Qaeda's movements forwarded an alarming report to their U.S. counterparts: Al Qaeda and the Taliban were quietly shipping large quantities of gold through Karachi, Pakistan, to Sudan. The gold was being sent by boat to either Iran or Dubai, where it was mixed with other goods and flown by charter airplanes to remote airstrips in Sudan. Even more alarming, the intelligence reports said, some of the aircraft being used to move the money belonged to Victor Bout, the weapons merchant who serviced both Taylor in Liberia and the Taliban in Afghanistan. Although living in Moscow, Bout continued to run his operation through his brother Sergei, the Europeans reported. One of his new hubs was Islamabad, Pakistan.

The gold was obtained through a "commodity-for-commodity exchange," Pakistani intelligence officials said, meaning heroin and opium stashed by the Taliban and al Qaeda was traded to drug traffickers for the precious metal. The gold was packed in boxes and represented only a small portion of the cargo on each charter flight. Estimates of the value of the gold ranged from several hundred thousand dollars to several million.

But just as important as the amount was what the gold signified: the ability of al Qaeda and the Taliban to replenish their financial coffers in the face of global efforts to disrupt their network. It also signaled the importance of Sudan, a putative U.S. ally in the war on terror, in collusion with bin Laden.

•

Sudan was familiar territory for bin Laden. In April 1991, he had moved there with a small group of trusted aides, welcomed by the fundamentalist Islamic government. Bin Laden had spent the previous two years in Saudi Arabia, where he had returned when the war in Afghanistan ended. But in 1991 the Saudi government allowed U.S. military personnel to be based in Saudi Arabia, for the first Gulf War. Bin Laden deeply opposed the move so he sought hospitality in Khartoum. He brought with him the remains of his inheritance, estimated to have been about $30 million. He invested liberally in the impoverished nation, buying the political goodwill of the ruling National Islamic Front (NIF), the radical Islamist government led by Hasan al Turabi. Bin Laden had known Turabi in Afghanistan and the two shared a vision of eradicating secular governments in the Muslim world. Bin Laden even married into Turabi's family, wedding Turabi's niece. Bin Laden's construction company, Al-Hijira for Construction and Development, built the road linking Khartoum and Port Sudan, as well as a modern international airport near Port Sudan.

Bin Laden also set up the Taba Investment Company and its subsidiary export-import firm, Wadi al-Aqiq Company Ltd. Through those investments he was able to secure a near monopoly on Sudan's major exports, including gum arabic, corn, and sunflower and sesame products. The investments were made in cooperation with senior NIF officials. His al-Hemar al-Mubarak-ah Agricultural Company Ltd. purchased large tracts of land near Khartoum and in eastern Sudan. One of his biggest investments was to jointly capitalize, with NIF officials, the al-Shamal Islamic Bank. Bin Laden's investment in the bank was $50 million. The bank continues to operate today. Its owners deny any connection to terrorists.

In May 1993, bin Laden paid for the travel to Sudan of 480 militant Afghan war veterans who were expelled from Pakistan for extremist activities. Among them was Abdullah Ahmed Abdullah, who a few years later established the first al Qaeda contacts in Liberia to purchase diamonds. Soon bin Laden's businesses expanded. By January 1994, with the blessing of the NIF, bin Laden set up at least three terrorist training camps in northern Sudan and many of his farms doubled as shooting ranges. His construction company worked with the Sudanese military to transport provisions and visitors to the camps.

Bin Laden used the money he was generating from his commercial activities in Sudan to expand his reach and his vision. He began financing Egyptian extremists and other groups. He hosted Egyptian, Tunisian, Algerian, and Palestinian combatants at his camps and funded safe houses in Pakistan and Afghanistan.

It was also during his time in Sudan that bin Laden made a historic but much overlooked decision with far-reaching implications. As part of his emerging strategy, he set aside the deep historical religious rift between his own Sunni Muslim group, which dominates Saudi Arabia, and those of the Shi'ite Muslim, who dominate Iran, Syria, and Lebanon. For centuries the two groups have remained hostile to and warred with each other.

In a 1998 affidavit, FBI agent Daniel Coleman, investigating the embassy bombings in east Africa, said bin Laden's group was willing to "put aside its differences with the Shi'ite Muslim terrorist organizations, including the government of Iran and its affiliated terrorist group, Hezbollah, to cooperate against the perceived common enemy, the United States and its allies."

Rohan Gunaratna, an expert on al Qaeda's history and structure, called the Hezbollah–al Qaeda alliance engineered by bin Laden "a strategic partnership, indicative of a major shift in terrorist thinking. Throughout the 1990s, ethno-nationalist Muslim groups were supplanted or fell by, or fell under the influence of, Islamist groups, thereby paving the way for further ideological tolerance and inter-group cohesion as a means of confronting a common enemy."

In fact, bin Laden was a staunch admirer of Imad Fayez Mugniyeh, the Hezbollah leader who, until he was supplanted by bin Laden after the 1998 embassy bombings, was the most wanted ter-rorist in the world. Mugniyeh, operating with the funding and back-ing of Syria and Iran, masterminded the 1983 bombing of the U.S. Embassy in Beirut, which killed sixty-three people, and the truck bombing six months later that destroyed the U.S. Marine barracks in Beirut, killing 190 American soldiers. He also ordered the kidnap-ping, torture, and execution of CIA operative William Buckley and the assassination of Col. Richard Higgins, who was serving in Lebanon with the United Nations. With ample financing from Iran and other state sponsors, Hezbollah grew into a formidable terrorist and military force. Sen. Bob Graham, the Florida Democrat who chaired the Senate Intelligence Committee in the summer of 2002, was regularly briefed on the emerging alliance and called Hezbollah "the A-team of terrorism."

It was the truck bombs that most impressed bin Laden, because they led to the U.S. withdrawal from Lebanon. He was hoping simi-lar attacks could drive the United States from Saudi Arabia.

To approach Hezbollah and arrange the meetings with Mug-niyeh, bin Laden turned to one of the most colorful but least known of his lieutenants: Ali Abdelseoud Mohammed, a former major in the Egyptian army who had received Special Forces training in the United States. Arrested in the United States on September 10, 1998, for participating in the embassy bombings, Mohammed was con-victed and is serving a life sentence. A naturalized U.S. citizen, Mo-hammed joined the U.S. military in 1986, received a security clearance of "secret," and rose to the rank of sergeant. He was as-signed to U.S. Special Operations at Ft. Bragg, North Carolina, home of the Green Berets and the Delta Force. He left the army in 1989, after stealing secret military documents and passing them on to bin Laden loyalists. The documents included the location of Special Operations forces in the Middle East, training schedules, and U.S. intelligence estimates of Soviet strength in Afghanistan.

After leaving the U.S. army, Mohammed emerged as a senior aide to bin Laden. He traveled extensively to Afghanistan to supervise training camps and instruct recruits, and oversaw bin Laden's move to Sudan in 1991. In Sudan, Mohammed arranged several meetings between bin Laden and Mugniyeh and provided the security for those get-togethers. According to Mohammed's own court testimony, the agreement reached between Mugniyeh and bin Laden was that Hezbollah would provide explosives, training, and other military expertise to the newly minted al Qaeda organization, while al Qaeda provided money and foot soldiers for Hezbollah operations.

In May 1996, under heavy pressure from the United States and anxious to rehabilitate its international image, Sudan asked bin Laden to leave. He returned to Afghanistan after Mohammed again made the necessary arrangements. However, many of bin Laden's businesses in Sudan remained active and he remained close, economically and politically, to many leaders of the NIF. Bin Laden's primary protector, al Turabi, lost an internal power struggle within his party and was placed under house arrest but remains a powerful force. Sudan's financial structure is dominated by those who enjoyed bin Laden's largesse and remain sympathetic to his vision.

From Afghanistan, bin Laden retained stakes in Sudan's banking system, a tannery, his construction business, and other endeavors. Because of that surviving infrastructure, Sudan was a logical place to turn as a new financial hub as the global pressure on al Qaeda's financial structure grew when the group was driven from Afghanistan after 9/11. With financial transactions in Dubai and elsewhere under growing scrutiny, a less visible location was needed. Bin Laden "has banking contacts there, he has business contacts there and he is intimately familiar with the political and intelligence structure there," said a European intelligence official. "He never fully left Sudan despite moving to Afghanistan."

That assessment was shared in a report by the Canadian Security Intelligence Service made public in November 2001. It disclosed that Sudanese leaders agreed in 1998 to use their diplomatic staff in New York, London, and Rome to raise funds for bin Laden. The intelligence finding also says the Sudanese agreed to provide diplomatic credentials to bin Laden supporters, allowing them unfettered travel around the world.

•

Just as troubling as the Sudanese destination for the gold was the routing of some of the gold through Iran, which the CIA thought for many years was hostile to bin Laden. As the bastion of Shi'ite Muslims, Iran was initially hostile toward al Qaeda and its Sunni Muslim creed. But the new world order brought new alliances. Now Iran's revolutionary leaders, already at odds with the United States and backing Hezbollah, offered the terrorist organization another avenue to replenish its coffers. The movement of the gold was a further indication that the alliance between al Qaeda and Hezbollah was stronger and deeper than ever. Shortly before the reports of the gold movements surfaced in the summer of 2002, Arab intelligence agencies were warning the CIA that Iran was harboring senior al Qaeda operatives in towns near the borders of Turkmenistan and Afghanistan.

The al Qaeda members were protected by Iranian intelligence services and security forces, perhaps operating outside the control of the civilian government. The flights that helped carry the gold flew out of the border region where the leaders were being sheltered. Among those being harbored in Iran were bin Laden's son and heir apparent, Saad, along with other top-tier leaders.

"Iran is not a monolith, there are different groups, and some seem to be directly helping with these [gold] transfers," said a European intelligence official. "It doesn't mean it is a decision of the government, but they do not have full control over what the security forces do."

At about the same time, U.S. and European intelligence officials were receiving intelligence reports that Hezbollah and al Qaeda were teaming up on logistics, finances, money laundering, weapons smuggling, and training. The new strength of the alliance alarmed the CIA and FBI. Intelligence reports show that when al Qaeda was driven from Afghanistan, bin Laden sanctioned his operatives to ally themselves with helpful Muslim groups without first seeking approval from above. In practice this meant that for the first time mid-level and low-level members of the terrorist groups could operate with autonomy.

One of the areas where Hezbollah has helped al Qaeda, intelligence officials said, was in setting up Internet communications. The favorite method of communication among and between groups has become Internet chat rooms, because they can be easily moved. Constantly changing passwords make it difficult for law enforcement groups to monitor conversations. New recruits can only access rooms where "holy war" against America or other general topics are discussed. Only trusted and vetted operatives can gain access to rooms where more operational matters are discussed.

The al Qaeda–Hezbollah alliance was observed by intelligence operatives on the ground in Africa and Asia long before it was accepted by analysts in Washington. There, long after 9/11, the conventional wisdom remained that Shi'ites could never work on behalf of al Qaeda, despite evidence going back a decade that the hypothesis was wrong.

Larry Johnson, a former CIA officer who later headed the State Department's counterterrorism division, said the intelligence community's attitude was naive. "The mistake the CIA and others make is saying 'they don't work together because we say they don't work together,' " said Johnson, who still works on contract for different U.S. government agencies. "That is a very dangerous logic."

Field officers say that logic is greatly hampering the war on terrorism. "We have been screaming at them for more than a year now, and more since 9/11, that these guys all work together," said one frustrated U.S. intelligence official in Africa familiar with the diamond trade. "What we keep hearing back is that it can't be because al Qaeda doesn't work that way. That is bullshit."

The Canadian intelligence report on Iran's relationship to al Qaeda paints a picture of extensive cooperation, going back to the early 1990s. Iran paid for al Qaeda camps in Sudan and provided military trainers, the report said. Because of al Qaeda's pragmatism and unexpected capacity for coalition building, its financial empire continues to thrive. A report by a UN panel of experts monitoring the group's financial movements found that "a large portfolio of ostensibly legitimate businesses continue to be maintained on behalf of Osama bin Laden and al Qaeda by a number of, as yet, unidentified intermediaries and associates across North Africa, Middle East, Europe, and Asia. Estimates put the value of this portfolio at around $30 million."

CHAPTER SEVEN: "And Spend for God's Cause"

On March 22, 2002, Bosnian police raided the Sarajevo offices of the Benevolence International Foundation, a Muslim charity whose headquarters is in the suburbs of Chicago. The raid was requested by U.S. officials, who suspected the organization was funneling millions of dollars to al Qaeda. But police uncovered far more than a front operation for terrorist financing. Seized documents and computer hard drives yielded the most complete record ever found of al Qaeda's history, structure, and financial strategy. Among the most revealing documents was a file labeled "Tareekh Osama," Arabic for "Osama's History." This included the minutes of the 1988 meeting where al Qaeda was founded, as well as a list of wealthy Saudi sponsors of the movement at its inception.

It is now clear that bin Laden was planning his war against the existing world order even before the Soviet forces had completed their withdrawal from Afghanistan in 1989. The Afghan war had forged a new type of Islamic fighter, a holy warrior for the twenty-first century. The mujahideen attributed their victory over a global superpower to Allah. Confident of his blessing, they plotted their next mission, the destruction of the West and Israel.

As theological justification for his violence, bin Laden embraced Wahhabism, a strain of Islam based on the eighteenth-century teaching of Mohammad bin Abdul Wahhab. Wahhabism teaches that Muslims must return to the pure Islam practiced centuries ago, before the corruption brought by false teachings and Western influences. Wahhabism teaches that it is a Muslim's duty to fight Christians, Jews, and other Muslims who are not devout enough. Above all, it is every Muslim's duty to fight to establish a single Muslim state, governed by strict Islamic law. This radical interpretation of Islam was embodied by the Taliban in Afghanistan. There, it led to amputations, stonings, the banning of music, punishment for men who shaved their beards, and the banishment of women from education and all forms of public life. Jews are routinely referred to as "pigs" and Americans are vilified as infidels who practice incest, gambling, and fornication.

"You have been described in history as a nation that spreads diseases that were unknown to man in the past," bin Laden wrote in his November 2002 "Letter to America." "Go ahead and boast to the nations of man, that you brought them AIDS as a Satanic American invention."

Bin Laden's embrace of Wahhabism also brought easy access to huge sums of money that could be used to spread his Islamic revolution across the globe, because the Taliban were not the only ones to embrace this fanaticism. Decades ago the al Saud family that rules Saudi Arabia, in order to maintain its grip on political power, cut a deal with powerful, radical clerics. The clerics could make Wahhabism the desert kingdom's religion, as long as they did not preach the overthrow of the royal family. Bin Laden, as a wealthy, influential Saudi, was thoroughly familiar with the arrangement.

As a result of the agreement, the Saudi government spends hun-

dreds of millions of dollars a year to spread Wahhabism. Much of
that money flows around the world to charities sponsored by the
Saudi government. The charities, which operate with little oversight
or accountability, make it easy for those who would divert money to
terrorism. For years the United States ignored the river of state-
sponsored Wahhabi hate for the West that poured out of Saudi
Arabia. Both countries pretended that Wahhabism was unimportant
in relation to the political alliance built on the U.S. need for Saudi oil
and the Saudi desire for American products, especially fighter jets
and other sophisticated weapons.

•

Minutes of a meeting of al Qaeda's founders in August 1988
show they planned a special military camp for a new, elite group of
fighters. A group of fifteen men met at bin Laden's house in
Afghanistan and agreed that a select group of fighters would enter a
"testing camp and the best brothers of them are chosen, in preparation to enter *al Qaeda al Askariaya* [the Military Base]."

Included in the minutes are the requirements for admission to
the new al Qaeda brotherhood: "listening," "being obedient," "good
manners," and "referred from a trusted side." The oath of loyalty that
members took says: "The pledge of God and His covenant is upon
me, to listen and obey the superiors who are doing this work, in en-
ergy, early-rising, difficulty and easiness, and for his superiority upon
us, so that the word of God will be the highest and His religion victorious."

When the meeting ended on August 20, 1988, al Qaeda was
born. The screening of new recruits was rigorous. Probably not more
than about one thousand men of the estimated seventeen thousand
men who passed through the terrorist training camps in the following thirteen years were allowed to take the oath. Only one of the
nineteen 9/11 hijackers, Mohammed Atta, was an actual member of
the organization.

For its divine mission, al Qaeda members needed money and

ways to move it around the globe. A special financial committee was set up to solve the problem.

The committee, presided over by bin Laden or his closest associates, turned to charities. Charities were crucial to funding the mujahideen during the anti-Soviet struggle. Now their role expanded.

Bin Laden hated the United States not only for its secular values but because it had defiled Islam's two holiest sites by stationing troops in Saudi Arabia during the Gulf War. But he also understood that significant sums could be raised there and that American recruits were valuable because they could travel more freely than others.

Al Qaeda also came to understand, much as it did with the diamond trade, that conventional money flows were easy to trace. America offered cover. Who was going to look for al Qaeda money flowing through seemingly legitimate groups in the United States?

By 9/11, bin Laden had built a network on American soil, its tentacles spreading from the suburbs of Washington, D.C., to Chicago, New York, Oregon, and Arizona.

As far back as 1993 bin Laden identified three Muslim charities as vital to his operations, according to conversations later recounted by a senior al Qaeda official. They were the Benevolence International Foundation, raided in Sarajevo; the Muslim World League, a globe-spanning charity funded by the Saudi government; and the Qatar Charitable Society. While much of these charities' money was used for relief activities, a portion was diverted to al Qaeda operations. The money for al Qaeda was accounted for in the charities' books as expenses for building mosques or schools, or feeding the poor. The charities have said that, while individual branches of their operations may have helped terrorists, the organizations did not.

●

Western intelligence agencies were unprepared for al Qaeda's marriage of religious zeal with violence, and its ability to use charities.

With the deep cuts in the CIA's budget and a rapidly shifting world order after the Cold War, most of the vast intelligence apparatus that supported the anti-Soviet efforts in Afghanistan evaporated. Those counting on U.S. support were cut loose, baffled and embittered by the dramatic reversal in their fortunes.

In the new world order, the United States showed little interest in Afghanistan's affairs. Few understood or cared what it meant in 1996 when the Taliban swept across the country and established a national Wahhabist government under the most extreme interpretation of Muslim Koranic law. Except for the occasional condemnation of the Taliban and fragmented attempts to get bin Laden, Afghanistan and its lessons were shelved with the Cold War.

All that changed after 9/11. Tracking al Qaeda's finances was suddenly one of the U.S. government's highest priorities, and almost nothing was known. Said David Aufhauser, the Treasury Department's general counsel and head of terrorist finance investigations: "We had been looking at the world from the wrong end of the telescope." Instead of searching for dirty money that businesses were trying to present as legitimate cash, as in the drug war, investigators had a harder task: tracking clean money that was "spirited around the world, intended to kill."

Charities offered several advantages to would-be patrons of terror. The donations were virtually untraceable because there was no oversight. Even large sums aroused little suspicion because they were given as part of *zakat*, one of the pillars of the Islamic faith that requires the donation of 2.5 percent of all income. The amount of money donated through *zakat* in Saudi Arabia skyrocketed in the early 1970s when OPEC oil price hikes initiated the largest transfer of wealth in the twentieth century.

Jean-Charles Brisard, a French expert on terrorist financing, estimates that al Qaeda has received "between $300 million and $500 million over the past decade, through *zakat* and direct donations by wealthy individuals."

•

Freed from fighting the Soviets by 1989, al Qaeda moved rapidly to extend its reach into Muslim enclaves in the Philippines, Malaysia, Bosnia, Indonesia, Chechnya, and elsewhere.

The terrorist network's penetration of the Philippines, using Saudi-sponsored charities as fronts, is a model of how the symbiotic relationship works and ties to the United States. The terrorist networks in Bosnia, Chechnya, and Asia operated in a similar fashion.

Two related Saudi charities, the Muslim World League and the International Islamic Relief Organization, registered with the Philippine Securities and Exchange Commission on September 20, 1991. The president of both was Mohammad Jamal Khalifah, who a few years earlier had married one of bin Laden's sisters, the second of his four wives. Khalifah channeled millions of dollars from the charities to terrorist activities, including the formation of two Islamic guerrilla groups in the southern part of the archipelago. The groups, the Moro National Liberation Front and Abu Sayyaf, remain active.

"The IIRO, which claims to be a relief institution, is being utilized by foreign extremists as a pipeline through which funding for the local extremists is being coursed," said a 1999 Philippine military intelligence report. It added that through Khalifah, "bin Laden's network is already deeply entrenched in the Philippines."

One of al Qaeda's main operatives there was Ramzi Yousef, a pioneer in al Qaeda's use of terror. He had plotted the first attack on the World Trade Center in 1993 that killed six people and wounded more than one thousand. In New York, Yousef was an acolyte of Omar Abdul Rahman, the "Blind Sheik," who was a spiritual adviser to al Qaeda and leader of a mosque in Brooklyn. Shortly before the 1993 bombing, Rahman delivered a prophetic sermon, declaring "There is no solution for our problems except jihad for the sake of God. . . . If those who have the right to have something are terrorists, then we are terrorists. And we welcome being terrorists."

In October 1995, the Blind Sheik was convicted of plotting a "Day of Terror" for New York. The plan included simultaneous strikes on UN headquarters, the Holland and Lincoln tunnels, the George Washington Bridge, and other landmarks.

Yousef fled the United States immediately after the 1993 attack and set up shop in Manila, working with Khalifah. Yousef's money came from the charities Khalifah controlled. With the backing of bin Laden and Khalifah, Yousef began preparing what would have been the most lethal attack ever on American soil, and a forerunner of 9/11. Code-named Operation Bojinka, the plot called for eleven airliners to be simultaneously hijacked in Southeast Asia. The airplanes were to be crashed into strategic U.S. targets including the Pentagon, the World Trade Center, and CIA headquarters. To carry out the attacks, the Kuwaiti-born Yousef developed undetectable liquid nitroglycerine bombs that could be hidden in contact lens bottles. The explosives would have easily slipped through the existing airport security. He also planned to assassinate Pope John Paul II and President Bill Clinton, who were scheduled to visit the Philippines in 1995.

Bojinka unraveled on January 10, 1995, when the bomb-making chemicals Yousef was mixing in his apartment caught fire. Yousef and an accomplice fled amid the billowing smoke, but their computer hard drive gave them away. It contained not only details of the Bojinka plan but telephone numbers for Khalifah and the charities he directed. The Yousef associate was arrested a few days after the fire; his phone book and cellular phone contained five numbers for Khalifah as well as Khalifah's business card. Yousef was arrested in Pakistan in February 1995 and deported to the United States. His address book and encrypted computer files contained Khalifah's phone numbers and those of his charities.

Yousef was convicted in 1996 for the Bojinka plot. Khalifah is an indicted fugitive in that case. Yousef was also convicted for the World Trade Center bombings.

But Khalifah lived a charmed life. On December 16, 1994, just three weeks before the Bojinka plot was discovered, U.S. officials arrested Khalifah in San Francisco for giving false information on his visa application. He was traveling with a director of the Chicago-based Benevolence International Foundation. Khalifah had contact numbers for bin Laden and Yousef, along with documents referring to the assassination of bishops and bombings of churches.

Even with a limited understanding at the time of what al Qaeda was, U.S. officials kept Khalifah in prison for four months because they feared he was a terrorist. In the end, officials decided it would be easier to extradite him to Jordan, where he was wanted on murder charges, than to try him in the United States. In arguing for his extradition, the State Department said Khalifah "has engaged in a repeated pattern of providing financial, logistical and training assistance to international terrorists." Khalifah was acquitted of the charges in Jordan and returned to Saudi Arabia.

Immediately after 9/11, Saudi officials said Khalifah had been arrested. At the same time, Khalifah was giving interviews from his home in Saudi Arabia to Philippine radio stations.

In a lengthy interview with the London newspaper *Al-Sharq al-Awsat* on May 4, 2002, Khalifah said he was an employee of the Saudi government while working with the charities in the Philippines, but denied any association with terrorists. He said he had never been arrested by Saudi authorities. Asked if he thought bin Laden was behind the 9/11 attacks, Khalifah replied: "All I can say is that Osama is not capable of planning for a sea cruise. So how could he have done all this?"

•

U.S. intelligence agencies were not completely oblivious to the shifting venues of terrorist finances. A 1996 CIA report said that, of the more than fifty Islamic nongovernmental organizations then in existence, "approximately one-third support terrorist groups or employ individuals suspected of terrorist connections."

The analysis noted that Saudis had contributed $150 million to aid Muslim NGOs in Bosnia in 1994.

While there was some intelligence on the use of charities by Islamic militants overseas, the growth of extremist Islamic operations in the United States went largely unnoticed. The FBI and IRS seldom scrutinized religious charities, fearful of violating constitutional protections of religious freedom. The Justice Department feared that any rigorous action against Muslim groups would spark charges of ethnic profiling.

Hiding in plain sight in the United States worked for al Qaeda. Dennis Lormel, head of the FBI's Terrorist Financing Operations Section, said that "as far as raising money, what better place than the United States? No one ever thought they were operational here."

All told, U.S. officials now estimate that Islamic extremist groups operating in the United States have raised hundreds of millions of dollars—and perhaps more than a billion—since the mid-1980s.

"Looking back, we just lay there and let this happen," said a former senior U.S. intelligence officer. "It was a truly massive intelligence failure."

•

Bin Laden is a relative newcomer among Islamic terrorists operating in the United States. Over the past two decades, Hamas, Hezbollah, the Palestinian Islamic Jihad, and others have used charities, think tanks, and religious studies programs in the United States to raise tens of millions of dollars. Al Qaeda soon joined in.

"Key people control where the funding goes and decided that al Qaeda was worthy of being funded, along with other terrorist organizations, mostly related to the Israel-Palestine issue," said Robert C. Bonner, the head of U.S. Customs. "How did this come about? There is an extreme Sunni Wahhabist mentality, and there is a request to someone who controls purse strings, usually a Saudi. That connection must be severed."

Bonner, the slow-talking, soft-spoken former administrator of the Drug Enforcement Administration, said that there are fewer than twenty "very wealthy, prominent" Saudis responsible for a "very significant amount of funds" going to al Qaeda.

Concern about Saudi funding of terror through the Wahhabi movement goes back to the last years of the Clinton administration. While several high-level delegations went to Saudi Arabia after 1998 to demand a cutoff of terrorist funding, they got nowhere.

David Aufhauser, the Treasury counsel, said that trying to cut off the rivers of money the Saudis spend annually on Wahhabi charities and missionary work around the world is "one of our most bedeviling problems."

Aufhauser said that the Saudi practice of spending tens of millions of dollars spreading Wahhabism around the world, yet abdicating responsibility for the violence that might ensue, is "akin to lighting a match in a parched forest."

The Sarajevo raid yielded a list of who the elite Saudi donors to al Qaeda were in the early days. In the "Osama's History" file was a document labeled the "Golden Chain," a list of twenty wealthy Saudis who gave generously to al Qaeda. Above the list, which was written in 1988, is a Koranic verse that translates: "And spend for God's cause."

Among the names on the Golden Chain list were the cream of Saudi society, including bin Laden's brothers, billionaire bankers and construction magnates, all close to the Saudi royal family. Beside each name was the name of the al Qaeda leader responsible for collecting the donations. Bin Laden personally collected the donations from seven of the donors. Those on the list have been named in a class action suit against alleged terrorist financiers, filed by family members of those killed in the 9/11 attacks.

After 9/11, U.S. officials grew increasingly frustrated with the Saudi government's unwillingness to seriously clamp down on terrorist financing. By late 2002, tensions between the two countries came to a boil. U.S. officials had worked quietly for months with Saudi Arabia to get Wa'el Julaidan, a Saudi citizen and officer on several al Qaeda–related charities, designated a terrorist sponsor so his assets could be frozen. Julaidan attended the 1988 meeting where al Qaeda was founded and was on al Qaeda's first finance committee. In a 1999 interview with al-Jazeera television, bin Laden referred to Julaidan as "our brother."

On September 6, 2002, with great fanfare, the two nations finally announced Julaidan's joint designation. Julaidan was the 236th person designated by U.S. officials in the year following 9/11, but only the second for Saudi Arabia. Still, the Treasury press release praised Saudi Arabia's "unprecedented cooperation."

But the façade broke down almost immediately as Julaidan's ties to charities funded by the Saudi royal family came into play. Within twenty-four hours two senior Saudi officials publicly disowned the designation. U.S. officials were apoplectic. One called the Saudi government "nothing short of schizophrenic." A few days later, under intense U.S. pressure, Saudi officials said the disavowals were the result of a "misunderstanding." The designation went ahead.

The Saudi waffling on Julaidan was the last straw for many in the Bush administration. Within weeks, a National Security Task Force, led by Treasury's Aufhauser, recommended that the U.S. government present the Saudis with hard intelligence on specific individuals and give them ninety days to act. The United States focused on nine individuals identified as al Qaeda's core group of financiers: seven Saudis, a Pakistani businessman, and an Egyptian businessman. Most were on the Golden Chain list of early al Qaeda financiers.

In December, senior U.S. officials quietly delivered a strong message, but without a specific time ultimatum.

"What we told them was, we don't care how it happens," one of the U.S. officials said. "They can freeze his accounts, call him in for an audience with the prince and tell him to stop, or stuff him in a box." As a result, a senior-level working group was set up to share intelligence on suspected financiers.

But, U.S. officials said, Saudi cooperation remained "selective" until the May 12, 2003, suicide bombings by al Qaeda in Riyadh brought a new Saudi resolve.

"The terrorism is directed against us," said Adel al Jubeir, a senior Saudi official. "We are convinced the United States and Saudi Arabia are the two countries that are in the crosshairs of this murderous organization called al Qaeda."

Tensions heated up again in mid-2003, when a joint congressional investigation into 9/11 found evidence that the Saudi government may have provided funds to some of the hijackers. The content remains a mystery because in the nine-hundred-page report, the twenty-eight pages detailing the Saudi government's alleged role were classified and blacked out.

•

Charities were not the sole avenue bin Laden and other Muslim terrorists had in the United States to raise and move funds. There was another vital link in the terrorist money chain that had long been overlooked by U.S. intelligence agencies, a link that has been crucial to several Muslim terrorist organizations, and one that bin Laden was intimately acquainted with. This link has a name: the Muslim Brotherhood.

•

In 1946, after visiting the United States, an Egyptian Islamic fundamentalist named Sayd Qutb was disgusted.

"All these Westerners are the same: a rotten conscience, a false civilization. How I hate these Westerners, how I despise all of them without exception," he wrote in 1946 in the Egyptian cultural magazine *Al-Risala*.

Qutb was the leader of the Muslim Brotherhood, a religious-political movement founded in 1928. As much an ideology as a religious credo, the Brotherhood calls for the establishment of one Islamic state governed by Koranic law. Like the Wahabbis, the Brotherhood believes the state should be ruled by a single caliph, the title bestowed upon the successors of the Prophet Muhammad at the beginning of the Islam. The Brotherhood's creed is: "God is our objective; the Koran is our constitution; the Prophet is our leader; Struggle is our way; and death for the sake of God is the highest of our aspirations."

The Brotherhood spread throughout the Arab world in the wake of the European colonization of much of the Middle East. Soon it was viewed as a threat to the secular states that emerged. Brotherhood members were persecuted and jailed in Egypt, Syria, and Iraq in the 1950s and 1960s, as pan-Arabic movements in those countries became increasingly non-Islamic. Brotherhood leaders often sought shelter in Saudi Arabia, where they were welcomed.

Qutb brought a particularly harsh anti-American slant to the Brotherhood. His writing fanned the growing anti-American feelings brought on by Washington's support for Israel and secular Arab leaders like Anwar Sadat.

Over seven decades the Brotherhood has grown into a network of businesses, banks, and charities spanning the globe. The mostly legitimate operations are also used as a cover to move terrorist funds, weapons, and personnel. Intelligence officials view the Brotherhood as a unique threat because it provides a crucial international political and financial framework to violent Islamic groups, a framework that cuts across geographic lines and Sunni–Shi'ite differences.

Hassan al-Turabi, bin Laden's benefactor during his stay in Sudan, was a leader of the Brotherhood. Hamas, the Resistance Movement of Palestine, is a direct offshoot of the Brotherhood. The Brotherhood is also tied to neo-Nazi groups in Europe. And the Brotherhood has ties to al Qaeda.

"It is a network of fairly prominent, well-established business people, ones that have one foot in the Western world and one foot in the radical Muslim world," said Juan C. Zarate, the Treasury Department's chief of terrorist investigations. "Al Qaeda took advantage of the existing organization because the Brotherhood matched al Qaeda's motivation to go international."

•

Bin Laden and other senior al Qaeda leaders had strong personal ties to the Brotherhood. During his university days in Saudi Arabia, bin Laden was taught Islamic studies by Brotherhood leaders. His theology teacher, Abdullah Azzam, was a stalwart of the Jordanian Muslim Brotherhood. Azzam soon became bin Laden's mentor, and the two fought together in Afghanistan. In 1984 they jointly set up a charity called the Afghan Service Bureau, which eventually formed the core group of al Qaeda.

Between 1980 and 1989 Azzam visited more than fifty U.S. cities. He got a visa because of the staunch U.S. support for his anti-Soviet efforts in Afghanistan. But he spent his tours of America urging holy war against the West. In one 1987 speech in Brooklyn, Azzam said that *"jihad* means fighting the infidels with the sword until they convert to Islam or agree to pay a tribute tax and be humiliated."

Azzam was killed by a car bomb in Pakistan in 1989 but bin Laden continued to tap into the Brotherhood's vast resources.

•

The ties between the Brotherhood and al Qaeda were little studied before 9/11. But afterward, links emerged from several investigations.

The Treasury Department and CIA dusted off the old files of a tiny offshore bank based in Nassau, Bahamas. Bank al Taqwa, which means "Fear of God," was founded in 1988 by leaders of the Brotherhood. It had drawn the interest of the CIA in the mid-1990s because of its ties to bin Laden. U.S. intelligence agencies had tracked telephone contacts between Bank al Taqwa and members of bin Laden's inner circle, who would call the bank as they traveled around the world. But the bank secrecy laws in the Bahamas and complex financial structuring made it difficult to prove where the money ended up. The investigation remained a relatively low priority until after 9/11.

The bank was part of the sprawling business empire of Yousef Nada, an Egyptian and naturalized Italian citizen who is a senior member of the Brotherhood. U.S. and European investigators now say Nada's bank was used to funnel tens of millions of dollars to Muslim fundamentalist groups around the world, including al Qaeda. But it was much more than that. The bank and Nada's other financial services companies provided al Qaeda with Internet services and access to encrypted telephones. They even arranged for weapons shipments.

The bank, while handling hundreds of millions of dollars, retained only a handful of employees, a few in Switzerland, and a few in Nassau, manning computers and telephones. On November 7, 2001, Nada was designated a terrorist financier by the United States. The assets of more than a dozen of his companies were frozen and the Bahamas bank shut down.

With a Bahamian-registered bank, al Taqwa users could open commercial correspondent accounts with established European banks. This allowed the transactions of al Taqwa to appear to originate in an established European bank, where they would draw far less scrutiny. This strategy kept Bank al Taqwa out of the public eye for almost a decade. One of the few public references to the bank came in 1999 when one of bin Laden's brothers sued it for refusing to pay $2.5 million he said he was owed. The suit was dismissed.

The bank served groups besides al Qaeda. In February 2002 Juan Zarate of Treasury told a congressional hearing that in 1997 "the $60 million collected annually for Hamas was moved to accounts with Bank al Taqwa." Zarate said that in October 2000, al Taqwa provided a clandestine line of credit to a close associate of bin Laden. But most damning, Zarate said, was that in late September 2001, after the attacks, "bin Laden and his al Qaeda organization received financial assistance from the chairman of that bank," Yousef Nada. Nada called the allegations "nonsense."

•

Besides Nada, other senior members of the Brotherhood who have been designated terrorist financiers were on the board of Bank al Taqwa. Among the most prominent was Ahmed Idris Nasreddin, a wealthy Eritrean in his late seventies and a longtime business partner of Nada. Nasreddin ran another bank out of the same Nassau office as Bank al Taqwa—Akida Bank Private Ltd. Like Bank al Taqwa, Akida provided a host of services to terrorist organizatons.

Nasreddin attracted the interest of European investigators in the early 1990s because of his sponsorship of the Islamic Cultural Institute of Milan, Italy. Intelligence agencies targeted the institute because it was a gathering place for Islamic radicals, including al Qaeda members. In October 2001, the Treasury Department described the institute as "the main al Qaeda station house in Europe. It is used to facilitate the movement of weapons, men and money across the world." Nasreddin's lawyer, P. F. Barchi, said Nasreddin paid the rent and utilities for the center but had nothing to do with terrorism.

European investigators first became interested in al Taqwa not because of its ties to Islamic terrorism but because of ties to the neo-Nazi movement. Albert Huber was the link, operating at the center of both worlds. Huber, a retired journalist, is best known as leader of Switzerland's neo-Nazi movement. Silver-haired and blue-eyed, Huber converted to Islam more than thirty years ago and changed his name to Ahmad. Born a Christian, Huber now preaches that Muslims and neo-Nazis must join forces to defeat Israel. He claims the United States "is now controlled by a small Jewish faction."

Huber acknowledges meeting bin Laden associates at Muslim conferences in Tehran and Beirut and described them as "young and highly intelligent people." But he denies any connection to terrorism.

•

The post-9/11 rush to uncover al Qaeda's infrastructure in this country found more than just the ties to the Brotherhood, and the discoveries left U.S. investigators shaken. Rather than finding a few individuals and businesses tied to the terrorist network, they found an intricate web of charities, businesses, and individuals funneling money to a variety of violent Islamic groups. Many of the groups had been under investigation for years, but the magnitude of their activities had not been understood.

Among the investigations of suspected terrorist financial backers pursued after 9/11, two stand out: the Benevolence International Foundation near Chicago and the Safa Group, in the suburbs of Washington, D.C.

•

The roots of Benevolence, which quietly set up offices in the United States in the early 1990s, can be traced back almost to the inception of al Qaeda. Founded on March 30, 1992, in Palos Hills, Illinois, Benevolence's stated purpose was to fund charitable work among Muslims worldwide. The president was a Saudi named Mohamed Loay Bayazeed. Another Saudi, Adel Batterjee, was also on the board of directors. A year later Enaam M. Arnaout, a Syrian-born naturalized American citizen, was named executive director.

The three were associates of Osama bin Laden. Bayazeed was a cofounder of al Qaeda. Batterjee has been designated a terrorist financier by the U.S. government and had his assets frozen. Arnaout was a confidant of bin Laden and helped manage al Qaeda camps in Afghanistan before moving to the United States.

The charity was an American incarnation of a Saudi relief organization famous in the Arab world for aiding bin Laden in Afghanistan. In the decade after its founding, unhindered by law enforcement officials, Benevolence quietly grew into one of the largest Muslim charities in the United States. The organization collected more than $12.8 million in the United States from 1993 to 1999. Much of the money allegedly went to support radical Muslim fighters in Chechnya, Bosnia, and Afghanistan.

Benevolence had been the target of a low-priority intelligence probe by the FBI since at least 1998. Like many others, it withered among competing interests and fears of charges of ethnic profiling.

But after 9/11, with the USA Patriot Act relaxing rules for wiretapping and restrictions on information sharing between espionage and law enforcement officials, the FBI and Customs redoubled their efforts.

On December 14, 2001, the Treasury Department froze the Foundation's financial assets and raided the group's offices, carting away files, computer hard drives, and financial records. Benevolence vehemently protested its innocence. In October 2002, Arnaout was indicted on charges of supporting terrorism.

On November 19, 2002, the government formally designated Benevolence a financier of terror and asked the United Nations to block the group's assets worldwide, which it did a few days later.

Arnaout denied any links to terrorism. On February 10, 2003, with jury selection set to begin, he reached a plea bargain with the government. He admitted illegally funneling large donations to pay for military equipment for rebel fighters in Bosnia and Chechnya in the 1990s.

•

In an affidavit, FBI special agent Robert Walker laid out the government's case. Among the charges were that Benevolence founder Bayazeed in 1993 and 1994 tried to obtain "uranium for Osama bin Laden for the purpose of developing a nuclear weapon." The information had been in FBI files for years, but compartmentalized on the intelligence side, walled off by law from criminal investigators.

Walker also outlined the relationship between Benevolence

leaders and Mamdouh Salim, a close associate of bin Laden's who was known for fatwas, or religious rulings, authorizing the killing of innocent civilians. In one edict Salim ruled that if an attack on an American building killed Americans, that was beneficial. If Muslims working with the Americans were also killed, it was punishment for helping the infidels. The innocent Muslims would be martyrs and go straight to heaven. They would be grateful, Salim argued.

In May 1998 Benevolence arranged a Bosnian visa for Salim and paid his hotel bills there. Arnaout signed a letter identifying Salim as a Benevolence director. In September 1998, Salim was arrested in Germany and extradited to the United States. While in the Metropolitan Correctional Center in New York, he tried to murder a corrections officer and stabbed him in the eye with a homemade knife.

One of the big breaks in linking Benevolence to al Qaeda came on March 22, 2002, when Bosnian police raided the Benevolence offices in Sarajevo, Bosnia-Herzegovina, where bin Laden's file and the Golden Chain list were found.

The file also contained a letter from bin Laden to "Generous Brother Abu al-Raida," an alias of Mohamed Loay Bayazeed, who later served as the Benevolence president. Although the letter was from bin Laden, it was signed by Arnaout. "[Bin Laden] is far away from me and he authorized me through a communication to sign on his behalf," Arnaout wrote. "My apology."

From the beginning the foundation tried to obscure the charity's ties to Saudi Arabia and especially to Adel Batterjee, a well-known Saudi fundamentalist fund-raiser. While Batterjee was no longer registered as an official of the foundation in 1994, he went on to become the director and primary stockholder in the al-Shamal Islamic Bank in Sudan, the same bank bin Laden capitalized with $50 million.

By early 2002, Arnaout knew that he and Benevolence were under close federal scrutiny and began to take precautions. On February 12, 2002, Arnaout told his brother Hisham that Benevolence's problems with law enforcement officials centered on Arnaout's relationship to wealthy Saudis, according to intercepted telephone conversations.

Arnaout asked Hisham to tell Batterjee to stop sending money via wire transfers. "If I receive one wire transfer from him, to any office of the offices, my home is destroyed," Arnaout said. "Tell him, 'Enaam is telling you, oh beloved brother, the scrutiny now is on a Saudi connection.' "

On April 15, 2002, Arnaout spoke to a man who called from the Benevolence office in Pakistan to say Pakistani intelligence agents were asking about him. Arnaout instructed the man to take all of the Benevolence funds, including the "orphan money," and flee to Afghanistan immediately. Arnaout warned the man his telephone conversations, e-mail communications, and bank transactions could be monitored. "I prefer that you travel to the inside and to put everything in boxes, and let your brother, or your two or three brothers, every one or two days, one of them to travel with a box."

•

In the early morning hours of Wednesday, March 20, 2002, 150 federal agents—many with their guns drawn—raided fourteen offices and homes in the suburbs of Washington, D.C. FBI and Customs agents loaded seven panel trucks with more than five hundred boxes of documents, computers, and financial records of more than one hundred charities, think tanks, and businesses affiliated with the Herndon, Virginia–based SAAR Foundation. Most of the interrelated businesses and charities were run out of a single office at 555 Grove Street, a brown brick and glass three-story office complex on a quiet street.

The SAAR Foundation, the backbone of the cluster, takes its name from Sulaiman Abdul Aziz al Rajhi, head of one of Saudi Arabia's wealthiest families, who funneled millions of dollars through the cluster of businesses and charities. The al Rajhi name was on the

Golden Chain list of early al Qaeda supporters that was found in the Benevolence files in Sarajevo.

The SAAR Foundation was incorporated in Herndon, Virginia, on July 29, 1983, and formally dissolved on December 28, 2000. However, many of the foundation's functions were taken over by the Safa Trust, an organization registered at the same address and run by several of the same board members.

Law enforcement officials dubbed the maze of the overlapping companies, with shared directors, the Safa Group. The groups often financed each other, sending the money in circles. The scores of Safa organizations are controlled by about fifteen Middle Eastern and Pakistani men who serve with each other on a host of institutional boards. Four senior leaders of the network are Iraqis who had lived in Saudi Arabia and have been members of the Muslim Brotherhood.

In the United States, the men used Saudi money to launch some of the nation's leading Muslim organizations. In 1983, with money from the al Rajhi family, the SAAR Foundation was born. The director was Yaqub Mirza, a Pakistani native with a Ph.D. in physics from the University of Texas. Other groups were formed shortly afterward. Five of the top Safa executives live in spacious homes on adjoining lots in Safa Court in Herndon, a twenty-two-acre parcel of land bought by one of the SAAR-affiliated firms in 1987.

In time, the Safa network owned or invested in scores of businesses worldwide: dairy farms in Zimbabwe; schools in Ivory Coast; a huge poultry business in the state of Georgia; an Islamic mutual fund in Washington state; an investment company in Malaysia; shell companies in Panama; and commercial apple orchards in Chile.

By the late 1980s the SAAR Foundation had become one of the Washington, D.C., region's biggest landlords. "The funds came very easily," said a businessman who dealt with SAAR. "If they wanted a few million dollars, they called the al Rajhis, who would send it along."

At the same time, the leaders of the SAAR Foundation incorporated and sat on the boards of charities and nonprofit organizations. Many were branches of Saudi charities that operate worldwide.

For years the Safa leaders were viewed as moderates in the American Islamic community. One of the raided institutions had issued a religious ruling that allowed U.S. Muslims to fight in Afghanistan. Another trained ten of the U.S. military's fourteen Muslim chaplains. "I'm moderate, I'm serving my country, and I'm innocent of these suspicions," said Taha Jabir Alalwani, the only Safa Group leader who agreed to be interviewed, even though his lawyer advised against it. "I'm trying to convince Muslims in the U.S. this is our home; we must defend this country." A stocky man with a flowing brown robe, Alalwani said the raids on his home and office reminded him of the tactics used by the secret police in his native Iraq.

The search warrant and affidavit requesting the searches laid out the government's contrasting view of the Safa network: a channel that passed money from wealthy Saudi donors to front groups that directed the money to al Qaeda and other radical groups.

The affidavit alleges that "individuals associated with the Safa Group use or have used over 100 organizations, which were interrelated through corporate officers and holding-company-subsidiary relationships, to facilitate the funding of terrorist activities."

Lawyers for the Safa leaders called the search a witch-hunt. Nancy Luque said her clients were "absolutely not involved in any way in supporting terrorism. It's a smearing."

•

Operation Green Quest was launched in October 2001 as part of the Customs Service initiative to track bin Laden's financial empire. In a small, windowless conference room Green Quest agents charted the byzantine relationships among the more than one hundred Safa network entities, a spiderweb of overlapping names and organizations. Green Quest investigators also charted the relationship among the Safa network entities and the Muslim Brotherhood through the al Taqwa Management empire of Yousef Nada. U.S. officials said they had tracked about $20 million from Safa entities flowing through Nada's Bank al Taqwa, but said the total could be much higher.

The ties between Nada and Safa leaders were many and long-standing, as were their ties to other Brotherhood leaders. Two members of the Safa Group helped set up Bank al Taqwa in the Bahamas and several Safa leaders loaned Nada money.

In 1976, two other men who later became prominent in the Safa Group founded Nada International, a Brotherhood bank in Liechtenstein. For a time, Sulaiman Abdul al Rajhi, the SAAR Foundation founder, worked for Nada at that bank. Nada International was designated a terrorist financier by the Treasury Department after 9/11.

After the Virginia raids, the magnitude of the investigators' task became evident. With only two full-time Arabic translators and no road map through the maze of documents, progress was slow. Swiss authorities had also seized thousands of documents from the al Taqwa headquarters in Lugano. Almost two years after the raids, no criminal charges had been filed. Investigators are still grappling with the undecipherable nature of the groups' finances.

Millions of dollars from the various Safa Group companies simply disappeared or were shifted among the different organizations in the network. For example, in its 1998 tax return, the SAAR Foundation said it moved $9 million to the Humana Charitable Trust, based in the Isle of Man. U.S. investigators said the Humana Trust never existed. And the money is gone. Millions of dollars more vanished in similar fashion over the years.

An IRS examination of the Safa Group charities found the groups received $54 million in grants from 1996 to 2000. Of that money, $26 million was transferred to the Isle of Man and $20 million stayed within the organizations. Only $7.7 million went to charitable works, the affidavit says.

"Looking into their finances is like looking into a black hole," said one U.S. official involved in the probe. "There is no way you can tell what their tax reports mean because they are gibberish. You can't figure out anything unless someone inside tells you what they mean."

The strangest transaction was reported on the SAAR Foundation's own, final 990 form, the report all charities must file with the IRS. In December 2000, as the foundation was dissolving, it reported receiving almost $1.8 *billion* in donations in 1998. That would make SAAR one of the largest recipients of charitable donations ever. For years the foundation had operated on reported annual budgets of about $1.5 million. In its initial tax return for 1998, the SAAR Foundation reported receiving no contributions at all that year.

SAAR lawyers said the $1.8 billion was reported because of a clerical error, despite the fact that the ten-digit number, $1,783,545,883, was repeated at least seven times on the form. Cherif Sedky, the foundation's treasurer, said that he "did not recall" that amount of money flowing through the company.

"It is a staggering sum," said one U.S. investigator. "We are still looking at it as a real transaction. We believe the money was spread around in pieces, like taking a salami and slicing it thinly and passing it all around."

In February 2002 the SAAR Foundation formally amended its tax return yet again, reporting no income to the foundation in 1998. As if the $1.8 billion never existed.

•

There is another complicated thread in the Safa network that has drawn scrutiny from federal investigators. For the last five years of its existence, the treasurer of the SAAR Foundation, the group's central entity, was Cherif Sedky, an American lawyer representing the al Rajhi family.

Sedky is also the representative and business partner of Khalid bin Mahfouz, one of the wealthiest men in the world and longtime banker to the Saudi royal family. Bin Mahfouz gave a $20 million endowment to a charity called the Muwaffaq, or Blessed Relief, Foundation in 1991. A month after 9/11, U.S. officials said Muwaffaq was an "al Qaeda front that receives funding from wealthy Saudi businessmen. Saudi businessmen have been transferring millions of dollars to bin Laden through Blessed Relief." Sedky acknowledged his client's role in founding the charity, but said the money was intended solely for humanitarian purposes. At the same time, the Treasury Department froze the assets of Yassin Qadi, a wealthy Saudi who had directed the Muwaffaq charity for most of its five-year life. Both the United States and UN designated Qadi as a terrorist financier.

Muwaffaq was initially set up as a for-profit company on the Isle of Man on June 25, 1991, with Qadi as a director. It then registered as a charity on the island of Jersey in 1992 and opened offices in Muslim enclaves around the world, including Afghanistan. It even registered an office in the state of Delaware in February 1992, with Qadi listed as the chairman of the board. The Delaware branch was dissolved two years later because of nonpayment of taxes.

The 1996 CIA report on charities stated that Muwaffaq funded terrorists in Bosnia and that it also "fund[ed] at least one training camp in Afghanistan."

While the charity supposedly went out of business in 1996, it was never officially dissolved.

•

Bin Mahfouz was no stranger to U.S. officials. In the 1980s he was a heavy investor in and also a director of the rogue Bank of Credit and Commerce International (BCCI). BCCI became notorious for ripping off its depositors and laundering money for terrorists, gunrunners, and drug dealers. In 1995 bin Mahfouz paid $225 million in a settlement with U.S. prosecutors for his role in that scandal. Bin Mahfouz's name was also on the Golden Chain list in Sarajevo.

In 1996 bin Mahfouz took over his father's bank, the National Commercial Bank in Saudi Arabia, the one used by the royal family. A 1998 audit of the bank found widespread irregularities, including an unauthorized $3 million transfer to Muwaffaq. U.S. officials had requested the audit, and after the review of the bank's books bin Mahfouz was forced to surrender his management position and the Saudi government bought a controlling interest in the bank. Sedky, bin Mahfouz's lawyer, denies the audit ever took place.

To pacify the Americans, the Saudi government told a high level U.S. delegation that bin Mahfouz had been placed under house arrest in early 1999. The Clinton administration pressed hard for access to the banker to question him and was rebuffed. Saudi officials "weren't willing to let us talk to him," said one official directly involved in events. "And we asked at a very senior level." Sedky denies bin Mahfouz was ever placed under house arrest.

•

The Safa Group might have escaped scrutiny in 2001 if not for a raid that occurred seven years earlier, leading to another thread of investigation.

In 1995, the FBI raided the home and offices of Sami al Arian, a Kuwaiti-Palestinian computer science professor at the University of South Florida in Tampa. The feds suspected al Arian, a slight, bearded, and balding man, was secretly funneling money to terrorists. They believed he was a senior member of the Palestinian Islamic Jihad, a group that unleashes suicide bombers against Israelis.

Al Arian was a vocal activist on Palestinian causes, and he frequently spoke at Islamic conferences. At one 1991 conference, al Arian, dressed in the flowing robes of an imam, was videotaped shouting in Arabic "Let us damn America, let us damn Israel. Let us damn their allies until death."

In the early 1990s al Arian set up organizations to raise money for orphans and widows and the study of Islam. He used the organizations to sponsor Muslim conferences, including one that featured Omar Abdul Rahman, the Blind Sheik who instigated the 1993 World Trade Center attack.

Al Arian also sponsored the U.S. visa of Ramadan Abdullah

Shallah, who joined al Arian on the university faculty from 1992 to 1994. But Shallah suddenly disappeared in October 1995, immediately following the assassination of PIJ leader Fat'hi Ibrahim Shikaki. Shallah resurfaced a few days later at Shikaki's funeral in Damascus, Syria, where the slain leader's body was taken with full military honors. Shallah, standing by the casket, had been named Shikaki's successor. Al Arian said he was "shocked" at Shallah's ties to PIJ. But the FBI finally swooped in.

The raid on al Arian led to the Safa Group. The FBI found letters documenting Safa entities' financial support of al Arian to the tune of tens of thousands of dollars a year. In a September 7, 1993, letter, Safa Group leaders told one al Arian–led group: "We consider you a part of us and an extension of us and we as a part of you," adding that their financial donation of tens of thousands of dollars was "for you as a group, regardless of the party or façade you use the donation for."

But the al Arian and Safa Group investigations languished. In the 2000 elections al Arian supported George W. Bush, urging Muslims to vote Republican as the best hope of ending discrimination against Arab-Americans. Al Arian and his family were photographed with a beaming Bush and his wife, Laura, during a Florida campaign stop. Al Arian liked to boast that he had delivered "considerably more" than the 537 votes that gave Bush his victory in Florida and allowed him to capture the White House. On June 20, 2001, al Arian was invited to the White House as part of a large delegation of Muslims to be briefed by presidential adviser Karl Rove.

But the FBI had never formally closed the investigation into al Arian and 9/11 ended his grace period. In December 2001, the University of South Florida's board of trustees voted twelve to one to fire al Arian. On February 20, 2003, al Arian was arrested and charged with conspiracy to commit murder through suicide attacks in Israel and with secretly leading the Palestinian Islamic Jihad for many years.

The fifty-count indictment, unsealed in Tampa, charged that al Arian had served on the Shura Council, or governing body of PIJ, since the 1980s. The indictment contained transcripts of telephone calls and faxes al Arian had sent through the years that the government said showed he was engaged in a wide-ranging conspiracy to funnel money to terrorists. Much of the al Arian indictment is based on intelligence wiretaps that were kept from the prosecution prior to the USA Patriot Act. Al Arian's lawyer, Nicholas M. Matassini, called the indictment a "work of fiction" and said his client "is a political prisoner." Al Arian later decided to represent himself.

•

In June 2003 the FBI arrested Soliman S. Bahiri and held him as a material witness in the Safa investigation. Two months later, federal agents, in arguing that Bahiri should remain in custody, for the first time laid out in open court the various ties of Bahiri to the Muslim Brotherhood, leaders of the Safa Group, and other suspected terrorists. It is a network that prosecutors contend stretches from Virginia to New Jersey, from Switzerland to Saudi Arabia. To make its case, the government used bank statements, canceled checks, tax records, wire transfer records, and public incorporation documents. Bahiri's attorney, James Clark, did not dispute most of the specifics of the government claims, but said there was "not a shred of evidence" his client supported terrorists. Judge T. E. Ellis III disagreed and ordered Bahiri held, saying there was plenty of evidence he did business with terrorists. Bahiri was convicted on immigration charges in October 2003.

The nexus of the complicated case that ties all the actors together is BMI Inc., a private Islamic investment company in New Jersey that Bahiri administered. Through BMI, Bahiri handled investments for several designated terrorists, including Yasin Qadi, who ran the Muwaffaq charity; Mousa Abu Marzook, a leader of Hamas; and Sheik Youssef al Qaradawi, a radical cleric banned from the United States since 1999 for his alleged support of terrorism. Qaradawi was also a shareholder in Bank al Taqwa, the Bahamian bank shut down because of its terrorist ties. David Kane, the agent from the Bureau of Immigration and Customs who testified against Bahiri, said BMI used Bank al Taqwa to move money.

BMI also took almost $4 million from businesses in the Safa Group and from other groups founded by Safa leaders, according to an affidavit. Nancy Luque, the defense attorney, denied her clients had any dealings with Bahiri, or gave him the money. Bahiri was also a close friend of Sami al Arian, the Florida college professor charged with funding terrorists. Another investor in BMI was Abdullah bin Laden, a nephew of the al Qaeda leader, who put $500,000 into the firm. At the time Abdullah ran the U.S. branch of a Saudi charity called the World Association of Muslim Youth, or WAMY. Federal officials say WAMY is under investigation as a suspected terrorist front.

"These cases are incredibly complicated to make, but in this one company you have everyone together," said a federal investigator. "Most investors were tied to the Muslim Brotherhood and designated terrorists, using a lot of Saudi money to invest in a small, opaque company that could move the cash to a variety of terrorist organizations. That is the modus operandi we find again and again."

D uring the day, Bob Fromme worked as a detective sergeant for the Iredell County, North Carolina, police department. At night he moonlighted as a security guard at a JR Tobacco warehouse that sold discount cigarettes in bulk. In 1996, while working the security job, Fromme grew suspicious of two Middle Eastern men who would arrive several times a week carrying plastic trash bags and wads of cash tightly wrapped in rubber bands. They would each purchase sixty thousand cigarettes—thirty cartons—the legal limit of bulk cigarettes; buying more would trigger reporting requirements. The two men would stash the smokes in large trash bags, load them into rental vans, and drive away, heading north. Unsure whether this was illegal, Fromme contacted a friend at the federal Bureau of Alcohol, Tobacco and Firearms. Together they set up a joint federal and state investigation into what they thought was a routine cigarette-smuggling case and dubbed it Operation

Smoke Screen. Instead, it turned out to be a groundbreaking case in exposing terrorist finances in the United States.

The two men making the purchases were brothers Mohammed and Chawki Hammoud. The scam was to buy van loads of cigarettes in North Carolina, where the cigarette tax was 5 cents a pack, the lowest in the country. They would then illegally transport the cigarettes to Michigan, where the tax is 75 cents per pack, one of the highest in the country, for resale. The brothers could clear $8 to $10 per carton, and each van load netted them up to $13,000. Surveillance, wiretaps, and financial records showed the brothers and a small group of associates were also tied to a crime spree that had been plaguing the Charlotte area.

The brothers, according to court documents, entered the country illegally, then paid American women to marry them in order to obtain citizenship. They then helped other Lebanese enter the country by arranging phony marriages.

The brothers and their friends relied on fraudulent Social Security numbers to fabricate identities, forge credit cards, pass bad checks, and illegally buy and sell millions of dollars' worth of cigarettes. In 1997 Mohammed Hammoud and the woman he fraudulently married, Angela Tsioumas, reported total wages of $24,693. But they made bank deposits totaling more than $737,000. A favorite scam was to obtain credit cards using false names, quickly max out the card, then dump it for another, stiffing the credit card companies for hundreds of thousands of dollars.

In 1999, as the U.S. attorney's office was preparing a case against the Hammouds and others for prosecution, the FBI stepped in. The bureau told the prosecutors that its agents had been conducting an intelligence probe into the fund-raising activities of a militant Hezbollah cell in Charlotte. The main targets were the Hammouds. Hezbollah was designated a terrorist entity by the U.S. government in 1996. Operating in Lebanon but sponsored by Syria and Iran, Hezbollah for years targeted Americans in the Middle East. Until 9/11, Hezbollah was the terrorist group that had killed the most Americans.

In addition to his criminal activities, Mohammed Hammoud hosted weekly meetings for a dozen or two fellow Lebanese in his two-story blue-slate home on a quiet street on the outskirts of Charlotte. At the meetings, the men watched videos of Hezbollah attacks against Israeli targets, listened to sermons by Hezbollah imams, and collected money for the movement. Court documents show that much of the money the Hammouds raised was sent straight back to Beirut to keep the terrorist network running.

The money was also used to acquire dual-use equipment for Hezbollah operatives in the field. The equipment included night-vision goggles, advanced aircraft analysis and design software, mine and metal detection equipment, stun guns, radars, ultrasonic dog repellers, and laser range finders. But not all the money went to the cause. The brothers lived upper-middle-class lives, with luxury cars, electronic gadgets, and nice houses.

With the FBI intervention, the case was reworked. The Hezbollah tie relied in part on telephone intercepts by the Canadian Security Intelligence Service showing the Charlotte group was in touch with and receiving instructions from Hezbollah leaders in Canada. Mohammed Hammoud, the intercepts showed, had a close relationship with Ayatollah Mohammed Hussein Fadlallah, Hezbollah's spiritual leader.

On July 21, 2000, some 250 law enforcement officers swarmed over the Charlotte suburb where the Hammouds lived, arresting the brothers and fifteen others. Another person was picked up in Michigan. Eleven of those apprehended were Lebanese, and seven were Americans who took money for the phony marriages that got the Lebanese into the country. By the time the ring was broken up the group had sold $7.5 million in cigarettes and committed credit card and identity-theft frauds worth millions more.

Following 9/11 and the passage of the Patriot Act, the prosecution successfully introduced FBI wiretaps as evidence. And, in the cigarette case, for the first time in U.S. legal history, prosecutors were allowed to introduce as evidence foreign electronic intercepts, including the Canadian intelligence wiretaps. On February 28, 2003, in a landmark terrorist prosecution, the Hammouds were convicted of smuggling, fraud, money laundering, and racketeering. Mohammed, the ringleader who knowingly funneled money to Hezbollah, was sentenced to 155 years in prison. Chawki received a fifty-one-month sentence for his role. Fifteen others pleaded guilty to various charges.

•

The crimes revealed in the cigarette case are among the scores of small-time scams and petty crimes that terrorist sympathizers in the United States use to raise money. The crimes include skimming the profits from drug sales, stealing and reselling baby formula, illegally redeeming large quantities of grocery coupons, swiping credit card numbers, and selling unlicensed T-shirts. While each scam alone raises only a relatively small amount of money, taken together they add up to tens of millions of dollars each year, a significant sum in the terrorist world.

Most of the groups began operating in the United States long before al Qaeda had established any presence here. Hamas, Hezbollah, the Palestinian Islamic Jihad, and other groups had been working here for decades. Most were affiliated with the Muslim Brotherhood, the radical group that has long financed radical causes.

But the crimes drew little attention from Washington despite numerous cases in which local law enforcement officials working separately reported links to international terrorist organizations. The local cops were almost universally ignored at a time when the war on drugs was the top priority and prosecuting infractions such as coupon fraud seemed a waste of time. The petty crime prosecutions were time-consuming, expensive, and difficult to make. Even if convictions were obtained, the punishment usually amounted to little more than a slap on the wrist. Why waste time and resources when it seemed like bigger challenges awaited?

"It wasn't until after 9/11 that we understood the magnitude of the [terrorist] fund-raising from our shores," said John Forbes, a retired U.S. Customs official who directed a financial crimes task force in New York in the early 1990s. "We were always looking to catch the big rats, we want to catch rats. That was what we focused on. But in looking for rats we let thousands of ants get by."

•

One of those chasing the ants was former New York police detective Ben Jacobson, who was hired in 1987 by NCH, the nation's leading coupon clearinghouse, to investigate coupon fraud in the New York area.

Coupon scams usually involve the perpetrators collecting thousands of coupons from Dumpsters, recycling centers, and printing plants. Soiled coupons are cleaned up and new coupons are made to look old. The coupons are then taken to stores participating in the scam, usually small grocery stores or minimarts. Although no purchases have been made, the stores send the coupons in for redemption. The profits are then divided between the storeowner and the scammers. About $3.5 billion worth of coupons are redeemed every year and industry officials say almost 10 percent of that—$300 million—is fraudulent.

Jacobson said he took the job expecting to arrest a few crooked storeowners. Instead, he stumbled on a lucrative scheme that was funding the radical cleric Omar Abdul Rahman, who helped plan the first World Trade Center bombing in 1993.

Jacobson found that a network of stores owned by Middle Eastern men were working together in the fraud, which stretched from New York City to New Jersey and Pennsylvania. Stores that had been doing $200 a month in coupon redemptions were suddenly redeeming tens of thousands of dollars' worth. Many of the storeowners never even saw the coupons, they just collected their checks. Jacobson said the scheme, involving hundreds of stores, was reaping millions of dollars a month in the late 1980s and early 1990s.

The coupons were packaged for mailing at 7912 Fifth Avenue in Brooklyn, a storefront identified as Hamada Video. Hamada was redeeming some $13,000 a month in grocery coupons even though it sold no groceries at all. One of the Hamada Video employees was Mahmud Abouhalima, who lived above the store. Abouhalima, an Egyptian, was the driver and chief aide to Rahman. He was also the main architect of the first World Trade Center bombing, working with Ramzi Yousef, who later planned Operation Bojinka. Abouhalima was convicted in the World Trade Center case and is serving a 240-year sentence.

But prosecution of the coupon fraud scheme foundered. Jacobson told a congressional committee in 1998 that "after more than five years of tracking, documenting and formulating a strategy for criminal prosecution in this New York scheme, I was unable to enlist the substantive aid of any law enforcement agency or prosecutor's office . . . This was despite the fact that during this period, hundreds of stores, businesses and individuals were identified . . . Today the fraud schemes continue unabated, unchallenged and facilitated by computers and the Internet."

Jacobson said that in his efforts to interest the FBI and others he was told repeatedly, "It's not guns, it's not drugs. We don't have the manpower." Until after 9/11. Then, Jacobson said, federal agents were suddenly calling him.

"I try not to make it an 'I told you so' conversation, but I do say that to myself," Jacobson said. "Did I bring them the bomber of the building, of the flight, the fellow flying the airplane? No. I brought them the network financing this."

•

Another scheme used by Sheik Omar Abdul Rahman and his followers to raise money was the sale of counterfeit name-brand clothing, mostly T-shirts. Easy to manufacture and highly profitable, knockoff clothing is a multibillion-dollar industry in the United States. The link was discovered with the bust of one of the biggest knockoff rings in history, a case of counterfeit Nike merchandise destined for the 1996 Atlanta Olympics.

The markup on fake T-shirts is especially high because making them is so cheap and easy. All an experienced criminal needs is a large enough workspace to set up commercial-quality silk printing. Knockoff shirts cost about $2 apiece to make and sell for about $10 instead of the $20 or so that legitimate merchandise fetches. So a knockoff artist can make $7 or $8 per shirt.

In 1995, Dempster Leech, a private investigator who specialized in finding counterfeit products, tracked the group of Middle Eastern men who were involved in the scheme to sell the fake shirts in Atlanta. The FBI and local police carried out the raids while most of the merchandise was still in New York. Leech was there when the raids went down.

"There were about three floors' worth of merchandise, already on pallets and stacked about seven feet high," Leech told me. "My little heart stopped right there."

In all the FBI found about twenty warehouses of merchandise, either fake Olympic stuff or products counterfeiting those of Olympic sponsors. The FBI confiscated about 100,000 T-shirts with the Nike "swoosh" symbol or the Olympic torch stenciled on. An informant in the case tied those responsible for the load to the Blind Sheik, as did telephone records. But, though the merchandise was confiscated, no one was arrested or charged in the case.

"A lot of money from that large and sophisticated ring was going to the Blind Sheik," said one knowledgeable official, citing telephone records and intelligence information. "But in the end the FBI and others lost interest because there were other things, like drugs, that were much hotter at the time."

•

Immediately after 9/11, the law enforcement community began to scrub their files for anything related to terrorism. Robert Bonner, the head of the Customs Service, scrambled to assemble a group of financial experts to begin tracking terrorist money inside the United States. The group became Operation Green Quest and what the group found astonished them. The agents were stunned to find dozens of cases over the previous decade involving terrorist groups.

In some ways, Bonner was suited by background and temperament to the new challenge of finally focusing attention on that illicit flow of money. He led the Drug Enforcement Administration during the cocaine wars with the Medellín and Cali cartels in the early 1990s and sat as a federal judge before taking the Customs job. Financial investigators widely credited the slow-speaking Bonner for developing a strategic framework to attack terrorist financing after 9/11.

Bonner said that in his new job he drew heavily on his experience from the drug wars. Those who worked for him at the DEA said Bonner constantly pushed them to come up with new ways of attacking the problems of drug trafficking and money laundering. The push to innovate carried over into the Customs investigations.

"Bonner turned us loose and wanted us to think outside the box; he wasn't afraid of that," said a veteran law enforcement official still in government service. "He is one of the few leaders who could deal with an immediate problem and still look down the road and develop a strategic vision of where we should be going."

Robert J. Nieves, who worked closely with Bonner during his tenure at the DEA, said Bonner was "not at all threatened" by new ways of doing things. "He had an uncanny ability to absorb data, he was a vacuum cleaner for knowledge," Nieves said. "He could be briefed, read, assimilate and come up with conclusions very quickly and demand action. Plans didn't sit in his in-box for weeks or months. He radically changed the way DEA operated."

Bonner acknowledged that the United States had a lot of catching up to do on terrorist financing, and little time to do it.

"Before September 11, this type of [petty criminal] activity was not high on the radar screen because it didn't involve a whole lot of money," Bonner said. "When it became interesting was when it had ties to terrorists."

One of the things Bonner did was shift the Customs supercomputer's NIPS program, which traces the import and export of commodities, away from tracking drug money to trying to find patterns in fraud used to fund terrorists.

In early 2002 the program detected an unusual discrepancy. It found that Intrigue Jewelers, a Florida jewelry company, was importing significantly more gold than it sold as jewelry in its franchise stores. Many of the franchise's owners were Pakistani. The anomaly prompted suspicions some of the gold was being diverted to al Qaeda or other terrorist groups. Customs officers swept down and raided seventy-five kiosks in seven states and removed documents and computer disks. Intrigue Jewelers maintains that it is innocent of any terrorist contacts. The investigation continues.

While worried about charges of racial profiling, Bonner and other law enforcement officials vastly expanded probes into suspected fonts of terrorist financing. Several different task forces across the country were quietly set up and began investigating hundreds of Muslim- and Arab-owned businesses to see if they were illegally funneling money to terrorist groups. The investigations have been designed both to stanch the flow of funding for terrorist groups and to follow money that could lead to terrorist suspects.

The controversial decision to target those groups for investigation drew a sharp response from Muslim leaders, who said they were unaware of the policy. "It wouldn't surprise me that authorities are singling out Arab and Muslim businesses for scrutiny, given the presumption of guilt we've confronted since September 11," said Ibrahim Hooper, a spokesperson for the Council on American-Islamic Relations.

But investigators said they had no choice after 9/11.

"The fact is that al Qaeda, Hezbollah, and Hamas are Middle Eastern groups and people from the Middle East here send their money back to the Middle East," said one senior official. "So of course we have to look at them. Who else is going to be sending them money? Pakistanis send money to Pakistan. Salvadorans send money to El Salvador. It isn't racial profiling, it is necessary."

•

Another new trend in terrorist financing was uncovered in a series of DEA busts of Mexican methamphetamine rings. Commonly known as meth, speed, or crank, the drug retails on the street for about $200 a gram.

The principal chemical needed to make meth—a multibillion-dollar illegal business in the United States—is pseudoephedrine, an ingredient in over-the-counter cold medicine. Because Canada has no law regulating the sale of pseudoephedrine, Mexican drug traffickers contract with Canadian criminal groups to truck huge shipments of the product into the United States. With the pseudoephedrine in hand and other ingredients readily available in pharmacies or hardware stores in hand, meth is easy to cook up.

On January 10, 2002, Operation Mountain Express, a joint undercover case operation between the DEA and Customs, brought down two large meth rings. The raids swept through Michigan, California, Arizona, Texas, Ohio, and Illinois, netting fifty-four suspects, hundreds of thousands in cash, and nine large methamphetamine laboratories. While Mexican drug gangs controlled the methamphetamine manufacture and sale, investigators found that most of the pseudoephedrine suppliers were from the Middle East, particularly Yemen. Using tractor trailers that crossed the Canadian border, the groups would store the pseudoephedrine in Detroit then transship it to meth laboratories across the United States. Often the trucks were disguised as Federal Express or U.S. Postal Service trucks. So far, law enforcement officials say, they have traced about $10 million sent from the meth group to bank accounts controlled by Hezbollah. Much of the cash was shipped in bulk.

"This is the first time we have seen drug proceeds going back [from the United States] to a terrorist organization," said Asa Hutchinson, the DEA administrator and former Republican congressman from Arkansas. "I don't know if this is a new phenomenon or if we are following this more closely since 9/11."

"Our concern," Hutchinson added, "is an alliance of sophisticated Mexican organized crime groups and Middle Eastern organized crime groups. Our concern is the growing alliance between the two."

One of the favorite ways for the pseudoephedrine dealers and other suspected terrorist sympathizers to send money back to the Middle East is through bulk cash shipments. The cash is simply hidden in different containers and shipped by express mail or packed in suitcases that are hand-carried. One of those arrested in Operation Mountain Express tried to ship $50,000 home by stuffing it in a box of Honeycomb cereal.

While there is no limit to the amount of money a person can legally bring into or take out of the United States, any amount above $10,000 must be declared, something criminals and terrorists are loath to do. And, because of its bulk and weight, moving cash is difficult. For example, $1 million in $20 bills weighs 110 pounds. To combat bulk cash smuggling by terrorist sympathizers, Customs again shifted resources from the war on drugs to create a new effort, dubbed Operation Oasis.

Specially trained dogs are among the most effective weapons against bulk cash smuggling. Rather than sniffing for cocaine or marijuana, the dogs are trained to smell for the particular odor of dye and ink on currency. Dogs helped find $659,000 stuffed in a suitcase at New York's John F. Kennedy airport on April 30, 2002. The cash, in $20, $50, and $100 bills, was found jammed into boxes of baby wipes and oatmeal on a flight bound for Egypt. On July 17, 2002, officials charged Alaa al-Sadawi, an Egyptian-born imam at a mosque in Jersey City, with currency reporting violations and opened an investigation into the origin and destination of the money. Operation Oasis seized more than $16 million in bulk cash shipments in the first nine months of its existence. "Operation Oasis is making it more difficult for terrorist organizations and other criminal groups to smuggle currency across our borders," Bonner said. "The operation is also generating significant intelligence that is being used to investigate suspected terrorist finance networks across the United States."

•

There are other ingenious scams that have been operating for years but are only now being tied to terrorist financing. Just after noon on a lazy Saturday in April 2002, in the small town of Conroe, Texas, Sgt. Harvey Smitherman of the Montgomery County Police Department spotted a van speeding through town at 91 mph. When he finally pulled the vehicle over, he found four people and piles of boxes with hundreds of cans of Enfamil, an infant formula that retails for about $10 a can. When he asked why they were speeding, one of the women responded that she was pregnant and they were rushing to find a hospital. When an ambulance arrived, the woman refused treatment. That raised Smitherman's suspicions. When he checked the idenfication of the others in the car, he found that two of the men had outstanding arrest warrants. Smitherman then asked to see the receipts for the boxes of baby formula. The occupants produced receipts from several Wal-Marts from Conroe to Waco. But Smitherman noticed the papers showed the cans were sold for 57 cents per can. Knowing that couldn't be right, Smitherman detained the entire group.

The county police were soon joined by the FBI, Customs, and other national agencies. The investigation found the group had been hired by a Middle Eastern man, who gave them the money to buy the infant formula. But first the group altered the bar codes on the cans, leading to a net profit of almost $9 per can.

"There is a very, very strong connection with what's going on here in relation to money going over to the Middle Eastern countries to fund terrorist groups over there," Montgomery County Police lieutenant Michael White said. "We're just a little, bitty town here. You'd never think something like this would happen."

But the widespread smuggling of baby formula to finance terror had already been discovered several years before, in Fort Worth. In the late 1990s, Det. Scott Campbell discovered an organized shoplifting ring that trafficked in stolen baby formula in the Dallas area. The ring had hit dozens of stores in the area. Campbell found that the gang would pay drug addicts and indigent people to steal thousands of cans of the formula. The thieves received a dollar or two per can. The cans would then be repackaged in counterfeit cardboard boxes and shipped to unsuspecting stores across the United States. Suspecting there was an overseas connection, Campbell asked for federal help. Customs agent Scott Springer was assigned to the case. Campbell and Springer found the gang had contracted a company called Nightingale Rehabilitation Center to package the formula for them. The center employed mentally and physically handicapped people for the work. In the end the shoplifting ring didn't pay the center for the work they performed, stiffing them for thousands of dollars.

Springer estimated the group netted tens of millions of dollars by the time the warehouses were raided and fourteen people arrested in 1997. Campbell said the scam "was probably more lucrative than any cocaine investigation I have ever investigated."

The potential ties to terrorism were not discovered until after the arrests. Officials found that a portion of the money was flowing to Jordan and Egypt, and into the account of a man named Adel Saadat. One of Saadat's sons, Mohammed Saadat, was arrested in the raids. It turned out Mohammed had been recruited by al Qaeda and trained in Afghanistan. The younger Saadat was recruited by Moataz al-Hallak, an imam the FBI linked to bin Laden. Al-Hallak was the imam at the Dallas mosque attended by Saadat. It was also the mosque attended by Wadih el Hage, bin Laden's personal secretary, who was later convicted of helping plan the 1998 U.S. embassy bombings. Officials said some of the money also appeared to be going to the Popular Front for the Liberation of Palestine, a Marxist-Leninist splinter of the Palestine Liberation Organization. The Front was designated a terrorist entity by the United States.

Alarmed by their findings, Campbell and Springer went to the FBI with the information. They ended up returning to the bureau four times to try to generate some interest. To no avail.

"At this point I think the person we were assigned to speak with didn't deem this case that important," Campbell said. "At the time they were kind of either shorthanded, busy . . . I couldn't tell you."

After 9/11, the case received renewed attention. Springer and Campbell were assigned to Operation Green Quest and are now involved in the probe of Arab businesses.

Since 9/11, massive baby formula scams have been uncovered in California, Kentucky, Colorado, and North Carolina. The largest operation appears to be the one run out of Lexington. Police say that group netted $44 million in just eighteen months of operation in the late 1990s.

"The total amount of the criminal activities we are investigating for ties to terrorism is well over $1 billion," said a senior law enforcement official. "It is hard to know how much goes to terrorists, but we guess it is in the tens of millions, at least. We are not finding a great pot of gold anywhere. It is all in smallish amounts, but it adds up."

•

There seems to have been one pot of gold, though. On November 18, 1992, the Holy Land Foundation for Relief and Development registered as a tax-exempt charity in Richardson, Texas. Over the next nine years Holy Land took in more than $25 million, making it the largest Muslim charity in the United States. Much of the money went straight to the Islamic Resistance Movement of Palestine, known as Hamas. On December 4, 2001, the Treasury Department designated Holy Land a terrorist support entity and shut it down.

Hamas was founded in 1987 as a violent offshoot of the radical, pan-Arab Muslim Brotherhood and has since pursued a sophisticated two-prong strategy aimed at destroying Israel and replacing it with a Palestinian state. Hamas is a proponent of violence and the use of suicide bombers. It also has used its financial resources to build schools, hospitals, and orphanages for Palestinians in Gaza and other territories where such services are virtually nonexistent. The social programs have helped Hamas win broad popularity among Palestinians even as suicide bombers have become the group's trademark. In its public statements the group routinely calls Jews monkeys and pigs. From October 1, 2000, to September 10, 2001, Hamas took credit for at least twenty suicide bombings that killed seventy-seven people, including three Americans.

The establishment of Holy Land was almost simultaneous with the founding of Benevolence in Chicago. In the diary of Wadih el Hage, bin Laden's secretary, there is a mention of a "joint venture" with Holy Land and the name and number of a Hamas figure working for the charity.

Like Benevolence, Holy Land managed to operate for years despite FBI investigations and a consensus in the law enforcement and intelligence communities that it was funding a group designated as a terrorist entity in 1995. Initially set up in 1989 as the Occupied Land Fund in California, the charity moved to Texas two years later. By 1998, Holy Land reported raising $5.2 million. That climbed to $6.3 million in 1999 before surging to $13 million in 2000.

In a memorandum from the FBI to Treasury laying out why Holy Land should be designated a terrorist entity, Dale Watson, the FBI's assistant director for counterterrorism, revealed that the charity had been founded by Hamas and shipped most of the money it raised back to Hamas. Mousa Abu Marzook, the leader of Hamas's political wing who was designated a terrorist by the U.S. government in 1995, gave the charity $200,000 in start-up money. "FBI investigations revealed . . . that [Holy Land] is the primary fund-raising entity for Hamas and that a significant portion of the funds raised by [Holy Land] are clearly being used by the Hamas organization," the FBI document said.

Like the Benevolence, Safa, and Sami al Arian investigations, the Holy Land case was years in the making. And like the previous investigations, it was initially given a low priority. Many of the wiretaps that were presented as evidence for shutting down Holy Land in December 2001 were recorded in 1993 and not translated until after 9/11.

Because of the Marzook connection and other suspected ties to Hamas, FBI surveillance of Holy Land leaders began in at least 1993. But the request for the surveillance came from the British and Israelis. The bureau bugged at least two meetings between senior Hamas officials and Holy Land directors. One of the meetings took place from October 1 to 3, 1993, at the Courtyard by Marriott Hotel, 8900 Bartram Avenue, in Philadelphia.

The intercepts show that the overall purpose of the meeting was to develop a strategy to defeat the Oslo Accords, the Israeli-Palestinian peace plan that had been negotiated by moderates on both sides with the hope of leading to a lasting peace in the Middle East. The meeting focused on U.S. fund-raising and the need to position Hamas as an alternative to Yasser Arafat's PLO.

"During the meeting the participants went to great lengths and spent much effort hiding their association with Hamas," the FBI report said. "Instead, they referred to Hamas as 'Samah,' which is Hamas spelled backward. Most of the time the participants referred to Hamas as 'The Movement.' "

Among those attending the meeting were Shukri Abu Baker, Holy Land's CEO; Haitham Maghawri, Holy Land's executive director; and Ghassan Elashi, the chairman of Holy Land's board.

By early 1994, Holy Land and another Hamas front, the Al-Aqsa Educational Fund, were in a conflict over fund-raising issues. Marzook flew to the United States and personally intervened in the dispute, finally designating Holy Land as Hamas's primary fund-raiser in the United States.

According to the FBI, much of the money sent to Hamas is used to encourage suicide bombers by paying large sums to their families. The bureau also alleges Hamas schools, supported by Holy Land, teach children, beginning in kindergarten or earlier, the virtues of being suicide bombers.

The FBI also suspected Hamas was receiving money through an Internet business that was closely tied to Holy Land. Five days before 9/11, FBI and Customs agents raided the offices of InfoCom Corp., located just across the street from the charity. The company, with about five hundred clients, was founded at the same time as Holy Land and did about $7 million a year in business. Its clients included some of the largest Islamic organizations in the United States. Ghassan Elashi, the cofounder and chairman of Holy Land's board, is also InfoCom's vice president for sales and marketing. His brother, Bayan, is InfoCom's president and CEO. Holy Land had a contract with InfoCom to maintain the foundation's website.

But what really concerned the agents was the tie between InfoCom and Marzook, the designated terrorist and Hamas leader. In 1993, Marzook's wife invested $250,000 in InfoCom and received an annual annuity from the company.

Both the InfoCom raid and the designation of Holy Land as a terrorist financier generated widespread anger in the Arab American community. The Council on American-Islamic Relations branded the InfoCom raid "an anti-Muslim witch-hunt promoted by the pro-Israel lobby in America."

In a joint statement, several of the nation's largest Muslim groups demanded Bush reverse the order to freeze Holy Land's assets. The statement said the action was "succumbing to politically motivated smear campaigns by those who would perpetuate Israel's brutal occupation."

"No relief group anywhere in the world should be asked to question hungry orphans about their parents' religious beliefs, political affiliations or legal status," the statement added. "Those questions are not asked of recipients of public assistance whose parents are imprisoned or executed in the United States and they should not be a litmus test for relief in Palestine."

But the FBI, in the memorandum to Treasury, said the newly translated wiretaps, now admissible in court, would show something else. "Hamas is a foreign terrorist group engaged in grave acts of violence . . . and constitutes an unusual and extraordinary threat to the national security, foreign policy and economy of the United States . . . The Holy Land Foundation for Relief and Development is acting for or on behalf of Hamas."

CHAPTER NINE: Fighting the Last War, Losing the New One

I t was Monday, March 17, 2003, when Rand Beers, the top White House counterterrorism adviser, finally did what his gut told him to do. After looking over the stack of classified threat memos from around the world, he wrote out a one-paragraph letter of resignation. After thirty-five years of public service—including senior positions in the NSC under both Ronald Reagan and Bush One—he was burned out, convinced the current Bush administration simply was not serious about winning the war on terrorism.

"As an insider, I saw things that weren't being done," Beers said after leaving. "And the longer I sat and watched, the more concerned I became, until I got up and walked out."

Beers's resignation was one of the strongest indicators of a counterterrorism policy in deep disarray. His absence shook the already-depleted ranks of counterterrorism experts in the government, many of whom shared Beers's frustration at the lack of coherence or innovation in the new war. Beers had replaced Wayne

Downing, a retired army general, following Downing's own abrupt departure in August 2002. Downing had replaced Richard Clarke, a holdover from the Clinton administration, in October 2001. Clarke spent ten years as the nation's terrorism czar. He was a pioneer in identifying al Qaeda and bin Laden as serious threats to the United States.

At the State Department, Pentagon, and other agencies, senior officials have walked out the door. The turnover has taken a toll on counterterrorism efforts. Decades of experience and knowledge have been lost at the time when they are most needed. The narrow field of true terrorism experts got narrower. Some of those who left blamed their dissatisfaction, in conversations with friends and colleagues, on the insular nature of Bush's inner circle, the inability to present unbiased intelligence, and the increasingly dysfunctional intelligence process itself.

As in the drug war before it—another war the United States never won—government rhetoric about the war on terror has masked a lack of sustained interest in fighting the threat on the ground. Afghanistan, Beers and others contended, has already been abandoned, only two years after being the epicenter of world terrorism. Bin Laden is still there and able to order up deadly operations around the world. The Taliban and al Qaeda have regrouped into mobile camps in Pakistan's lawless Tribal Territories, where the law of the land is in the hands of warlords and loyalty can be bought and sold. And the authority of Afghanistan's central government does not extend much beyond Kabul, yet there are no plans to improve the situation and little money to fulfill the promises made to rebuild the nation.

The war on Iraq siphoned resources and manpower from the overall counterterrorism strategy while also badly fracturing the international coalition vital to taking on the terrorists. Beers said many of his colleagues felt Iraq was "an ill-conceived and poorly executed strategy." In real terms, the Iraq war meant that Special Forces hunting al Qaeda, regional specialists, satellite resources to track movements and communications, and money were taken away from the counterterror strategy. Iraq has presented another problem as well. Rather than getting rid of a terrorist haven by toppling the regime of Saddam Hussein, the opposite occurred. Hundreds of radical Islamic fighters, some of them affiliated with al Qaeda, poured into Iraq after the U.S. occupation to fight the American forces. Where once the ties between Iraq and al Qaeda were tenuous at best, Islamic terrorists are now being welcomed with open arms.

"What is wrong?" Beers asked. "The administration is not only not giving the necessary money for combating terror, they are talking about a grand strategy without following through on it. These people have not got a systematic approach for the implementation of the war on terrorism. No money is a huge problem in and of itself. But they are also not starting the programs that need to be started."

Among the problems Beers ticked off were the lack of progress on immigration reform, cyberspace security, port protection, the protection of chemical plants, and the underfunding of Homeland Security. But what really makes the current system unworkable, according to Beers and others familiar with the process, is that the flood of raw intelligence gathered by intelligence agencies in the field is no longer analyzed and sifted before being sent on to superiors. Upper-level officials are simply overloaded now. Beers said that the number of pieces of "threat information" flowing into his ultrasecure in-box had swelled to between five hundred and one thousand pieces a day. Few of the threats would turn out to be real, but almost none had been filtered out on their way to his desk. He was expected to make a decision on each one, from reports of bombs on ships to threats to poison water supplies to suspicious surveillance of an embassy in Africa.

"No one wants to be discovered as the person who made the ultimate mistake, with thousands of people dying," Beers said. "So there is a constant pressure to push stuff up. The filters have gone. The sheer volume alone makes the system dysfunctional."

There were other deep-seated problems that had hamstrung the Bush administration since before 9/11. The Clinton administration had begun to take the threat of al Qaeda and international terrorism seriously, but all its efforts were viewed with disdain and suspicion by the Bush team. Even without the pervasive suspicion of Clinton policies, terrorism was not a priority for the Bush administration when it came into power. Every new administration tries to put its own stamp on foreign policy, and the enunciated priorities of the Bush team were the construction of a national missile defense system and dealing with China, viewed as a strategic competitor of the United States. The foreign policy team of Colin Powell at State, Vice President Dick Cheney, and Donald Rumsfeld at Defense were experienced and had a clear idea of where they wanted U.S. policy to go. Fighting terrorism was not among their priorities.

Former senior Clinton administration officials warned the Bush team of the terrorist threat. NSC chief Sandy Berger told his replacement, Condoleezza Rice, that "You are going to spend more time during your four years on terrorism generally and al Qaeda specifically than any other [issue]." Brian Sheridan, a former CIA analyst in charge of terrorism issues at the Pentagon, offered to brief anyone on the new team, anytime, on the issues his office dealt with. No one took up the offer.

Beers stayed longer than most and went one step further than the other career civil servants who left in dismay. After quietly consulting with friends, he joined the presidential campaign of Sen. John Kerry of Massachusetts, a liberal Democratic hopeful, in a bid to oust his former boss. The move was shocking, given Beers's years of loyal government service across party lines. A Vietnam veteran, he replaced Oliver North as director for counterterrorism and counternarcotics in the Reagan NSC. He was respected as smart, intellectually honest, and a team player with little ego. He was no pushover, but he did not publicly humiliate subordinates or seek the limelight.

"Rand's leaving should have been a wake-up call to Bush and

his senior people, but it wasn't," said a senior counterterrorism official. "They viewed it as just another malcontent heading out the door."

•

The efforts to cut off the flow of money to terrorists have not been exempt from the dysfunctionality. For twenty months after 9/11, efforts to track and freeze terrorist funds were hampered by a bitter and bruising bureaucratic turf battle over which government agency would be responsible for investigating terrorist financing. The fight didn't end until May 13, 2003, with an agreement between the FBI at the Justice Department and Operation Green Quest at the Treasury Department. The Memorandum of Understanding between Attorney General Ashcroft and Homeland Security secretary Tom Ridge finally gave the FBI sole control over the terrorist-related financial investigations.

In the vast government reshuffle after 9/11, Customs had fallen under Ridge's new Homeland domain. Bonner, the head of Customs and Green Quest's architect, was moved to the newly created position of head of the Customs and Border Protection Bureau. In the end, Ridge didn't want to spend political capital saving Green Quest. It was formally dissolved on June 30.

The Green Quest dispute was one of the most visible of the myriad government turf fights that hampered efforts to track and cut off terrorist funding dating back to the mid-1990s. Even in the post-9/11 world, where the need for broad-based cooperation became painfully evident, the squabbles continued. The government infighting was much broader than the FBI–Customs feud. The FBI and CIA were extremely reluctant to share intelligence. FBI field offices were loathe to share information with FBI headquarters in Washington and vice versa. The State Department was often out of the loop on investigations that touched overseas. Separate watch lists of suspected terrorists were kept by a host of different agencies; there was no centralization. Two years after 9/11 there was still no single database on terrorist finance accessible to the multiple agencies involved in investigations. Rather, each group maintained its own data on computers that were often incompatible with those of other agencies.

"For a few weeks after 9/11 the bureaucratic walls came down," said one veteran of the interagency process. "But within a month or so most of the walls were back up. It's like being in kindergarten and trying to get all the kids to go the same direction."

Green Quest was formed immediately after the attacks and was targeted at tracking al Qaeda's money. At the same time the FBI set up its own terrorist financial unit. With two groups pursuing almost identical mandates, a clash was inevitable. The FBI claimed expertise in terrorism; Green Quest claimed financial expertise, pointing out that many of the current financial terrorist investigations had been under the FBI's jurisdiction for years with little progress.

The truth was that neither side had much experience. The U.S. government was almost completely unequipped to go after bin Laden's elaborate financial structure. Before 9/11, neither Treasury nor the FBI had financial groups dedicated to studying or tracking terrorist assets. After 9/11, most of al Qaeda's resources were already beyond reach, in the form of diamonds, tanzanite, gold, or other commodities.

While both Treasury and the FBI stood up their terrorist finance units immediately after 9/11, the Customs expertise lay in tracking the billions of dollars in the drug war. The FBI specialized in building cases after crimes occurred and carrying out lengthy intelligence probes of suspected criminal and espionage activity. The information they collected often gathered dust in folders for years and much of the intelligence from the probes could not be shared with criminal prosecutors or case agents.

Those whose job it became to lead efforts to track al Qaeda's money did not have experience in tracking terrorist money. Dennis Lormel at the FBI had worked on the BCCI bank fraud case in the 1980s and was on the financial crimes unit. In Treasury, David

Aufhauser, as general counsel, was a skilled lawyer but had no experience finding or tracking terrorist funds. Juan Zarate, in charge of the Treasury operations, came from the Justice Department. His current job had been created only after 9/11. While he had worked on some terrorism cases, he had no experience in tracking the cash.

Immediately after 9/11, fear of another attack was paramount in the intelligence and law enforcement communities. In the FBI, the financial crimes unit dropped almost everything it was doing and tried to get a handle on how the money moved. Bonner argued for Green Quest as a way to attack terrorist financial systems, such as *hawala* and gold transfers. Green Quest, he felt, could draw on years of uncovering schemes used by drug traffickers. Bonner immediately shifted resources to special financial intelligence units with computers used to track drug money. Lormel's FBI group focused in on the precise movement of the money that funded 9/11.

But the FBI and Green Quest could not avoid conflict. Customs agents did not have clearance to look at much of the FBI's intelligence gleaned from the wiretaps and surveillance of suspected terrorist organizations. Jurisdictional battles raged in several high-profile cases, like the Northern Virginia raids on the Safa network and the Holy Land Foundation, as well as in smaller cases.

"If we were trying to build a new police force in another country, we would have to tell them, 'Look at us and don't do what we do,' " said one senior U.S. official. "We compartmentalize, we don't share intelligence among agencies and no one seems to have the authority to make that happen. We are very much a Third World country in how we are doing this."

Both Green Quest and the FBI set up joint working groups to track terrorist assets, in which the Pentagon and the CIA were also supposed to participate. But the sides remained so resistant to cooperation that the FBI and Green Quest did not send people to each other's meetings for months after 9/11. In an effort to ease the tension, the Foreign Terrorist Asset Tracking Center, established under

Treasury's auspices in late September 2001, was moved to CIA headquarters in Langley.

The tensions continued to fester almost two years after the terrorist attacks. As new information flowed in from captured al Qaeda
financial operatives and, in some cases, from their computer hard
drives and other sources, the information was fought over and compartmentalized.

By April 2003 senior law enforcement officials were calling the
ongoing feud intolerable. The FBI made its pitch to the White House
to take over all terror financing investigations, a move pushed by
Michael Chertoff, Justice's Criminal Division chief, and Deputy
Attorney General Larry Thompson. The move enraged Green Quest
operatives, who felt the FBI was big-footing them. They also com-
plained of the FBI's unwillingness to turn over critical information to
Customs agents. One official said the FBI "won't share anything with
us, then they go to the White House and accuse us of not sharing . . .
If they can't take it over, they want to kill it."

The FBI responded with accusations that Green Quest had bun-
gled several key operations, including the Safa Group raids, by not
properly preparing for the actions and by casting too wide a net.

As tension grew, supporters of Green Quest in Homeland Security struck back at the FBI by questioning the validity of the FBI's
power to arrest terror suspects under immigration laws. Ashcroft had
signed a special order granting the FBI that power in the wake of
9/11. Homeland officials said the attorney general's order became
invalid when the INS moved from the Justice Department to Homeland in the reorganization. Unless Homeland secretary Ridge reauthorized the arrest power, they said, any immigration arrests by the
FBI could be deemed illegal.

After weeks of negotiation, the FBI won. The May 13 agreement
states that Homeland Security agents can examine terrorist financing
and terrorism cases "only with the consent of the FBI." Homeland
Security investigators were thrown the bone of being assigned to the

national and regional Joint Terrorism Task Forces, where their expertise could be used. The deputy director in the FBI's terrorist finance unit would be a Homeland official detailed to the bureau. The final blow was the agreement that "no later than June 30, 2003, Operation Green Quest will no longer exist."

The reaction among those outside the FBI was bitter.

W. Ralph Basham, director of the Secret Service, which was also folded into Homeland Security, wrote Ridge a letter asking the secretary to rescind the agreement, arguing that it "would severely jeopardize thousands of ongoing investigations and could compromise the federal government's ability to effectively prevent future attacks against our financial and critical infrastructure."

Some Green Quest agents said they would retire or move to other agencies rather than work under the new agreement. "The FBI is calling this a major victory," said one disgruntled Homeland Security official. "You would think we were the terrorists. There is very little incentive for anyone to work on important cases anymore." Beers, who was involved in making the decision to end Green Quest, said it was the right decision. "The question now is whether the FBI integrates the Green Quest agents into investigations in the field," Beers said. "If they do, it will work. If they don't, they risk losing more than they gained."

•

Interagency fighting over how to handle and fund counterterrorist initiatives, especially financial investigations, goes back years. Early in Clinton's second term, his administration had begun to seriously focus on terrorism as the primary threat to the United States. Clinton himself devoted his marquee speech of October 22, 1995, marking the fiftieth anniversary of the United Nations, to the transnational threats of drug trafficking, organized crime, and terrorism. He warned of the dangers of terrorist attacks, including those from terrorists "who plotted to destroy the very hall we gather in today." The Clinton administration also began to devote vastly increased resources to counterterrorism efforts. Figures from the Office of Management and Budget show that spending doubled in Clinton's second term, from $5.7 billion in fiscal 1996 to $11.1 billion in fiscal 2001. The money went to a host of programs across the federal bureaucracy. Counterterrorism, which had accounted for less than 4 percent of the FBI's budget in 1996, increased to more than 10 percent five years later. The CIA's counterterrorism center nearly tripled its budget and personnel.

But the money did not translate into quick progress. Much of the money went to shore up security at embassies abroad. Another large chunk went to high-tech items such as satellites. Human intelligence, the key component in tracking money, went begging. At the same time, the diplomatic corps around the world was being slashed and foreign aid declined steeply. In Clinton's early years, former senior officials acknowledge, there were few people in the administration who cared about or understood intelligence. But by the end of Clinton's first term, terrorism was designated a Tier 1-A threat, the highest possible ranking. But by then the neglect had taken its toll.

"We didn't have the human intel we needed, and we didn't have many goodies to give to liaison agencies (in other countries) because aid was slashed," said Jonathan Winer, who served five years as the deputy assistant secretary of International Narcotics and Law Enforcement. "To get something, you have to give something. It is the same in intelligence. And we didn't have much to give."

When the budget increases did come, they couldn't ensure that all government agencies worked in concert. For one thing, House Republicans blocked some of the Clinton-backed initiatives for improving terrorism tracking by integrating it with other enforcement priorities. The Republicans, fearing such moves would weaken the commitment to fighting drugs, refused to allow the State Department to combine counterterrorism with its bureau looking at international drug trafficking and organized crime.

"Not every drug trafficker is a terrorist, but almost every terrorist group is tied to drug trafficking," said Winer. "We wanted to look at the twilight zone where criminals, terrorists, and intelligence operatives meet and greet. But we were forced to keep drugs and terrorism apart, and that had a huge impact."

Even when some consensus existed among government agencies on the action to be taken, things did not always get done.

In March 1996, for example, the Treasury Department, with the unusual and strong support of the State Department, was about to name the Holy Land Foundation and two of its leaders "specially designated terrorist" financiers and block all their funds because of their suspected ties to Hamas. Richard Clarke, the Clinton administration's counterterrorism director at the National Security Council, had been pushing for the action.

Clarke, a hard-charging, dynamic man who inspired great loyalty among his team, had brought the first sustained focus at senior levels in the White House on terrorist money movements. Richard Newcomb at Treasury, in charge of seizing designated terrorist funds, had written the blocking order for Holy Land. At almost the last possible second, though, Attorney General Janet Reno blocked the move. It was not the first time.

According to sources with direct knowledge of events, the primary reason was not lack of evidence, but lack of political will and Reno and the leadership of the FBI's fear of a public backlash. Reno's Justice Department argued that the International Emergency Economic Powers Act, used by Clinton to freeze the assets of Colombia's Cali cocaine cartel and other criminal groups, did not empower authorities to target charities operating in the United States. The NSC and FBI feuded over that legal interpretation until late 1995, when the Justice Department drafted a legal opinion backing the FBI. Clarke and his team were infuriated. While Clarke had carte blanche from national security advisers Anthony Lake and then Sandy Berger to fight interagency battles—and make a lot of enemies in the process—he couldn't push forward on this point.

"The first thing you have to understand is that the FBI and the intelligence community didn't want us to know what was going on," said one member of Clarke's group. "Terrorism and terrorist finance were a much lower priority for them than it was for us. And they didn't like being asked to produce information by the executive branch."

A second reason was that the FBI and police at the time "were getting hammered on racial profiling," said one official with direct knowledge of events. "The FBI was not going to run the risk of being seen as profiling. And Janet Reno carried Louis Freeh's water on that issue."

To get around the Justice Department's legal reservations, Clarke successfully pushed for the passage of the 1996 Antiterrorism and Effective Death Penalty Act, a cumbersomely worded law that, for the first time, specifically made it a crime to fund terrorist activities from the United States. It also made it much easier to deport suspected terrorists from the United States and to bar the entry of terrorist suspects into the country.

Still, Reno and Freeh refused to take action against U.S.-based charities. After the 1998 embassy bombings, Clarke renewed his quest to shut some of them down. The most prominent ones he targeted were Holy Land and the Safa group. Clarke's team also took seriously the information on gold and the *hawala* system, generated by the Treasury Department's Patrick Jost and others, and pressed for action on that front.

"I remember Dick literally pounding on the table, demanding to know why Holy Land wasn't shut down and what the plan of action was," said one participant in many of Clarke's meetings. "But of course we weren't in charge of law enforcement. Dick would also pound the table demanding to know what was being done to shut down *hawala*s. Of course, nothing was being done."

Sources with direct knowledge of events said the bottleneck was not with FBI agents on the ground, who were willing, even anxious, to provide information. But they, along with the NSC, were stymied by senior levels of the Justice Department that did not share the same sense of urgency on terrorist matters.

"There was a lack of political will to follow through and allow investigators to proceed on the case, despite the fact that all the *i*'s were dotted and the *t*'s were crossed," said a government analyst who reviewed the case against Holy Land. "When I say political I mean we can't have the public come out and say we are bashing Muslims."

Winer, who worked closely with Clarke's group, was harsher. "The FBI under Freeh simply refused to share information or work with anyone else in government," he said. "People developed relationships of trust with individuals of great integrity at the FBI, but it wasn't institutional. Clinton was fighting the war with one arm tied behind his back, and maybe two."

That deep split between the rest of the government and the FBI was passed on from the Clinton administration to the Bush administration. It only began to change after Robert Mueller was named the bureau's director in July 2001. Mueller, though new to the job, was already trying to repair the damage inflicted by Freeh's refusal to work with other branches of the government when he faced the crisis of 9/11. Faced with charges of intelligence failures and incompetence, Mueller publicly acknowledged the need for a radical "culture change" at the bureau and set about to remake the FBI.

There was other intramural wrangling that hindered the hunt for terrorist funds. In the fall of 1999, the State Department's counterterrorism director, Michael Sheehan, wanted the United States to begin pressuring other governments to crack down on charities and relief organizations that were aiding terrorist networks. He wrote a long, forceful cable instructing a number of ambassadors to tackle the matter with their host countries. The cable acknowledged that some agencies played a vital humanitarian role, but pointed out that others did not. The cable asked the ambassadors to press the governments for genuine oversight of the groups to prevent them from aiding terrorists. But the State Department's regional bureaus demanded the cable not be sent. After weeks of attempted compromises and negotiations, and despite strong White House support, the cable was spiked.

In 1999 Clarke also persuaded Clinton to set up an interagency terrorist asset-tracking center, headquartered at Treasury. It was to be the first group of its kind, designed to draw and feed intelligence to and from different agencies. On May 17, 2000, at the Coast Guard Academy in New London, Connecticut, Clinton publicly announced the initiative. To combat the terrorist threat, Clinton announced $300 million in additional funds, of which more than $100 million was to go to the asset-tracking center. But nothing happened. It wasn't until the week after 9/11 that the team for the new center was actually formed and put in place. After a brief time at Treasury it was moved to the CIA.

Efforts to more effectively monitor foreign students in the United States also foundered. A pilot program that would have instituted a tracking program was cut after only eighteen months. The INS remained an antiquated backwater of the federal bureaucracy, where it could easily take two years to identify visa frauds, by which time the perpetrators were long gone.

There were other hitches, often due to the tradition of separating church and state. Under existing laws, federal agents could not monitor mosques or other religious centers to see if they were being used for terrorist fund-raising activities.

In the wake of the failed terrorist attacks—a would-be terrorist bomber tied to al Qaeda was caught on December 14, 1999, while crossing into the Pacific Northwest with plans to set off bombs in Los Angeles—Clarke grew even more agitated. He was convinced there were al Qaeda sleeper cells in the United States that probably wouldn't be uncovered because of the prohibitions placed on federal agents. The question of attacks inside the United States was "not a matter of if, but when," Clarke warned his boss, National Security Adviser Berger, in 1999.

•

With the change of administration in January 2001 came the inevitable changes in personnel.

Clarke remained in his job as counterterrorism czar in the Bush administration, and was there on 9/11. Then, many of his recommendations, especially regarding charities, were implemented. *Hawalas* were targeted. His pet project, arming unmanned Predator aircraft to track terrorist leaders, was finally given the green light and used effectively in Afghanistan and Yemen to attack al Qaeda forces. For years the CIA had resisted using the Predators for that purpose.

"Dick Clarke was the most effective guy I have seen in government, ever," Winer said. "But the integration he brought about was with everyone kicking and screaming every step of the way."

In 2002 Clarke was moved to lead the White House office of cyberspace security. When Homeland Security was formed he was offered a mid-level job there, which he declined, viewing the move as a demotion. He resigned from public service on March 12, 2003.

•

Just how little Customs and other law enforcement officials knew after 9/11 about the radical Islamic financial network in the United States was shown by their almost complete reliance upon private citizens and groups for information.

While the FBI had accumulated some intelligence, it did not share it with other agencies. In fact, the information was closely held within the bureau itself. Immediately following 9/11, many officials felt they were in a race against time. But they didn't have a reliable database to find potential targets or to identify suspected donors. In their desperate search for information, first Customs and then others turned to a small group of private investigators who had been trying for years to focus government attention on the activities of radical

Islamists in the United States. These investigators came to wield un-usually wide influence in shaping investigations. The documents, videos, and databases collected by these investigators in the years be-fore 9/11 would prove to be invaluable resources for the government and journalists alike as they sought to make sense of the alphabet soup of names, acronyms, and businesses that were suddenly under investigation. Never before, in a major crisis, have intelligence agen-cies and journalists relied so heavily on so few for so much informa-tion and analysis.

The best known was Steven Emerson, the copper-haired, hyper-active director of the Investigative Project. Emerson, a former inves-tigative journalist, had been compiling information on and writing about the activities of most of the charities that were eventually shut down a full decade before the U.S. government took any action. His 1994 PBS documentary, *Jihad in America,* was the first to publicly ex-pose the presence in the United States of Muslim militants who raised money for Hamas and other groups and preached the destruc-tion of the West. The film won a George Polk Award for journalism and gained Emerson widespread notice. In the documentary and in his later writings and speeches, Emerson named names and organi-zations, infuriating many groups. American Muslim rights coalitions have denounced him as a racist and an anti-Arab hate-monger. Before 9/11, many journalists shunned him as well, viewing him as a controversial advocate and "radioactive" if quoted.

Aggressive and confrontational, Emerson occasionally hurt him-self, such as when he publicly and erroneously speculated shortly af-ter the 1995 Oklahoma City bombing that the attack was the work of Muslim extremists. But over the years his group, funded by grants from foundations and individual donors, amassed the largest data-base in the country on radical Middle Eastern groups and their ac-tivities in the United States. With a largely young staff, including Arabic speakers, his outfit subscribes to Arab-language publications, surfs the Internet to visit radical sites, and uses public documents to track overlapping directorships among different groups. He also collected an impressive array of tapes, videos, and literature distributed by the groups, full of calls for jihad against the West and solicitations for cash.

Emerson was thinking about going into another line of work before 9/11 suddenly thrust him into the limelight. "Going after jihadis certainly was frustrating," he said. "Islamic groups would scream 'racism' every time I would say something, and the government wouldn't take action. It's like the proverbial pounding your head against the wall. The wall doesn't crumble, your head does. There is only so long you can say the world is crazy before you begin to think maybe it's you who is crazy."

While Emerson had good contacts in the law enforcement community, he said there was no recognition that radical Islam was a threat to the United States before 9/11. There was little incentive for anyone in law enforcement to focus on the groups, he said, because "all you got was grief. They [radical Islamists] controlled the debate until 9/11. It comes down to naming names because these groups had a veneer of respectability."

After 9/11, Emerson said, his work has been "like shooting fish in a barrel." The government sent all 535 members of Congress copies of Emerson's *Jihad in America* and he has frequently briefed the Justice Department, Treasury, the FBI, NSC, and numerous committees in both houses of Congress. His book, *American Jihad: The Terrorists Living Among Us*, made it onto the *New York Times* bestseller list.

A former colleague of Emerson's, Rita Katz, also came to exercise great influence when she left Emerson's operation to start her own organization, the Search for International Terrorist Entities (SITE) Institute, in the summer of 2002.

A native Arabic speaker, over the past decade Katz has gone to many of the conferences where jihad was discussed and where Emerson's group gathered its information. Wearing the full, traditional dress that covered her from head to toe, Katz secretly recorded, then translated many of the sermons that showed that jihad was the goal of many of the Islamic organizations in America. Often, the English parts of the meetings were much more moderate than the Arabic portions.

Because of this, and her knowledge of how to comb public records and monitor Arab-language websites, her Washington-based group had a contract to consult with Green Quest to help with financial investigations. She also has been retained by Ness, Motley, LLC, the law firm suing leading Saudi officials and financiers for aiding and abetting terrorism on behalf of the families of those killed on 9/11. Her group also has contracts with the FBI.

Fast-talking, effusive, and driven, Katz is also surrounded by a hungry young staff that spends its days tracing ties among business and individuals, scouring registration records, combing Arabic magazines, and, on more than one occasion, Dumpster-diving to find information on suspected terrorist activities in this country.

Katz's book, *Terrorist Hunter*, describes not only her current work in investigating suspected terrorist supporters, but her Jewish family's escape from Iraq when she was a child. Saddam Hussein had her father hanged as an Israeli spy. Her book generated a libel suit for her allegations against members of the Safa network of terrorist financing.

"In tracing terrorist funds, you are not going to find a check written to al Qaeda or Hamas," Katz said. "You need to tie people together through documents. That is why we are playing a major role. We can get the documents and understand them. Otherwise, cases are only intelligence cases and take forever."

Journalists—myself included—also dealt extensively with Katz and Emerson when stories broke and reliable information was needed quickly.

A senior law enforcement official said that relying on information provided by Emerson and Katz, who are not government employees and may have personal axes to grind, was "problematic," but he added that the government had no choice. "Their ability to fill in the blanks and give us hard information was essential, although not conventional," the official said. "They knew so much more than we did after 9/11, and knew how to find information, which was even more important. We would have been even farther behind on tracking money here if we had not been able to turn to them."

•

Still, knowledgeable sources say, more than two years after 9/11 the United States remains far behind in the race to cut off the flow of money, the lifeblood of terrorism, although cooperation among some government agencies has improved. The CIA and FBI have ironed out many of their differences. Attention is slowly being focused on the Wahhabi influence in the United States. Saudi Arabia, shocked by al Qaeda bombings at home, is finally beginning to crack down on terrorist money flows. A raft of senior al Qaeda leaders have been arrested.

But tremendous obstacles remain.

"Despite these strikes against the leadership of al Qaeda, it remains a potent, highly capable, and extremely dangerous terrorist network," said Larry Mefford, the FBI chief of counterterrorism. "It is the number-one terrorist threat to the United States today. Al Qaeda as a network has shown itself to be adaptive and resilient."

Such rhetoric is fine, said former NSC official Rand Beers wearily as we wrapped up our last conversation. But the current counterterrorist strategy, he repeated heavily, was "a rhetorical policy. You can't say you don't care about three thousand people dead in Washington and New York." But in reality, he said, the Bush team was greatly underestimating al Qaeda and other terrorist threats.

Beers said that, at the time of 9/11, "we didn't know anything" about terrorist financing. "We know a hell of a lot more now, but we don't know what we don't know," he said. "We have to have the humility to say we don't know. And it is very easy to forget that."

NOTES

Unless otherwise noted, the quotes and information in this book came from personal interviews with those directly involved in the events described. Material from published sources is cited in the following notes. The titles of individuals cited were current at the time of the interviews. Publication information about those sources and other relevant documents is contained in the Bibliography.

INTRODUCTION: The Money Trail

2 *Intelligence officials . . . the United States:* Mark Hosenball and Michael Isikoff, "Al Qaeda's Money Man," *Newsweek*, March 24, 2003, 13.

3 *"There were no slip-ups . . .":* Testimony of Robert Mueller, Joint Intelligence Committee Inquiry, September 25, 2002. Statement for the Record, 14. 107th Congress, First Session.

CHAPTER ONE: Blood from Stones

15 *Taylor got his start . . . :* Taylor's embezzlement and escape are described by Stephen Ellis, *The Mask of Anarchy: The Destruction of Liberia and the Religious Dimension of an African Civil War* (New York: New York University Press, 2001), 58.

15 *Taylor, his family . . . :* The sanctions are contained in *United Nations Security Council Resolution 1343 (2001) on Liberia.*

16 *stashed some $3.8 billion . . . :* Global Witness, "The Usual Suspects: Weapons and Mercenaries in Cote d'Ivoire and Sierra Leone: Why

It's Still Possible, How It Works and How to Break the Trend," March 2003, 18.

16 *"May I . . . It is terrible"*: Charles Taylor. Author interview, January 19, 2001, Monrovia, Liberia.

20 *"chaos . . . terrorist syndicates"*: Robert Cooper, "Reordering the World: Post-Modern States," *The Foreign Policy Centre*, London, April 2002, 18.

21 *"Tradition, certainly, supports . . . "*: Matthew Hart, *Diamond: A Journey to the Heart of an Obsession* (New York: Walker and Company, 2001), 139.

22 *Even before . . . in 1954:* Ian Smillie, Lansana Gberie, and Ralph Hazleton, *The Heart of the Matter: Sierra Leone, Diamonds and Human Security* (Ottawa, Canada: Partnership Africa Canada, 2000), 4.

23 *As President Stevens built . . . parliament:* Lansana Gberie, *War and Peace in Sierra Leone: Diamonds, Corruption and the Lebanese Connection*, The Diamonds and Human Security Project, *Occasional Paper 6*, (Ottawa, Canada: Partnership Africa Canada) January 2003, 12–13.

23 *Berri has distinguished . . . "allies":* Daniel Nassif, "Nabih Berri: Lebanese Parliament Speaker," *Middle East Intelligence Bulletin*, December 2000, http/www.meib.org/articles/0012–ldi.htm.

24 *"the Harvard and . . . revolutionaries":* Ellis, *The Mask of Anarchy*, 72.

24 *He was born on March 31 . . . :* Accounts of Bah's history come from author interviews with Bah associates and intelligence services.

26 *The outfits, so . . . worlds*: Stephen Ellis e-mail to author, May 26, 2003.

27 *"any reason to confirm the reports"*: Chuck Fager, "Robertson Takes Flack for Gold Mining Venture," *Christianity Today*, February 4, 2002, http:/www.christianitytoday.com/ct/2002/002/14.18.htm.

28 *Bockerie, revered by his men . . . :* Accounts of Bockerie's organizational skills and magical powers came from author interviews with Bockerie and other RUF combatants. Several said they had witnessed Bockerie being struck by bullets and suffering only minor bruises.

28 *On May 6 . . . children:* Douglas Farah, "Tribunal Indicts Liberian Leader," *Washington Post,* June 5, 2003, A22.

30 *"characterized by systematic . . .":* Smillie and Gberie, *The Heart of the Matter*.

33 *"Estimates of the . . . level"*: UN Panel of Experts, *UN Report on Liberia*, December 2000, paragraphs 1–2.

34 *"handled much of . . ."*: Ibid., paragraph 198.

34 *The diamonds were usually sold . . . :* Descriptions of the diamond bidding process come from author interviews and e-mail communication with Cindor Reeves.

CHAPTER TWO: The Merchant of Death

36 *Born in Tajikistan . . . :* Accounts of Bout's early activities come from several sources, including interviews; International Consortium of Journalists, *Making a Killing: The Business of War* (Washington, D.C.: Public Integrity Books, 2003); and *Los Angeles Times* staff, "On the Trail of the Man Behind Taliban's Air Fleet," *Los Angeles Times*, May 19, 2002, A1.

37 *"can locate its . . ."*: UN Panel of Experts, *UN Report on Liberia*, December 2000, paragraph 222.

38 *"Bout would fly . . ."*: ICIJ, *Making a Killing*, 145.

38 *Between July 1997 . . . :* Bout's dealings in Angola are documented in the *UN Security Council Report on Angolan Sanctions*, December 21, 2000.

39 *"Africa's chief merchant . . ."*: ICIJ, "Merchant of Death," 143.

39 *Bout's entrée into Liberia . . . :* Accounts of the dealings of Bout and Ruprah come from the *UN Report on Liberia*, December 2000, and author interviews.

40 *"It is difficult . . ."*: *UN Report on Liberia*, December 2000, paragraph 233.

40 *He had even tried . . . :* ICIJ, "Africa's 'Merchant of Death' Sold Arms to the Taliban," January 31, 2002.

42 *"He was working . . ."*: *Los Angeles Times* staff, "On the Trail of the Man Behind Taliban's Air Fleet."

42 *"selling heavy ordnance . . ."*: Document provided to author by ICIJ.

42 *lucrative deals with . . . :* *Los Angeles Times* staff, "On the Trail of the Man Behind Taliban's Air Fleet."

42 *"close business associate of Bout" . . . :* *UN Report on Liberia*, December 2000.

42 *acting on behalf . . . :* *Los Angeles Times* staff, "On the Trail of the Man Behind Taliban's Air Fleet."

44 *"What have I done . . ."*: Victor Bout. Echo Moskvy radio station, February 28, 2002, translation by *Washington Post*.

44 *"I have never . . . :* Victor Bout. CNN interview by Jill Dougherty, March 3, 2002.

45 *When he was arrested . . . :* Accounts of Menin's activity are drawn from several studies of his operation, including: *Drugs, Diamonds and Deadly Cargoes*, ICIJ Investigative Reports, November 18, 2002 (Washington, D.C.: Public Integrity Books, 2003) and the *UN Report on Liberia*, December 2000.

CHAPTER THREE: The al Qaeda Connection

48 *Due to recent fighting . . . :* This account of events is based on extensive interviews and e-mail communication with Cindor Reeves and other RUF and Liberian sources who asked not to be identified for fear of retaliation.

54 *Taylor was especially angry . . . :* A detailed report on the operations of OTC and other logging companies can be found in Global Witness, "Logging Off: How the Liberian Timber Industry Fuels Liberia's Humanitarian Disaster and Threatens Sierra Leone," September 2002.

CHAPTER FOUR: Roots of the al Qaeda Connection

63 *While plotting the bombing . . . :* Benjamin Weiser, *New York Times*, September 18, 1998.

64 *El Hage's file of . . . :* Information on the trial documents and transcripts is taken from *The United States v. Usama bin Laden et al.*, U.S. District Court, Southern District of New York.

64 *"Yes, el Hage . . .":* Bundeskriminalamt interview of Mamoun Darkazanli, September 15, 2001. Signed by Schmitz, KHK and Brock-muller, KHK. Provided and translated by SITE Institute, Washington, D.C., February 24, 2003.

65 *Before the Taliban . . . :* Akram Walizhada, *Afghan Emeralds That Fed War May Now Fund Peace*, Reuters News Service, June 3, 2002.

65 *An extensive November 2001 . . .:* Robert Block and Daniel Pearl, "Underground Trade: Much Smuggled Gem Called Tanzanite

Helps bin Laden Supporters," *Wall Street Journal*, November 16, 2001, A1.

68 *Caldwell set up . . . :* Kenneth R. Timmerman, *Shakedown* (New York: Regency Publishing, 2002), chap. 13.

71 *Nassour boasted of . . . :* BBC documentary, "Blood Diamonds," February 10, 2003.

71 *Even after Laurent . . . :* Lansana Gberie, *War and Peace in Sierra Leone: Diamonds, Corruption, and the Lebanese Connection*, The Diamonds and Human Security Project, Occasional Paper 6, January 2003, 14.

71 *Osailly had appeared . . . :* Ibid.

72 *With his contacts . . . :* The account of Osailly's arrival, the trip to Sierra Leone, and the rental of the house is taken from interviews with Cindor Reeves, Allie Darwish, Samih Osailly, and RUF commanders. It was first reported by me in the *Washington Post* on December 30, 2002. Nassour maintains he only traveled to Ouagadougou one time, in May 2001.

73 *About ten days . . . :* Telephone records obtained by author.

75 *On May 2, 2001 . . . :* *Wall Street Journal*, January 2002.

75 *to Afghanistan and Pakistan . . . :* Douglas Farah, "Reports Says Africans Harbored al Qaeda," *Washington Post*, December 30, 2002, A1.

76 *On June 16 . . . :* Ibid.

76 *In July 2001 . . . :* Farah, "Report Says Africans Harbored al Qaeda," A1 (based on a European intelligence report).

76 *"Sir, we write . . .":* RUF document obtained by author.

80 *But what was . . . :* End-user certificate obtained by author.

81 *"The likelihood these . . .":* Farah, "Report Says Africans Harbored al Qaeda."

82 *"in the presidential . . .":* Ibid.

83 *"But in the end . . .":* Ibid.

CHAPTER FIVE: The CIA Drops the Ball

87 *When the BBC . . . :* Rachel Morgan. Interview, February 7, 2003, producer, "Blood Diamonds," BBC.

89 *On June 4 . . . :* Indictment, The Special Court for Sierra Leone, *The Prosecutor v. Charles Ghankay Taylor*, Case Number SCSL-2003-01-I, March 7, 2003.

91 *Shortly after arriving . . . :* The account of Darwish's dealings comes from interviews with Darwish and two U.S. officials directly involved in the incident.

93 *On September 5 . . . :* This account is drawn from interviews and e-mails with Cindor Reeves as well as confidential author interviews with U.S. officials.

95 *According to the official . . . :* Confidential "Note de Renseignements," Direction Generale de la Police Nationale, November 29, 2001, obtained by author.

96 *"since Nov. 29 . . .":* Private letter, Ministry of Foreign Affairs, Burkina Faso, to UN Panel of Experts, April 18, 2002, obtained by author.

104 *it was the first time . . . :* Confidential author interviews with congressional and diamond industry sources.

105 *The efforts of Hall . . . :* Confidential author interviews with congressional and diamond industry sources.

106 *"an historic step . . .":* Joseph Kahn, "House Votes to Combat Sale of Diamonds for War," *New York Times*, November 29, 2001, B6.

CHAPTER SIX: The Golden Trail

108 *On October 16 . . . ". . . came and took it.":* Karl Vick, "Taliban Emptied Country's Banks: Millions Gone, with Little Accounting," *Washington Post*, January 8, 2002, A27.

109 *"Gold is a huge factor . . .":* Douglas Farah, "Al Qaeda's Road Paved with Gold," *Washington Post,* February 17, 2002, A1.

110 *"Yes . . . he . . .":* Civil Action Case 1:02 CV 01616 (JR), U.S. District Court for the District of Columbia, paragraph 401.

111 *The annual demand . . . States:* "Gold Smuggling and the Drug Trade in Southwest Asia," 1998 Interpol Report, obtained by author.

113 *"The Taliban took . . .":* Farah, "Al Qaeda's Road Paved with Gold."

113 *Unknown to most people . . . :* Descriptions of how *hawala*s operate socially come from interviews with *hawaladar*s and Patrick Jost.

114 *These people, sending small amounts . . . :* Nikos Passas, "*Hawala* and Other Informal Value Transfer Systems: How to Regulate Them?" U.S. National Institute of Justice, 2003, 4–5.

114 Hawalas *handle hundreds of billions . . . :* Ibid.

114 *Here is how . . . :* For an extended discussion of how *hawala*s operate, both legally and illegally, see Patrick M. Jost and Harjit Singh Sandhu, "The *Hawala* Alternative Remittance System and Its Role in Money Laundering," Interpol Report, January 2000.

116 Hawalas *have many friends . . . :* Passas, "*Hawala* and Other Informal Value Transfer Systems." Passas offers a wide-ranging explanation of *hawala* and its many uses.

116 *"if gold and silver smuggling . . .": Money Laundering: Special Problems of Parallel Economies,* Joint Meeting of Commonwealth Finance and Law Officials on Money Laundering, London, June 1, 1998, 16.

116 *"There are no traditional . . .":* Farah, "Al Qaeda's Road Paved with Gold."

121 *Shortly after Benazir Bhutto . . . :* John F. Burns, "Bhutto Clan Leaves Trail of Corruption in Pakistan," *New York Times,* January 9, 1998, A1.

122 *Dawood fled to Karachi . . . :* Nick Meo, "All Eyes on India's Most Wanted," *Sunday Herald* (New Delhi), January 27, 2002, A1.

125 *"ARY Gold, a branch . . .": Civil Action Case,* paragraphs 389–402.

125 *Al Qaeda and the Taliban were quietly shipping . . . :* Douglas Farah, "Al Qaeda Gold Moved to Sudan," *Washington Post,* September 3, 2002, A1.

126 *Bin Laden even married . . . :* Eric Reeves, leading Sudan expert, Smith College, North Hampton, Mass., e-mail communication, February 20, 2003.

127 *Among them was . . . :* Global Witness, "For a Few Dollars More: How al Qaeda Moved into the Diamond Trade," April 2003.

127 *By January 1994 . . . :* State Department Fact Sheet on bin Laden, August 14, 1996, and Rohan Gunaratna, *Inside al Qaeda: Global Network of Terror* (New York: Columbia University Press, 2002).

127 *"put aside its differences . . .":* United Press International (UPI), "Iran-Hezbollah Terror Connection," October 2, 2001.

127 *"a strategic partnership . . .":* Gunaratna, *Inside al Qaeda,* 148.

128 *Sen. Bob Graham . . . :* Dana Priest and Douglas Farah, "Terror Alliance Has U.S. Worried," *Washington Post,* June 30, 2002, A1.

128 *A naturalized U.S. citizen . . . :* Steven Emerson, *American Jihad: The Terrorists Living Among Us* (New York: The Free Press, 2002), 224.

129 *After leaving the U.S. army . . . :* United Press International (UPI), Iran-Hezbollah Terror Connection."

129 *Bin Laden "has banking . . .":* Farah, "Al Qaeda Gold Moved to Sudan."

130 *That assessment was shared . . . :* Canadian Security Intelligence Service Report to the Federal Court of Canada, in Relation to Mohammed Zeki Mahjoub, September 2001, paragraph 26. Report provided to author by Eric Reeves.

130 *"Iran is not a monolith . . .":* Farah, "Al Qaeda Gold Moved to Sudan."

131 *One of the areas where Hezbollah . . . :* Priest and Farah, "Terror Alliance Has U.S. Worried," A4.

132 *"a large portfolio of . . .":* Report of the Monitoring Group, United Nations, August 2002, paragraph 46.

CHAPTER SEVEN: "And Spend for God's Cause"

135 *Included in the minutes . . . : United States v. Enaam M. Arnaout,* Government Evidenciary Proffer Supporting the Admissibility of Coconspirator Statements, U.S. District Court, Northern District of Illinois, Eastern Division, Case 02 CR 892, January 31, 2003, 40–41.

136 *They were the Benevolence International . . . :* Testimony of Matthew Epstein and Evan Kohlmann before the House Committee on Financial Services, Subcommittee on Oversight and Investigations, March 11, 2003.

137 *"We had been looking . . .":* David Aufhauser testimony before Senate Judicial Committee, February 12, 2003.

137 *initiated the largest transfer . . . :* Nathan Vardi, "Sins of the Father?" Forbes.com, March 18, 2002.

137 *estimates that al Qaeda . . . :* Jean-Charles Brisard, "Terrorism Financing; Roots and Trends of Saudi Terrorism Financing," report prepared for the Presidency of the Security Council, United Nations, December 19, 2002, 11.

138 *"The IIRO, which claims . . .":* Christine Herrera, "Bin Laden Funds Abu Sayyaf Through Muslim Relief Group," *Philippine Daily Inquirer,* August 9, 2000, A1.

138 *"There is no solution . . .":* Daniel Benjamin and Steven Simon, *The Age of Sacred Terror* (New York: Random House, 2002), 16.

139 *The Yousef associate . . . :* Sworn affidavit of FBI Special Agent Robert Walker, *United States v. Benevolence International Foundation, Inc.,* District of Illinois, Eastern Division, Case 02 CR 0414, April 29, 2002, 18.

139 *contained Khalifah's phone numbers . . . :* Ibid., 21.

140 *"has engaged in . . .":* Seth Rosenfeld, "Saudi's In-Law Had U.S. Arrest: Bin Laden Kin Claims He Was a Victim of Paranoia," *San Francisco Examiner,* August 22, 1998.

140 *"All I can say . . .":* Al-Sharq al-Awsat (London) May 4, 2002, interview conducted by Muhamad Samman, translated by FBIS.

140 *"approximately one-third . . .":* Copy of the CIA report obtained by author.

142 *Golden Chain list . . . :* Copy of list and translation provided by SITE Institute, March 2003.

143 *But the façade . . . :* Douglas Farah, "Saudis Face U.S. Demand on Terrorism," *Washington Post,* November 26, 2002, A1.

144 *"The terrorism is . . .":* May 16 transcript of al Jubeir press conference at Saudi Arabian Embassy, Federal Document Clearing House, Inc.

144 *"All these Westerners . . .":* Emerson, *American Jihad: The Terrorists Living Among Us* (New York: The Free Press, 2002), p. 249.

145 *"God is our objective . . .":* Benjamin and Simon, *The Age of Sacred Terror,* 57.

145 *Hassan al-Turabi . . . :* Ibid., 109.

146 *"jihad means fighting . . .":* Emerson, *American Jihad,* 251.

146 *U.S. intelligence agencies . . . :* Mark Hosenball with Kevin Peraino and Catharine Skipp, "Is al Taqwa, a Shadowy Financial Network, a Secret Money Machine for Osama bin Laden?" *Newsweek,* March 25, 2002, 28.

147 *The bank and Nada's other . . . :* U.S. Treasury Department Statement on Terrorist Designations, August 12, 2002.

147 *This strategy kept . . . : Civil Action Case 1:02 CV 01616 (JR),* U.S. District Court for the District of Columbia, 252.

147 *One of the few . . . :* Mark Hosenball, "Periscope," *Newsweek,* November 12, 2001, 18–20

147 *"the $60 million . . .":* Testimony of Juan C. Zarate to the House

Financial Subcommittee on Oversight and Investigations, February 12, 2002.

148 *Nada called the allegations . . . :* Steve Scherer, "Italy Freezes 25 Bank Accounts Linked to al-Qaeda," Bloomberg News Service, August 29, 2002.

148 *Among the most prominent . . . :* U.S. Treasury Department Statement on Terrorist Designations, August 12, 2002.

148 *"the main al Qaeda station . . .":* U.S. Treasury Department press release, September 24, 2001.

148 *"is now controlled . . .":* Hosenball, "Is al Taqwa, a Shadowy Financial Network?" 18.

148 *"young and highly . . .":* Yaroslav Trofimov, "Bin Laden Trail Extends to Swiss Outfit—In Search of One Firm with Links to an Egyptian Group," *Wall Street Journal*, September 21, 2001, A9.

149 *But he denies . . . :* Hosenball, "Is al Taqwa, a Shadowy Financial Network, a Secret Money Machine for Osama bin Laden?" 19.

150 *The organization collected . . . :* Epstein testimony.

150 *Much of the money allegedly went . . . : United States v. Enaam M. Arnaout.*

150 *Benevolence vehemently protested . . . :* Press release of Benevolence International Foundation, January 30, 2002.

150 *On November 19, 2002 . . . :* "Treasury Designates Benevolence International Foundation and Related Entities as Financiers of Terrorism," Office of Public Affairs, Department of the Treasury, November 19, 2002.

150 *On February 10, 2003 . . . :* Eric Lichtblau, "Charity Leader Accepts Deal in a Terror Case," *New York Times*, February 11, 2003, A1.

150 *In an affidavit . . . :* Sworn affidavit of FBI Special Agent Robert Walker, 16.

151 *While in the Metropolitan . . . :* Ibid. 15–16.

151 *"Generous Brother Abu . . .":* Ibid.

152 *"If I receive one . . ." United States v. Enaam M. Arnaout*, 111.

152 *"I prefer that you travel . . .":* Ibid., 112–13.

153 *live in spacious homes . . . :* Public records obtained by the *Washington Post*.

153 *In time, the Safa . . . :* Douglas Farah and John Mintz, "U.S. Trails Va. Muslim Money, Ties," *Washington Post*, October 7, 2002, A1.

153 *"The funds came very . . . :* Ibid.

154 *A stocky man . . . :* Ibid.

154 *"individuals associated . . .":* Affidavit of Senior Special Agent David Kane, U.S. Customs Service, obtained by author.

154 *"absolutely not involved . . .":* Farah and Mintz, "U.S. Trails Va. Muslim Money, Ties."

155 *U.S. officials said they had . . . :* Ibid.

155 *Two members . . . :* The two are Samir Salah and Ibrahim Hassaballa, who incorporated Bank al Taqwa in the Bahamas, according to Treasury Department documents. Salah is also a founder of the Safa Trust and is an officer of Amana Mutual Funds Trust, both Safa Group entities. Hassaballa serves on the board of the Islamic Charitable Organization, a Safa-related charity. In 2001, according to Safa lawyers, several Safa Group leaders arranged a personal loan to Nada from a joint bank account. The lawyers would not say how much the loan was for or why Nada approached them for the money.

155 *in its 1998 tax return . . . :* Public records obtained by the *Washington Post*.

155 *"Looking into their finances . . .":* Farah and Mintz, "U.S. Trails Va. Muslim Money, Ties."

156 *"It is a staggering sum . . .":* Ibid.

156 *Bin Mahfouz gave . . . :* Jeff Gerth and Judith Miller, "Saudis Called Slow to Help Stem Terror Finances," *New York Times*, December 1, 2002.

157 *said the money . . . :* Ibid.

157 *Muwaffaq was initially . . . :* General Registry, Isle of Man, Certificate of Incorporation No. 54717C, provided to the author by the SITE Institute.

157 *It even registered an office . . . :* Sworn statement of Harriet Smith Windsor, secretary of state of Delaware, January 18, 2003, provided by the SITE Institute.

157 *also "fund[ed] at least . . .":* CIA report obtained by author.

157 *never officially dissolved . . . :* General Registry, Isle of Man, Certificate of Incorporation.

157 *A 1998 audit . . . :* Summary of "Saudi National Commercial Bank Audit Report," provided to author by the SITE Institute.

158 *was forced to surrender . . . :* Vardi, "Sins of the Father?"

158 *"weren't willing to let . . .":* Farah, "Al Qaeda's Road Paved with Gold," *Washington Post,* February 17, 2002, A1.

158 *"Let us damn America . . .":* Richard Leiby, "Talking Out of School: Was an Islamic Professor Exercising His Freedom or Promoting Terror?" *Washington Post,* July 28, 2002, F1.

158 *He used the organizations . . . :* Ibid.

159 *"We consider you a part . . .":* Farah and Mintz, "U.S. Trails Va. Muslim Money, Ties."

159 *Al Arian liked to boast . . . :* Leiby, "Talking Out of School."

160 *The fifty-count indictment . . . : The United States v. Sami Amin Al Arian et al.,* United States District Court, Middle District of Florida, Tampa Division.

160 *"not a shred . . .":* Glenn Simpson, "U.S. Provides Details of Terror-Financing Web: Defunct Firm in New Jersey Is the Hub," *Wall Street Journal,* September 15, 2003, A5.

161 *almost $4 million . . . :* Douglas Farah, "U.S. Links Islamic Charities, Terrorist Funding," *Washington Post,* August 20, 2003, A2.

CHAPTER EIGHT: The Terrorist Treasury

163 *The brothers could clear . . . :* Testimony of Robert J. Conrad, Jr., U.S. Attorney for the Western District of North Carolina, before the Senate Committee on the Judiciary, November 20, 2002.

163 *A favorite scam . . . :* Daniel Pipes, "Hezbollah in America: An Alarming Network," *The National Review,* August 28, 2000; John Mintz and Douglas Farah, "Small Scams Probed for Terror Ties," *Washington Post,* August 12, 2002, A1.

164 *The money was also used . . . :* Superseding bill of Indictment, *United States v. Mohamad Youseff Hammoud et al.,* U.S. District Court, Western District of North Carolina, Charlotte Division, March 28, 2001.

165 *Following 9/11 and the passage . . . :* Conrad testimony.

166 *"We were always looking . . .":* Mintz and Farah, "Small Scams Probed for Terror Ties."

167 *"after more than five years . . .":* Testimony of Ben Jacobson before the

Senate Judiciary Subcommittee on Technology, Terrorism and Government Information, 1998.

167 *"I try not to make . . .":* "How North America Fraud Funds Terrorism," Canadian Broadcast Corporation, November 26, 2001.

168 *So a knockoff artist . . . :* Mintz and Farah, "Small Scams Probed for Terror Ties."

170 *"It wouldn't surprise me . . .":* Ibid.

171 *Operation Mountain Express . . . :* Jerry Seper, "DEA Takes Down 2 Major Meth Rings; Agency Probes for Links to Terrorists," *Washington Times*, January 11, 2002, A8; Peter Eisler and Donna Leinwand, "Canada Top Source for Drug Chemical," *USA Today*, January 10, 2002, A3.

172 *"This is the first time . . .":* Mintz and Farah, "Small Scams Probed for Terror Ties."

172 *$1 million in $20 bills . . . :* Douglas Farah, "Moving Mountains of Illicit Cash," *Washington Post*, August 9, 1997, A27.

173 *"Operation Oasis is making . . .":* U.S. Customs press release, July 2, 2002.

173 *When an ambulance arrived . . . :* "Montgomery PD May Have Opened a Financial Link to al Qaeda Terrorist Group," *Montgomery County News,* April 4, 2002, A1.

174 *"We're just a little, bitty town . . .":* "Feds Looking into Operation with Possible Terrorist Ties," Associated Press, April 2, 2002.

174 *"was probably more lucrative . . .":* "How North American Fraud Funds Terrorism."

175 *"At this point I think . . .":* Ibid.

175 *Much of the money . . . :* Fact Sheet on Shutting Down the Terrorist Financial Network, White House Press Release, December 4, 2001.

176 *In the diary of Wadih el Hage . . . :* Glenn R. Simpson, "Hesitant Agents: Why the FBI Took Nine Years to Shut Group It Tied to Terror," *Wall Street Journal*, February 27, 2002, A1.

176 *By 1998, Holy Land reported . . . :* Action Memorandum from Dale L. Watson, assistant director, Counterterrorism Division, FBI, to R. Richard Newcomb, director, Office of Foreign Assets Control, Department of Treasury, November 5, 2001.

177 *"FBI investigations revealed . . .":* Ibid., 46.

177 *"During the meeting . . .":* Ibid., 11.

178 *The company, with about . . . :* Steve McGonigle, "Internet Business Targeted in Raid," *Dallas Morning News*, September 6, 2001, A7.

178 *"an anti-Muslim witch-hunt . . .":* Marcus Kabel, "FBI Denies Bias in U.S. Raid that Shut Qatar Web Site," Reuters, September 6, 2001.

178 *"succumbing to politically motivated . . .":* "Freeze on Holy Land Assets Questioned by US Muslims," CAIR, December 5, 2001.

179 *"Hamas is a foreign terrorist . . .":* Action Memorandum from Watson, 3.

CHAPTER NINE: Fighting the Last War, Losing the New One

180 *"As an insider . . .":* Laura Blumenfeld, "Former Aide Takes Aim at War on Terror," *Washington Post*, June 16, 2003, A1.

183 *"You are going to spend . . .":* Daniel Benjamin and Steven Simon, *The Age of Sacred Terror* (New York: Random House, 2003), 328–30.

183 *Brian Sheridan, a former . . . :* Ibid., 329.

184 *The Memorandum of Understanding . . . :* John Mintz and Dan Eggen, "Ashcroft, Ridge Settle Turf Battle," *Washington Post*, May 23, 2003, A7.

186 *"If we were trying . . .":* Karen DeYoung and Douglas Farah, "Infighting Slows Hunt for Hidden al Qaeda Assets," *Washington Post*, June 18, 2002, A1.

187 *"won't share anything . . .":* "Whose War on Terror?" *Newsweek* Web Exclusive, April 9, 2003.

187 *reauthorized the arrest power . . . :* Ibid.

188 *"no later than . . .":* Memorandum of Agreement Between the Department of Justice and the Department of Homeland Security Concerning Terrorism Financing Investigations, May 13, 2003.

188 *"would severely jeopardize . . .":* Mintz and Eggen, "Ashcroft, Ridge Settle Turf Battle."

188 *"who plotted to destroy . . .":* Barton Gellman, "Struggles Inside the Government Defined the Campaign," *Washington Post*, December 20, 2001, A1.

189 *Figures from the Office of Management . . . :* Ibid.

192 *"There was a lack of political will . . .":* Ibid.

192 *He wrote a long, forceful cable . . . :* Benjamin and Simon, *The Age of Sacred Terror*, 293–94.

193 *To combat the terrorist threat . . . :* Public papers of the President, Commencement Address at the United States Coast Guard Academy in New London, Connecticut, May 17, 2000.

194 *"not a matter of if, but when":* Benjamin and Simon, *The Age of Sacred Terror*, 313.

195 *The best known . . . :* Description of Emerson's work and background come from author interviews and John Mintz, "The Man Who Gave Terrorism a Name," *Washington Post*, November 14, 2001, C1.

198 *"Despite these strikes . . .":* Prepared Remarks of Larry A. Mefford, assistant director, FBI Counterterrorism Division, before the U.S. Senate Terrorism, Technology and Homeland Security subcommittee of the Committee on the Judiciary, June 26, 2003.

BIBLIOGRAPHY

Anonymous. *Terrorist Hunter: The Extraordinary Story of a Woman Who Went Underground to Infiltrate Radical Islamic Groups Operating in America*. New York, HarperCollins, 2003.

Benjamin, Daniel, and Steve Simon. *The Age of Sacred Terror*. New York: Random House, 2002.

Brisard, Jean-Charles, and Guillaume Dasquie, *Forbidden Truth: U.S.-Taliban Secret Oil Diplomacy and the Failed Hunt for bin Laden*, trans. Lucy Rounds. New York: Thunder Mouth Press/Nation Books, 2002.

Ellis, Stephen. *The Mask of Anarchy: The Destruction of Liberia and the Religious Dimension of an African Civil War*. New York: New York University Press, 1999.

Emerson, Steven. *American Jihad: The Terrorists Living Among Us*. New York: Free Press, 2002.

Global Witness. *For a Few Dollars More*. London, 2003.

———. *Logging Off: How the Liberian Timber Industry Fuels Liberia's Humanitarian Disaster and Threatens Sierra Leone*. London, 2002.

———. *The Usual Suspects: Liberia's Weapons and Mercenaries in Côte d'Ivoire and Sierra Leone*. London, 2003.

Gunaratna, Rohan. *Inside al Qaeda: Global Network of Terror*. New York: Columbia University Press, 2002.

Hart, Matthew. *Diamond: A Journey to the Heart of an Obsession*. New York: Walker and Company, 2001.

Making a Killing: The Business of War. The International Consortium of Investigative Journalists. Washington, D.C.: Public Integrity Books, 2003.

Reeve, Simon. *The New Jackals: Ramzi Yousef, Osama bin Laden, and the Future of Terrorism*. Boston: Northeastern University Press, 1999.

INDEX